Canoeing and Camping on the Historic Suwannee River:

A Paddler's Guide

Leslie Rose Knox
and Graham Schorb

CANOEING AND CAMPING ON
THE HISTORIC SUWANNEE RIVER:
A PADDLER'S GUIDE

Copyright © 2012 by Leslie Rose Knox and Graham Schorb

All rights reserved under International and Pan-American Copyright Conventions. No part of this book may be reproduced in any form or by any means, electronic or mechanical, including photocopying, recording, or by any information storage and retrieval system, without permission in writing from the publisher, except by a reviewer who may quote brief passages in a review.

Artistic Contributions by noted Florida Artists Joe Akerman, Johnny Dame Jr., Sue Knox, Theodore Morris, and Linda K. Della Poali

Cover image from a 1907 Hugh C. Leighton Company postcard, Ada Coates Parrish collection, Library of Florida History

All photographs, unless otherwise cited, are courtesy of Graham Schorb.

Second Impression, April 2013

ISBN 10: 1-886104-56-5
ISBN 13: 978-1-886104-56-3

The Florida Historical Society Press
435 Brevard Avenue
Cocoa, FL 32922
www.myfloridahistory.org/fhspress

P•R•E•S•S

Dedication

Jessica Blair Arnaudin, Shelby Daniel Knox, Samuel Herbert Schorb, John Parker Schorb, and Robert (Robby) Gregory Schorb, may you diligently perpetuate to others how our own fragile existence is inextricably intertwined upon Nature's delicate balance. Live to love, revere, and protect the Natural world.

—Leslie Rose Knox and Graham Schorb

Acknowledgements

Thanks to the late Joe Akerman, noted Florida author and my professor, mentor, and friend, for his advice, encouragement, and artwork; to Ben Brotemarkle, Kirsten Russell, and Paul Pruett at the Florida Historical Society Press in readying and compiling the work for publication; to North Florida Community College librarians Sheila Hiss, Kathy Sale, Kay Hogan, Kathy Smith, and Lynn Wyche for providing important books and information about Florida; to Sheila Hiss for questions concerning copyright laws; to the State Library and Archives of Florida for historic photographs of the Suwannee River and Basin; to Jason Welch, history professor, for his confirmation concerning the Appalachee and Timucuan tribes; to Graham Schorb for his photographic contributions and his efforts in showing me sections of the river I did not know; to Gina White of Winthrop University Special Collection's Department, Dacus Archival Library, for giving us permission to use the John R. Schorb photograph; to Chris Trowell, author, for his assistance in answering questions concerning the Okefenokee Swamp; to Jim Burkhart, ranger at Okefenokee National Wildlife Refuge, for information on the Sill; to Ms. Cherry of The Old Bookstore in Madison, Florida, for providing books about pioneer Florida; to noted Florida artists Sue Knox, Johnny Dame Jr., Joe Akerman, Theodore Morris, and Linda K. Della Poali for their artistic contributions; to Steve Baxter, owner of the Suwannee Canoe Outpost, for running shuttles; to Randy Smith and to David and Debbie Pharr for interviews and stories about the Suwannee River; to Greg Pflug for assistance in compiling a comprehensive gear list; to Eric Musgrove, historian and author, for his assistance with Rebecca Charles's grave and his willingness to share his knowledge of local river history about many locations, including the Ivey Cemetery; to Paul Camp and Frank Ilene of the Tampa Library Reference Archive

Department for their information concerning old maps; to Dr. Ryan Wheeler, chief archaeologist of Florida, for his attempts to help validate the authenticity of a dugout canoe found on the Suwannee River; to Vincent "Chip" Birdsong, Database Administrator at the division of Historical Resources in Tallahassee, Florida, for his assistance with information about archaeological finds on the Suwannee River; to Bivian and Murl Howell, cemetery researchers, and the Suwannee County Genealogical Society Library for their willingness to share with us the Charles's Papers and other significant historical information about the Suwannee River, including leads concerning pioneer and Confederate cemeteries; to David Cook, biologist with the Florida Fish and Wildlife Conservation Commission, for identification of the loggerhead musk turtle; to Martha J. Robinson, public information specialist with the Florida Department of Environmental Protection, for permission to use and to publish the *Madison* steamship at Troy Spring; to Madison County local public librarians April Brooks, Melanie Salyer, Katie Griffis, and Monnika Hopkins for providing books on Suwannee River history; to The Gilchrist County Chamber of Commerce and to Kyle Stone for book leads on North Florida history; to Cindy Bellot and the late Preston Chavous for information about the Lower Suwannee; to Junius M. Downing for Dixie County history leads; to Suwannee River Water Management District for use of their river maps; to the Robin Harper family, to the Delma Eugene Presley Collection of South Georgia History and Culture, to Marvin Goss of Georgia Southern University and Zach S. Henderson archival library, and to Dr. Karen Cook of the University of Kansas archives Harper Collection for assistance and permissions to use and to publish the Lee Family photograph; to Carol Christiansen, copyright manager at Random House, Inc., for permission to publish the Joseph Campbell quotation; to the University Press of Florida for permission to reprint a passage from Janisse Ray's story "Borderline" in *The Wild Heart of Florida*; to Chelsea Green Publishing Company for permission to reprint excerpts from Janisse Ray's *Pinhook: Finding Wholeness in a Fragmented Land;* to Danny and Kathy Breedlove, our friends, for providing electricity to charge the laptop while we collaborated in remote Appalachian locations; to Dennis Price for geological facts about the Big Shoals; to Dotty Price, yoga instructor, for illuminating the world of serenity that led to this guidebook's creative inspiration; to my twin brother and friend for his humorous stories; to Kelly Broderick, editor of Florida Wildlife Magazine, who showed faith in my early work; to the late coach Louis (Louie) Thompson for his informal history lessons; to John and Gayle Dickert and to Laura Larson for friendship and prayers; to John Dickert for photographic conversions; and to my students for tolerating my passion for this project. Special thanks to Frances Sanders, my fourth grade teacher, for introducing me to the mysteries of Nature and the wonder of poetry; and to Mama and Daddy for revealing to their five children the eternal spectacle of the Spiritual realm, which manifests in water and waves.

Table of Contents

Dedication iii

Acknowledgements iii

Preface 1

The purpose of this historical
river guidebook is to 5

Introduction:
Meet the River Guide 6

Preparing to Canoe Camp
on the River 12
    Best Months for River Camping 12
    Paddle Time Estimation 12
    Water Levels Defined as Gauged at White Springs
    Use on the Upper Suwannee 12
    Information for Checking Water Levels 12
    Directional Definition 12
    Important Contacts 13
    Distances Between Canoe/Boat Launches on the Suwannee River ... 13
  What Every Paddler Needs to Pack for Extended River Excursions 14
    Gear List 14
    Optional Items 15
    Cooking Utensils and Tools 15
    Menu Suggestions 15
    Packing the Ice Chest 16
    How to Load a Canoe for River Camping 16

Navigation Permit and Suggestions 17
  Important Contacts 17
  Navigation 17
  Using a Compass or a GPS System 18
  Portage 18
  Weather 18

Tips for Choosing a Campsite 19
   Protect the Wilderness with
   Environmentally Sound Practices 19

Tips for Building a Campfire 21

Section One Map 23
   Navigation Warnings 24
   Camping Information 24
   Topography 24
   Wildlife Spotted 24
   Points of Interest 24
   Billy's Island: Named After the Famous Seminole Indian Billy Bowlegs 29
   Stephen C. Foster Boat Launch and Sill: Paddling the Okefenokee Swamp 31
      Tips for Paddlers 33
      Information for Paddling Over the Sill: History of the Sill 33
   Canoe Camping on the Legendary Suwannee River: A Narrative 36
   Lem Griffis Fish Camp: Stay Here for a Small Fee 41
   Suwannee River Visitor's Center Interactive Display
   Revives Swamp/River History: Telling Stories of the Past 48
   The Legendary Suwannee River Whispers Echoes from History 50
   Bob's Bear Encounter: Somewhere near Fargo, Georgia 55

Section Two Map 59
   Navigation Warnings 60
   Camping Information 60
   Topography 60
   Wildlife Spotted 61
   Points of Interest 61
   Early Pioneers of the Okefenokee and the Suwannee River Basin 64
   Turpentine Camps and the Longleaf Pine Forests 66
   Fishing on the Suwannee 69
   The American Alligator: Prehistoric Creatures on the Suwannee River 72
   Live Oaks 75
   Bizarre, Unusual Wildlife Stories from Randy Smith,
   Avid North Florida Outdoorsman 77

Section Three Map 79

Navigation Warnings 80
Camping Information 80
Topography 80
Wildlife Spotted 81
Points of Interest 81
Restocking Supplies 81
Big Shoals: Only Class III Rapid in Florida 85
White Springs: Ancient Gathering Place for Native Americans
and Posh Resort Town in Late 1800s – Early 1900s 88
Stephen Collins Foster Folk Culture Center:
Songwriter's Historical Contributions Honored 94
Wall Murals: Johnny Dame's Nature Depictions 99
The Alligator-Snapping Turtle:
"Dinosaur of the Turtle World" Makes the Suwannee Home 107

Section Four Map 109
Navigation Warnings 110
Camping Information 110
Topography 110
Wildlife Spotted 111
Points of Interest 111
Restocking Supplies 111
An Experimental Dam at Suwannee Spring: Pilings Still Visible 116
Suwannee Spring:
War Fort, Popular Resort Location—Limestone Walls Remain 118
Suwannee Canoe Outpost: Floating Barge 127
The Florida Panther: History and Local Sightings 131
The Florida Sheriff's Boys Ranch Located Directly on the Suwannee:
A Good Place to Fill Water Bottles 134
The Alapaha River: A Tributary to the Suwannee 136
The Suwannee River Experience: A Solo Journey at High Water 140
Lime Sink Run: Breathtaking Excursion at Suwannee River State Park 144
Ferry Crossings, Cotton Gin Wheel, Old Stagecoach Road:
Visit Them in Suwannee River State Park 148
Confederate Railroad Bridge and Confederate Earthworks:
Men Died Protecting the Crossing 152
Bustling Trade Center:

Cemetery Marks History in the Suwannee River State Park 156
Steamboats Navigate the Suwannee 160
Drew Mansion at Ellaville: Famous Logging Location 167
Paddlers May Encounter Various Snakes on the Suwannee:
Story of Rattlesnake in Suwannee River State Park 176

Section Five Map 183
   Navigation Warnings 184
   Camping Information 184
   Topography 184
   Wildlife Spotted 184
   Points of Interest 184
   Restocking Supplies 185
   Native Americans on the Suwannee River:
   Ancient Indians and the Later Confederations 188
   Watch for Wild Boar: Ancestors of Hernando de Soto 196
   Dowling Park History:
   Lumber Town, Tourist Attraction, and Christian Retirement Community 199
   Ivey-McIntosh Cemetery 203
   Charles Spring: A Native American Christian Mission Site
   and Bustling Crossing in Pioneer Florida 206
   Converting the Timucua: Christian Missions on the Suwannee River 213
   Modern-Day Baptisms 215

Section Six Map 217
   Navigation Warnings 218
   Camping Information 218
   Topography 218
   Wildlife Spotted 218
   Points of Interest 218
   Restocking Supplies 219
   Hal Adams Bridge: First Suspension Bridge in Florida 223
   Irvine Ferry 225
   Old Drew Bridge (Some Call the Ghost Bridge):
   Abandoned in 1920s 226
   Peacock Springs: Where Native American Cultures,
   Pioneer Families, and Cave Divers Congregated 228

United States Army Forts Built on the Suwannee River:
Removal Declaration Causes Native American Retaliation 231

The Early Logging Industry in North Florida:
How Area Rivers Played a Role 234

Troy Spring: Captain Tucker's Steamship, the Madison, Rests Here 238

Little River Springs 240

Section Seven Map 241
    Navigation Warnings 242
    Camping Information 242
    Topography 242
    Wildlife Spotted 242
    Points of Interest 243
    Restocking Supplies 243
    Branford's Ivey Park: Named for Steamboat Captain 248
    Swamp Cabbage: Florida's Tree, Southern Savior, and Today a Delicacy 250
    450-Year-Old Dugout Canoe Pulled from River Near Confluence
    of the Suwannee and Santa Fe Rivers: An Unconfirmed Find 255
    Hatch Bend: Settlers Versus Native Americans 258
    Santa Fe River Major Tributary: Inspiration for Coleridge's Famous Poem 259
    The Rock Bluff Ferry: Often Called the "Free Ferry" 262
    Prehistoric Fish, Eight Feet, 200 Pounds: Swimming Under Canoe! 264

Section Eight Map 267
    Navigation Warnings 268
    Camping Information 268
    Topography 268
    Wildlife Spotted 268
    Points of Interest 269
    Restocking Supplies 269
    Hart Springs: Enjoy Nature Trails and Camping 271
    Seminoles on the Suwannee River: History Discovered at Old Town 273
    Myths of the Southeastern Native American Tribes 281
        From a Creek Myth 281
        From many southeastern tribes 282
        From the Cherokee 282
    Underwater Archaeological Preserve: Steamship Abandoned in 1922 284

Fanning Spring State Park: Once a Paleo-Indian Gathering Place,
Fort Location, Ferry and Steamboat Landing, Tourist Attraction,
and Manatee Refuge 285
A Seminole Indian Village Named Tallahascotte 292
The Loggerhead Musk Turtle: A Prodigious Climber 293
Muskogean Tribes Merge with Escaped Plantation Slaves:
Black Seminoles on the Lower Suwannee 295

Section Nine Map 297
   Navigation Warnings 298
   Camping Information 298
   Topography 299
   Wildlife Spotted 300
   Points of Interest 301
   At River's End 302
   Manatee Springs: Gulf Sturgeon and Manatees 304
   Fowler's Bluff and Pirate's Treasure 307
   Pirate's Treasure and a Ghost Story:
   Unconfirmed Tales of the Suwannee River Basin 311
   When the "Lazy" River Rises: The Mighty Suwannee Turns Deadly 315
   Pollution on the Suwannee River: The Human Toll 319
   Fragmentation and Wholeness: Isolation and Community 321

Graham's Outdoor Kitchen:
Recipes for Camp Cooking 325

Boat Ramp and Launches 335
   Upper Suwannee River 335
   Lower Suwannee River 337

Bibliography 341

About the Authors 349
   Rose Knox 349
   Graham Schorb 350

Preface

This paddler's guide chronicles one of America's most legendary rivers. However, the guidebook covers more than directional information, topography, and wildlife of the Suwannee River and basin. Instead, it takes an historical glimpse at the "River of Deer" from the perspective of the varied number of human beings who once occupied the ancient river's corridor.

While paddling the Suwannee's famous tannic currents, consider the Paleo-Indians, who once hunted giant mammoth, colossal land tortoises, and ferocious saber tooth tigers within this basin. Later tribes left evidence in middens and meticulously crafted tools. Those confederations of the Timucua and Apalachee gathered near crystal springs to conduct ceremonial rituals. Then the Spanish arrived. History reveals that

Rivers whisper age-old symphonies of celebration, laughter, sorrow, and death. Lend an ear to the music of rivers to hear humanity's story.

hundreds of suited, armed Spanish soldiers marched through the region somewhere near Charles Spring, eventually establishing Christian missions as they utilized regional springs for Baptismal waters to convert natives into the Christian faith. Also, fantastic tales of pirates and ghosts whisper stories of murder and of buried treasure.

Much later, the mighty Seminole Nation, with iconic warriors like Billy Bowlegs and his Black Seminoles, built expansive villages along these very shores but were violently forced from their lands by government decrees. Later still, powerful rich men began building sawmills and turpentine camps, and as a result, pioneer towns sprung up as the expansive virgin forests were razed to meet the country's demand for lumber. Around the same time, elegant steamships provided entertainment for wealthy tourists. Soon opulent resorts were constructed along the Suwannee, offering big game sportsmen exotic hunting grounds to kill alligators, panthers, and bears. Prominent people like Thomas Edison were drawn to the Suwannee to enjoy such succulent dishes as Suwannee catfish and gopher gumbo. Confederate soldiers, men and boys, spilled blood to protect one of the river's bridges. Pioneer and Confederate cemeteries are testament to those times of trial and hardship.

Today, the river is a recreational wonderland! Paddlers can enjoy scenic views of impressive million-year-old limestone outcroppings of an age-old sea bed, white sand shores, first and second magnitude springs, and centuries-old bald cypress trees. I have been privileged enough to swim in pristine springs, paddle gentle tea-colored currents, camp upon glorious beaches, hold in my hand primordial artifacts, walk where the Spanish and British trod, wonder where French pirates buried chests of gold, stand reverently near native ceremonial mounds and stare somberly over Confederate graves and pioneer cemeteries. Until now, no other book of this kind has been compiled to tell such a cultural history of the river and corridor. The legendary Suwannee River has a story to tell. Are you listening?

Rose Knox

Old Folks at Home
Way down on the Suwanee ribber, far, far away,
Dere's wha my heart is turning ebber,
Dere's wha de old folks stay . . . [1]

—Stephen Collins Foster

Notes
1. Housewright, Wiley. *An Anthology of Music in Early Florida.* Gainesville: University Press of Florida, 1999.

A Paddler's Guide

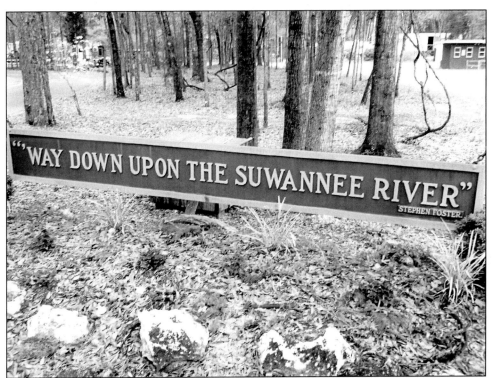

"Old Folks at Home": *Way down on the Suwanee ribber, far, far away, Dere's wha my heart is turning ebber, Dere's wha de old folks stay.* —Stephen Collins Foster

The purpose of this historical river guidebook is to . . .

1. offer practical advice for beginners and experts alike on camping, canoeing, cooking, exploring, and fishing on the Suwannee River.
2. provide fascinating historical information, including archival photos, as well as river stories about the Suwannee. We give tips on how paddlers may explore such sites from the river.
3. reveal the location and information about springs and creeks along the Suwannee.
4. offer comprehensive sections of river maps about camping, river miles, and boat launches.
5. tell paddlers where they may restock supplies and re-fill water bottles.
6. tell paddlers how they may find lodging on extended camping trips upon the Suwannee.
7. warn paddlers of difficult navigation areas such as dangerous shoals and places to portage on the river.
8. provide informative websites on checking water levels.
9. share practical advice on how to prepare for trips. We have included a gear list.
10. give pointers and recipes for outdoor cooking.
11. tell real life river stories and share wildlife photos of the Suwannee.

Place setting and loading the canoe.

12. perpetuate the cultural and historical legacy of the Suwannee.
13. share twenty-five years of wildlife experience, from a guide's perspective, on camping and paddling wilderness areas of North Florida.

The Historic Suwannee River.

Introduction: Meet the River Guide

In the American culture's harried age of omnipresent technologies—such as cell phones, I-pods, Internet, and big-screen plasma television sets—lives a North Florida man who has made a deliberate choice. He resides on the Suwannee River, where hammocks shade tannic waters of a winding river amid ancient limestone embankments. Graham Schorb, a river guide and self-studied naturalist with a pioneering spirit, shunned modern civilization as a boy, when he witnessed his own beloved tropical Florida landscape in Saint Petersburg overrun by developers. Saving money diligently by owning his own lawn and landscaping business, he was able to bring his lifelong dream to full fruition. In the 1980s, he relocated to North Florida close to the banks of the middle Suwannee River. There he lived in a camp tent for approximately six months, while he singly constructed his own rustic home within the piney woods and oak hammocks.

The primitive cabin beckons me to the front door. Shards of flint, partially worked ancient tools, and a large grey hornet's nest are all perfectly arranged on a dust-layered glass table. A beaver stick, elected now as a walking stick, leans against the framed entrance. I enter tentatively, attending to minute details; I feel as if I have stepped through some science fiction time-warped threshold, back to the pioneer Florida of the 1800s. The interior walls are rough-cut lumber, and a tanned deer hide hangs prominently over a modest saffron-colored sofa. Several other deer points adorn the walls. Near a set of antlers is displayed a golden framed image that draws me in. I move closer to examine a face that time captured. The depiction is of an elderly man wearing wire-

Interior view of Graham's cabin.

The unique smokestack is one Graham and Randy Smith built from limestone.

Graham bottle-feeds a day-old pig.

rimmed spectacles; the face next to it is of an innocent maiden. These likenesses are not photographs as we know them today. Instead, they are an early form of photography called daguerreotypes. The gentleman in spectacles is Graham's great-great-great-grandfather John R. Schorb. He was known as America's first traveling photographer. He trekked many states, chronicling the lives of people, including some of the Catawba Indians. A museum at Winthrop University in Rock Hill, South Carolina is dedicated to John R. Schorb's historical, photographic contributions.

Like his ancestor, Graham decidedly chooses to live a life most of us might consider foreign. He, in the words of the famous American poet Robert Frost, has pursued "the road less traveled." Graham lives off of the grid, relying on the sun's energy for electricity. Solar panels capture sunlight that is stored in a small bank of batteries an electrician friend has provided. Books are important to Graham, too; in one room, the weight of books burdens a sagging shelf. Curiously my eyes scan the titles. My philosophy has always been that I can learn a great deal about someone by the books they own. Those works that fill his shelves include such titles as *Five Acres of Independence*, *The Book of Survival,* and *How to Build Your Home in the Woods.*

"It is only by being obliged to think for himself that he acquires that greatness of mind that distinguishes so few." John R. Schorb, 1818-1908. Courtesy of Gina White and Winthrop University's Archival Dacus Library.

    For pleasure, Graham does not follow the desires of the commercially driven masses. He is not obsessed with running up credit cards at the nearest mall, nor does he consume himself with sporting trivia and events. On the contrary, he spends hours tilling, planting, and laboring in his own garden; caring for his livestock; hiking; canoeing; reading; and contemplating. Often he is quietly observing the sacred natural wonders of his North Florida paradise. Here is a man, like Henry David Thoreau, who in this time of fashion trends, commercialism, technological obsession, and greed, finds simple pleasures in the song of a mockingbird or the symphony of a brook.

Graham is a true native Floridian who, much like Thoreau, "went to the woods for he wished to live deliberately, to front only the essential facts of life, and see if he could not learn what it had to teach, and not, when he came to die, discover that he had not lived."[1] Graham will serve as river guide as he leads paddlers down the legendary Suwannee River. The information he offers comes from twenty-five years of his own wilderness experience in North Florida. Ponder his lifestyle. My wish is that every person reading this guidebook will strive to exist (if only for a few days) as Graham lives out his whole austere existence.[2]

As native Floridians, Graham and I envision people finding peace through Thoreauvian contemplation here. We believe, though you leave the river, she never leaves you. We hope to see you on the river!

Notes
1. Thoreau, Henry David. *Walden and Other Writings*. New York, New York: Bantam Books Inc., 1962.
2. Schorb, Graham. Personal interview at his cabin. March 2008.

Preparing to Canoe Camp on the River

Best Months for River Camping

October through April: Because there are fewer mosquitoes, yellow flies, and sand fleas, these months are more conducive for camping.

Paddle Time Estimation

Experienced canoeists can paddle fifteen to twenty miles easily in a day. Depending on water levels, time will vary. In high water, the river runs faster. However, a good formula to use is to calculate that one day equates to fifteen miles down-river.

Water Levels Defined as Gauged at White Springs Use on the Upper Suwannee

High Water: 60 and up—It is advisable to re-schedule at this level because of the danger involved. However, if paddlers decide they must go, they should proceed with great caution. The current is swift, and there are many overhanging branches and strainers.

Medium Water: 52 – 59—Good level for canoeing

Low Water: below 51—Navigation is still possible, but shallow water may present obstacles for canoeists.

Note: The middle Suwannee River beginning at Suwannee River State Park to Branford and the lower Suwannee River to the Gulf have water depths suitable for canoeing.

Information for Checking Water Levels

Suwannee River Management at 1-800-226-1066 or mysuwanneeriver.com to check real time river levels.

Directional Definition

River right and river left are the directions indicated as a canoeist paddles forward down the river.

A Paddler's Guide

Camping on the River: Refer to sectional maps. SRWMD indicates areas of Suwannee River Water Management District where camping is allowed. These areas have rules and alcohol is prohibited. Remember that some places on the river are privately owned. Camping below the one hundred year flood mark is allowed.

Important Contacts

Suwannee River Water Management: Call 1-800-226-1066 to inquire and make reservations about state river camps along the Suwannee River.

Distances Between Canoe/Boat Launches on the Suwannee River

Mileages are near approximations and no GPS device has been used in calculations. Refer to sectional maps for specific information on boat ramps and canoe launches.

Camping on a Suwannee River Beach. Water levels on the Suwannee River rise and fall season after season. Much of the upper river remains undeveloped by Man because of her constant fluctuations.

Campers experience a misty morning near Fargo, Georgia.

What Every Paddler Needs to Pack for Extended River Excursions

Though Graham has paddled the entire river in one long journey, including solo trips, some of his canoeing involves hosting guests for five days and four nights. Anyone who wishes to do the entire river in one trip can find useful information on towns along the river where paddlers may restock supplies and refill water bottles. At various places along the river, we have named towns and included places to restock. Also mentioned are restaurants and places of historical interest in the towns along the Suwannee River.

Gear List

A first aid kit, paddles for each person plus one extra for each canoe, personal flotation device (United States Coast Guard Approved for each person), paddling gloves, whistle attached to personal flotation vest, knee pads, bailer, sponge, ropes tied on each end of the canoe, canoe seats with back, small day pack or fanny pack, compass, duct tape, pain reliever, personal medical supplies (prescriptions, antibiotics, inhaler, etc.), water bottles, flashlight or head lamp, spare batteries, sunglasses, prescription glasses or contact lenses and supplies, tent, ground cloth, a tarp, bungee cords, sturdy string or small pieces of rope, sleeping bag (temperature appropriate), camp pillow or stuff bag to fill with clothing for use as pillow, sleeping pad, waterproof stuff bags for sleeping bag, waterproof stuff sacks for clothing and gear, equipment repair supplies, Leatherman Multi Tool™ sleeping pad, small ax, knife (Swiss Army Knife™ or good folding model), mosquito and insect repellents, water shoes, feminine hygiene products, toilet paper, trowel, toothbrush and toothpaste, hair brush and comb, biodegradable soap, antibacterial gel, pack towel or wash rag, moist towelettes, bandanas, brimmed hat, mosquito head net, rain gear, waterproof breathable jacket, fleece or wool shirt or wool sweater, lightweight camping pants, swim suit, shorts, t-shirt, long-sleeved shirt (lightweight—great for sun protection), gloves for paddling and warmth, sunscreen, sunburn cream, lip balm, camp stool, charged cell phone (cell phones are often **not** operable on the river, but some places can pick up service).

Optional Items

Candle lantern/candles, books, reading glasses, journal and pen, playing cards, binoculars, weather radio, camera and film, waterproof camera bag, fishing gear (must hold a valid fishing license), guide books, snorkeling gear, yoga mat.

Gear List Courtesy of Greg Pflug

Cooking Utensils and Tools

Non-disposable cups, plates, spoons, forks, knives, small cast iron pan, small grill, Dutch oven, heavy gloves for handling items from the fire, camping coffee pot, matches, two lighters, kindling, a can opener, paper towels, Bronner's soap™ for washing dishes, body, clothes, etc.—expect to use a half a gallon of water a day for rinsing, a small towel for drying dishes

Menu Suggestions

Graham prepares many meals on his personal and hosted extended river trips, including bacon, eggs, and homemade biscuits for breakfast. Lunch includes slices of sharp cheese, smoked oysters, crackers, and tuna fish on a tortilla. Dinners include pork chops, chicken, beef stew, and fresh salad, to name a few meals on Graham's outdoor menu. He sometimes brings canned vegetables, which he cooks over the hot ashes of the campfire.

Refer to camp recipes offered in the recipe section, "Graham's Outdoor Kitchen," for more detailed cooking information.

Packing the Ice Chest

For extended river trips, pack the ice chest with block ice. Well before the trip, freeze juice bottles, as they will remain frozen for longer periods. Also freeze all meat and pack it between frozen bottles. Keep the ice chest covered with a tarp and a thick towel to provide shade and insulation. Such a measure will preserve the ice longer. Open the ice chest only when necessary. Another ice chest filled with frozen bottled water and stocked with other drinks is a good idea. Using a second ice chest for drinks and snacks will allow the larger ice chest with meat items to stay frozen longer. Bring along several gallon jugs filled with water for drinking and rinsing.

How to Load a Canoe for River Camping

Place the heaviest items at the bottom center of the canoe. Items that are next in weight go on the top of the heaviest items. The lighter gear is positioned at each end of the canoe. Packing in such a way creates a well-balanced craft. Paddlers may find they need to reposition some objects; placing the heaviest objects at the bottom center is a good rule to follow. In addition, keeping gear under the gunwales of the canoe will contribute to a better center of gravity.

A loaded canoe on a Suwannee River beach.

A Paddler's Guide

Navigation Permit and Suggestions

Important Contacts

To apply for a permit to paddle in the Okefenokee Swamp at Stephen C. Foster State Park in Georgia, call (912) 637-5274.

Navigation

Study the river map, making approximate plans about how many river miles to cover in a day. Be familiar with the river. Know where takeout launches are located in case an outfitter or friend must find you. Always inform loved ones of where you will be putting in upon the river and where you plan to take out. Let them know what day you plan to get off of the river and what day you plan to return home.[1]

Graham applied for a required Sill permit in 1993. Road access is now available to the sill.

Using a Compass or a GPS System

Some paddlers will bring a compass, while others may rely on GPS systems to help them with directions. Others do not bring either. If using these devices, know how to operate them before launching. Graham and Rose have not found it necessary to use a GPS tracking device.[2]

Portage

Only extremely experienced white water paddlers should attempt to run the Class III rapids at Big Shoals near White Springs! However, we advise that all paddlers portage there. There are other shoals in various places on the Suwannee River, and paddlers should proceed with caution in shoal areas. Make sure everyone in the canoe party knows where the dangerous places are located. Also, be certain everyone knows where to get out and portage at Big Shoals Class III rapids. (See specific directions in Section Three Map under Navigation Warnings in this guidebook.) Good communication and planning make for a safe trip.

Weather

Know the extended weather forecast before launching. A weather radio is a good idea for extended trips. Bring extra batteries and keep them in a sealed bag or case.[3]

Notes
1. Chambers, Virgil, and Robert Kauffman. American Canoe Association Inc., Newington, VA.
2. Ibid.
3. Ibid.

A Paddler's Guide

Tips for Choosing a Campsite

Important Reminder: Always pull each canoe up high upon beaches or embankments and/or firmly tether the craft with ropes. The river current may take the canoe down-river if boats are not properly secured!

Canoe campers should begin searching for a campsite several hours before sundown. Ample time allows paddlers plenty of daylight to find a suitable site and set up camp. Early camp setup also offers time enough to prepare a meal over a fire or cook stove. Do not wait until exhaustion sets in or when it is very late in the day. The best campsites are those that are chosen NOT out of desperation or exhaustion. Attempt to pitch a tent on a flat sandy area. If camping under trees, survey them for dead branches, which may break in a wind or a storm and damage the tent or cause personal injury.

Protect the Wilderness with Environmentally Sound Practices

1. Canoe camp with only a few travelers.
2. Limit the nights on one beach.
3. Place tents in ground areas where plant life is not growing.

All responsible campers abide by such a motto.

4. If bathing, use only environmentally sound soap. Graham uses Dr. Bonners'™, which also cleans fabrics and dishes, and which has many other uses. The soap can also be utilized as a substitute for toothpaste.
5. Finding and collecting natural objects may seem like a creative souvenir idea, but remember to leave wilderness areas untouched. Collecting floating driftwood has many drawbacks, because insects, spiders, centipedes and other living organisms make dead wood home. If disturbed, they may exit their habitat and enter your canoe or tent!
6. Camp stoves are an efficient way to conveniently cook.
7. Always cover toilet paper and human waste with six inches of soil.
8. Plan to carry out all trash. Bring several large empty trash bags to house refuse.
9. Pick up trash left by other less courteous campers. Leave the site and the river cleaner than you found it.[1]
10. Avoid playing loud music, which carries long distances over water and is a nuisance to others. Instead, enjoy the sounds of chirping birds, splashes from leaping fish, and soft breezes blowing through branches.

Notes
1. Chambers, Virgil, and Robert Kauffman. American Canoe Association Inc. Newington, VA.

Micah Baxter can escape worldly distractions while camping on the river. Teach your children well.

A Paddler's Guide

Tips for Building a Campfire

- Supplies Needed: matches, fat lighter, small dry twigs and sticks, larger stick pieces to fuel the fire as flames rise, and cut, dry wood.
- When camping on a beach, locate a place where a campfire has already been extinguished. Use the area again instead of creating a new one. The practice will help maintain the natural beauty of the beach or wilderness area.
- Bring only locally cut fire wood to prevent the spread of invasive insects, or search surrounding camp area for dead trees and branches. Use the available dead wood. Never cut down a tree; green wood does not burn well.
- If the weather turns to rain, or if the ground area is wet from a recent downpour, and if finding dry wood is difficult, look in tree bows for dead branches that have fallen and remain trapped in bows. Such suspended wood is often dry enough for starting a small twig/stick fire, as it allows flames to sustain heat enough for other damp wood to burn.
- Build a fire only on sandy places and not near dry leaves or branches.
- Tips for Beginners: Start by putting a very small stack of fat lighter and dry twigs in a pile. Light the stack on the bottom. As the flame begins to rise, add more small twigs; then add incrementally larger sticks and branches as the flame grows hot. Last, add large logs or cut wood. Tend the flame often.
- Do not leave a fire unattended.
- Extinguish all fires before abandonment of any campsite.[1]
- Graham usually allows a fire to burn completely down to ash before he departs. Using his practice, the beach is not littered with wood-charcoal pieces, and the fire area is ready for the next camper.

Notes
1. Chambers, Virgil, and Robert Kauffman. American Canoe Association Inc. Newington, VA.

A campfire is an excellent gathering place for storytelling.

Grilling over an open fire is one of the great, indelible memories awaiting canoe campers.

Section One Map

Stephen C. Foster State Park to Roline Launch
Mile 242.0 – Mile 202.0

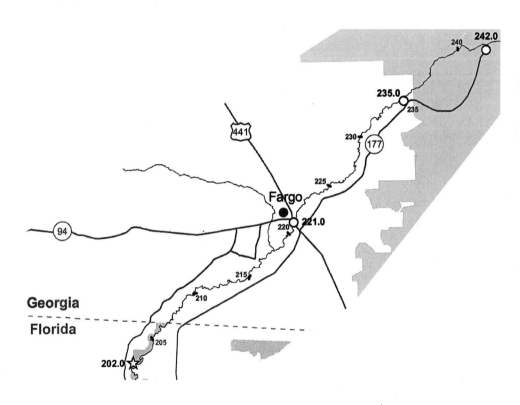

Navigation Warnings

Watch for strainers and low hanging branches at medium to high water levels. Be aware of trees in the center of the river, too. A sill crossing permit is necessary. Contact the Stephen C. Foster State Park for information at (912) 637-5274.

Camping Information

- Camp at Stephen C. Foster State Park for a fee.
- Stephen C. Foster State Park to the Sill: Paddle 4.3 miles; no camping on this stretch.
- The Sill to Lem Griffis Fish Camp: Paddle 2.7 miles; no camping on this stretch.
- Lem Griffis Fish Camp: Camping available for a small fee.
- Suwannee River Visitor's Center at Fargo, Georgia: Day use only; no camping available.
- In low-to-medium water there are various campsites, but they are not in great abundance on Section One. From Lem Griffis to the Florida state line, owners display signs here, and campers should respect private property.

Topography

Some of Section One looks much like the mysterious Okefenokee Swamp. Seek out unusual driftwood along the shore. Notice the century-old bald cypress trees.

Wildlife Spotted

Black bear (rare), white tail deer, Florida panther (rare), grey squirrel, bobcat, grey and red fox, wild boar, striped skunk, river otter, fox squirrel, raccoon, beaver, American alligator, osprey, cormorant, sand hill crane, and a variety of birds, bats, mice, and reptiles.

Points of Interest

The Okefenokee Swamp, the Sill crossing, the Suwannee River Narrows, headwaters of the Suwannee River, Lem Griffis Fish Camp, unusual driftwood, and the Suwannee River Visitor's Center at the launch in Fargo, Georgia.

A Paddler's Guide

River guides Greg Pflug (pictured) and Graham lead a kayak party out from the Okefenokee Swamp marina.

A directional sign helps paddlers navigate Billy's Lake.

Our friend Jim peers from behind a stand of cypress trees in Billy's Lake.

A sign announces the River Narrows and the upcoming sill crossing.

Leaving the refuge, looking back at the directional sign, the party paddles out of the Okefenokee Swamp refuge.

Suwannee River headed to Lem Griffis.

A Paddler's Guide

A maple tree grows out of a bald cypress tree in the passage between Lem Griffis and Fargo, Georgia.

Rail road bridge before Fargo, Georgia.

See the Suwannee River Visitor's Center on river right at Fargo, Georgia.

Highway 441 Bridge at Fargo, Georgia.

White sand beaches below Fargo, Georgia, make good camping sites.

A Florida-Georgia state boundary sign is located on river right before entering Florida.

Billy's Island: Named After the Famous Seminole Indian Billy Bowlegs

Billy's Island and Billy's Lake in the Okefenokee Swamp were named after the legendary Seminole Indian called Billy Bowlegs or Holata Micco. Micco lived in the Okefenokee Swamp with his tribe in the early eighteen hundreds. At first he was friendly with white settlers, learning their ways and even their language. In fact, he was extremely proud of his ability to sign his own name in the white man's language. However, he began to realize that the white man could eventually decimate his tribe's way of life, so he took revenge with raids on white settlers.

General Charles Floyd of the United States Army penetrated the Okefenokee Swamp, marching his troops to Billy's Island in an attempt to capture and remove Micco from the swamp. However, Micco had earlier fled the Okefenokee.[1] He and his tribe members were driven south, and in 1858 he finally surrendered along with 123 of his followers. He was exiled permanently to Oklahoma.[2]

Notes

1. Russell, Franklin. The Okefenokee Swamp: The American Wilderness. Alexandria: Time-Life Books Inc., 1973.
2. Morris, Theodore, and Jerald T. Milanich. *Florida's Lost Tribes*. Gainesville: University Press of Florida, 2004.

Holata Micco, a brave Seminole warrior, lived in the Okefenokee Swamp. Billy's Lake and Billy's Island were named after his American name of Billy Bowlegs. Micco and his followers were driven from the Okefenokee Swamp by the United States Army. Seminole Indian history chronicled later gives details of Bowlegs' relocation to the Suwannee River. Pictured above is Billy's Lake in the Okefenokee Swamp.

Stephen C. Foster Boat Launch and Sill: Paddling the Okefenokee Swamp

Motionless water sends mist from dark depths. On black nights, snakes find cover hiding in tangles of root systems. Confident alligators await unsuspecting prey beneath shadows cast by Spanish moss. Such eerie descriptions of impenetrable swamplands often fill people with intrigue and adventure. Paddling in the Okefenokee Swamp feels like going back in time to a primordial past! For those who love dark forests, voracious reptiles, and stillness, the swamp, like an ancient Greek siren, will call you to her.

The one-of-a-kind wetland was named "quivering earth" or "the land of the trembling earth" by Native Americans. The spectacular Okefenokee Swamp encompasses a half a million acres, and the name "trembling, or quivering earth," is a reference to floating peat, which will tremble if disturbed. Known as one of the nation's most fascinating eco-systems, no other topographical area like it exists in the world! The Okefenokee National Refuge is a 438,000-acre preserve established in 1936. In 1974, the interior 353,981 acres was designated as a national wilderness site to ensure the protection of such a fragile eco-system. Spanning thirty-eight miles from north to south and twenty-five miles east to west, the Okefenokee Swamp encompasses approximately 700 square miles and is one of the oldest and most intact freshwater systems in America.[1]

In wilderness, wonders of the swamp elicit gifts, in sights, sounds, and secrets. In spring and summer months, an enthusiastic multitude of frogs brings forth a hallelujah chorus. Their symphony is one to rival any world-class concert at Carnegie Hall. Grunts, those uncontrollable mating calls from bull gators, reverberate from mud banks, then drift through forests as the urgent summons help supplement the frogs' already rhythmic song. Largemouth bass and bream violently attack surface water, disturbing a glass-smooth grand mirror as they gobble writhing insects. Fall months offer mild breezes that drift though a palette of color. In winter months, discover supreme silence.

The swamp has evolved from an ancient past, but the mystery of her birth is still in question by scientists today. However, there are several theories on how the swamp was formed. One idea proposes that it was once a lagoon at the edge of the Atlantic. Some geologists believe the swamp was one of the Carolina Bay depressions. Scientific research to back the theory reveals that a few of the islands in the Okefenokee are remnants of sand ridges, much like southeastern edges of Carolina Bays. Other more recent theories from geologists claim that the swamp depression was formed as a result of the dissolution of limestone. Though no one knows for certain how the Okefenokee evolved, there is often a belief that it is an ancient place, an eternal wetland existing for millions of years. The idea, though curious to some who would like to imagine great dinosaurs foraging for food in such an impenetrable and mysterious place, is greatly misleading. For scientists know that the oldest peats, which lie at the bottom of the lining of the swamp, hold pollen grains that have been preserved for thousands of years by the acid of the water. The telling sign of the oldest of the small grains is not more than seven thousand years old, and reveals that, perhaps, just thousands of years ago, the early American Indians may have been present to see the birth of the Okefenokee. Although the swamp as we know it today is relatively young from a geological standpoint, all of the components are very old; the processes that have formed the Okefenokee wetland are ancient beyond our conception.

The history of human beings within the swamp is enveloped with rich, compelling stories; some include tales of how the Seminole Nation fought intrusion by ever-encroaching white pioneers as they fled raids conducted by the American government. Other stories tell of the rice farming era of the 1830s, when African slaves worked watery swamp plantations. As the nation's call for lumber increased, lumber companies began hiring loggers during the 1850s to the 1930s. These labor forces worked upon thousands of mucky acres, harvesting grand cypress trees. Paddlers can still see the forlorn crowd of stumps—those abandoned trees truncated by Man's need for ever more lumber.

Many early accounts have been written about the Okefenokee Swamp. For instance, people in the 1700s gained information about the Okefenokee from William Bartram, the Philadelphia naturalist. Because of Bartram's sensory descriptions, they thought of the Okefenokee as a place of fear and of death. Others, such as Oliver Goldsmith in his work *The Deserted Village*, wrote that the Okefenokee was a place "where the dark scorpion gathers death around . . . where birds forget to sing . . . where crouching tigers await their hapless prey."[2] And to those early Georgia pioneers, the swamp's elusive mystery must have held a great fascination while conjuring for them inconsolable fears. Francis Harper, the noted naturalist, entered the swamp in 1912. He lived among the swampers, and his colorful journals reveal how isolation created a rich cultural heritage, encompassing gator hunters, ballad singers, swamp philosophers, fiddlers, hollerers, and prognosticators.

The vastness of the swamp's desolation intrigues and horrifies tourists even today, just as the wetlands did when those early naturalists and writers explored, then wrote to speak of her wildness. Perhaps such duality of emotion is what compels thousands to visit the swamp each year. As Megan Kate Nelson reveals in her book *Trembling Earth*, "Through labyrinthine waterways, oppressive humidity, or mosquito bites, I can understand why it is so hard to love a swamp."[3]

Yet, the swamp allows people to commune with Eternal wisdom; the great swamp's stillness gives us interconnectivity with Nature. Other writers illustrate that point. For example, in his book *Okefenokee*, George W. Folkerts contemplates, "There is wisdom in the sounds of wild places. In our times, this knowledge is more vital than ever before. . . . There are comprehensions here beyond comprehension because they come from the primal places of nature and speak to the ancient within us. Listen for the lessons that the Swamp can teach."[4]

When paddling in the Okefenokee, lend an ear for the gentle voice of the siren as her message rises from obscure depths. Perhaps between paddle strokes, you may encounter her beckoning song.

Tips for Paddlers

A paddler may happen upon numerous thrilling wildlife opportunities in the magnificent swampland. Be on the lookout for American alligators. They congregate on downed logs, embankments, and hide in bogs as they are actively moving, swimming, seeking sustenance, or finding mates; however, they are most active in summer and spring months. Also, search out other wildlife such as frogs, snakes, and a variety of birds, including the sand hill crane. In the mysterious mist of the morning, look for dew-covered petals of a variety of spectacular wildflowers like the pitcher plant.[5] For a fascinating study of the swamp, see *Okefenokee,* George W. Folkerts' book of text and photographs.

Information for Paddling Over the Sill: History of the Sill

To cross over the sill located in the southwestern portion of the swamp, a permit is required for canoes and kayaks. Included in this guidebook is information on contacting the Stephen C. Foster Park for a permit; refer to the section "Navigation Permit and Suggestions." Paddlers will begin at Stephen C. Foster boat launch in Georgia. After traveling approximately four miles, see the large man-made structure. The sill, which was begun in 1950 and completed in 1962, was created for several reasons, all considered beneficial. It was once believed that fire burned out peat, which dammed the Okefenokee near where her waters flow out into the Suwannee River. To correct the problem, scientists surmised that the sill could be built to copy the effects of the peat masses. Yet another reason for the sill was that if the levels of water could stay high enough, no large fires could burn. At that time, humans did not realize that fire was significant in preserving natural eco-systems. With people living in the swamp, the fear of a wildfire consuming their world was enormous.

Other ideas for building a sill were that with more water, there would be an abundance of fish. Any time Man attempts to change a natural place, the results are not always positive. On the contrary, they usually render disastrous consequences. The damages caused by the sill are many, such as unnatural fluctuation, which compromises indigenous plant growth but promotes invasive, thriving plants. Some experts believe the ill effects of the sill may not be apparent for a hundred years.[6]

One of the places where Graham often encounters a multitude of alligators is upon the banks adjacent to the sill.

Notes

1. U.S. Fish & Wildlife Service. "Okefenokee National Wildlife Refuge." http://www.fws.gov/okefenokee/
2. Folkerts, George W. *Okefenokee.* Jackson: University Press of Mississippi; 2002.
3. Nelson, Megan Kate. *Trembling Earth: A Cultural History of the Okefenokee Swamp.* Athens: University of Georgia Press; 1972.
4. Folkerts, George W., *Okefenokee.*
5. Ibid.
6. Ibid.

Suggested Reading

The following titles will provide a more comprehensive study concerning subjects of Native Americans, early pioneers, and the Suwannee Canal Company.

Indians in the Okefenokee: The History and Prehistory by C. T. Trowell

Exploring the Okefenokee: Letters and Diaries from the Indian Wars, 1836-1842 by C. T. Trowell

Okefenokee Album by Francis Harper and Delma Presley

Jackson's Folly: The Suwannee Canal Company in the Okefenokee Swamp by C.T. Trowell, with artwork and maps by the author

The Sill channel.

Paddlers will need a permit to cross the Sill.

Canoe Camping on the Legendary Suwannee River: A Narrative

Fall leaves have donned shades of yellow, apricot, and plum. The season is mid-November in the South, a much-loved time in this neck of the woods. The first major cold front has finally pushed through the region, making conditions ideal for canoe camping. November through April is prime season for Southern adventures, and today the chill enlivens us as we load camp gear. I turn to gaze for a moment at dawn's mist rising from the glass-like surface waters of the Suwannee River. It looks like steam curling above black coffee. Days like this are what bring us to these legendary currents.

Immortalized by Stephen Collins Foster, the nineteenth century songwriter, the Suwannee River offers canoe campers a multitude of Nature experiences. Some come to paddle the 242 miles in one trip, while others choose to spend a week or so upon these shores. The river has hundreds of springs and several major tributaries. There are sharp shoals, hardwood forests, limestone walls, and glorious beaches; the river basin is a geological wonder! Many types of animals call the Suwannee home, including the black bear and the Florida panther. Culturally and historically, the Suwannee has witnessed compelling, often tragic stories of human occupation and navigation on her ancient currents. The past perpetuates tales and legends, but it is the beauty of her corridor and basin that still summons people today to her banks. For these reasons, people from all over the world come to the Suwannee.

Graham and I, with two camp dogs Marley and River, have made our way from North Florida to South Georgia, our destination, the locally famous Lem Griffis Fish Camp. The Griffis family can trace their ancestry to early Georgia pioneers; the camp has been open since the early 1900s. Our trip starts here at the headwaters of the Suwannee, where currents flow out of the vast wilderness of the Okefenokee Swamp. After securing gear and supplies, we launch from the Lem Griffis ramp. The brisk current takes hold of our loaded canoe. What an exhilarating moment! Though Graham and I love paddling numerous rivers in the southeast, what we especially like about the upper Suwannee River is her unique topography. We have done our homework on the internet, as always, and checked the water levels first! Though the Suwannee winds 242 miles through various counties and different terrain, ending at the Gulf of Mexico, the upper portion resembles the lush appearance of the adjacent Okefenokee Swamp. Bald cypress trees thrive along the river's bank, and tannic acid produced by their roots, gives the Suwannee its tea-like color. Soon after launching, we see one century-old cypress tree growing in the middle of the Suwannee, just down-river from where we started. Each extended branch is draped in Spanish moss, and the gray cover of epiphyte cloaks the tree, creating a primordial look. The same thick blanket envelopes most of the hardwood forest around us. Visitors often are charmed by the mystic appearance of moss, for it has a way of conjuring images of the romanticized deep South. Soon we are moving in the current. Along the low shoreline, I notice strangely shaped driftwood contorted in fantastic shapes.

Suddenly something up ahead captures both dogs' attention. We look on river left to see what might be breaking the smooth surface-water and creating a small wake. Paddling closer, we catch a glimpse of a monstrous American alligator! We think it must be ten to twelve feet long! As in the swamp, large alligators are prolific on the Suwannee and can often be seen basking on logs or swimming on the surface of the river. Especially observant paddlers might spy one. We know, too, that we need to watch our passengers, two brown and tan Chihuahuas, keeping them far from the Suwannee's edge. Dogs will attract a hungry alligator! But we feel lucky to have seen such a large creature.

Essential to all of us is our understanding of wildness. The river nudges me back to that idea. Coming here is like discovering an elemental truth. Graham and I believe in this truth. It has moved us both since childhood. That sort of internal quest—for something still, wild, immense, and immeasurable—draws us to the upper Suwannee River. Anyone who has spent time in wild places knows that the natural world is not a quiet place, either. The early morning chatter of kingfishers, cardinals, finches, mockingbirds, crows, and hawks explodes in a chorus of varied pitches and calls. A kingfisher is especially loud today as it takes flight, forging ahead of us, fussing as it dips over the corridor. Such music makes us calm, in contrast to sounds of a mechanized world.

A November breeze picks up and sweeps over the river; miniscule ripples appear. Then through branches of tupelo, cypress, hickory, and maple, sounds from rustling leaves, like a mother's prayer, reach us. A blast of air carries flurries of multi-colored leaves downward as they surf overhead, eventually landing in tannic waters. Paddling against wind, we soon come up on root systems of tupelo trees spectacularly adorned with green, yellow, and rust-colored leaves. Their undulating roots sprawl over the riverbank like a patchwork of snakes as soft wind turns each leaf into a rattling tambourine. Later, we stop to take pictures of four-foot cypress knees that line the left bank. They remind me of C.S. Lewis's mystical beings, frozen in time by some enraged forest nymph. Rarely have I seen cypress roots so tall! After paddling for a few hours, we stop to take a break on a beach. Sand beaches are abundant on the Suwannee River in low to medium river levels, and they are grand places to stop for a rest, to eat lunch, or to camp.

Snacking on apples and cheese, we hear rustling behind us. Beneath the shade of long leaf pines is a dense thicket. The noise, whatever it is, moves closer to the beach—still within the palmetto scrub. Finally, we see a large raccoon. Today she is alone. But there have been times when I have seen one like her with four clumsy babies lumbering behind. We watch her scurry away; then we launch the canoe again. Graham says we have paddled at least ten miles in four hours. Our plan is to camp below the launch at Fargo, Georgia. Near there are a few flat beaches, ideal for camping. Fargo is approximately fourteen miles from Lem Griffis Fish Camp, our original launch site.

During our trip, we have seen a few trickling tributaries and watched swallow tail kites soar. Soon, we come up on a nice camp area. The beach lures us after a long day on the river. I get out, pulling the canoe up to shore. Graham exits, firmly securing our canoe as we begin unloading gear. He sets up camp, while I explore the nearby hardwood forest. My mission: getting dry twigs, sticks, and downed logs to make a camp and cook fire. I think deliberately about each step, though, because diamondback rattlers are sometimes still moving. We have a few hours before Graham makes dinner, so we set camp chairs facing the current of the river as we breathe in the chill of mid-November. There are no hungry mosquitoes to swat! The lazy movement of water mesmerizes us.

A shadow of an airborne bird appears on the beach, breaking our hypnotic state. Graham and I look up, and we spy a great blue heron in flight. The scene reminds me of something I read once in a book by Marjorie Kinnan Rawlings. We are awed by the bird's four-foot wing span; then we hear the flapping from great wings as the bird flies over. The sound grows faint as the heron becomes a speck on the horizon. Growing quiet, we linger awhile near the river's edge. I am not sure how much time passes, but we spend a long time just gazing and soaking in wonders at the river's shoreline. Soon pre-dusk silence is broken by loud splashes. To our surprise, a creature's furry head pops above the surface. Graham whispers, "Rosie, look! There is an otter!" The little critter splashes, dives, and resurfaces. It seems to love to roll playfully from stomach to back. The gentle currents move the otter down to our river bend. When it gets right in front of us, it is intimidated. It dives, disappearing down into the murky depths.

The sun slips lower nearing the horizon. I light the campfire. I allow it to burn for forty-five minutes or so, until flames produce red-hot coals. Graham takes four of his own home-raised pork chops from an ice chest. From a box, he removes two foil-wrapped medium-sized Idaho potatoes, a can of baked beans, and some bagels. In a while, I hear sizzling over the grill. Enticing aromas of simmering pork fill the air, making my stomach growl like a bear. The potatoes and the can of beans cook over the glowing coals.

The sun is soon a fiery orb, turning the horizon shades of pink, lavender, and orange. The river mocks these colors, presenting a canvas of double images. The sight reminds

Sizzling pork, baked potatoes, and toasted bagels make for a hearty camp dinner.

me of paintings I have admired by Johnny Dame, local artist and friend, whose works are a testimony to his own reverence for the river. As the November day comes to a close, an immeasurable silence settles over the landscape, all the while a peace lingers over us. The colors of the sunset intensify, transforming a once-white canvas beach to hues of pinks and oranges. Graham and I are bathed, literally lit, in a heavenly glow of soft beams.

Dusk conjures stars that peek through a deepening blue sky. As darkness descends, their twinkling lights appear more defined in the heavens, against the night's vast backdrop. A full moon crawls high above pines, casting lavender shades over the Suwannee River as we take our first bite. Mouth-watering grilled pork, grilled over an open flame, fuels our bodies for tomorrow's adventure. Tonight, we look forward to sleeping under a sky lit by billions of stars as we dream of the river.

Bathed in soft beams, the sky and the river are illumined by multicolored splashes of orange and lavender.

Lem Griffis Fish Camp: Stay Here for a Small Fee

Far in the backwoods of South Georgia, nestled in shadows of seemingly endless pine forests, is an old fish camp. Ideal for canoe-campers intent on extended excursions, the launch lies just northeast of Fargo, near the boundary line of the Okefenokee Refuge. Lem Griffis Fish Camp, owned by the Griffis family, has been in operation since the 1930s.

On a shuttle trip to take three European paddlers to the camp launch, Graham and I unexpectedly met Al and Dot Griffis. Al happened to be standing in his yard as we were leaving the camp, so I grabbed my field notepad, climbed from the van, and asked if I could talk to him about the swamp. In true Southern hospitable fashion, he and his wife graciously invited us, total strangers, into their humble home. Dot made iced tea as we chatted a few moments, talking about nearby towns. It did not take long for Dot to realize that I was the niece of Gladys Raulerson. My own Aunt Gladys had been in a quilting circle with Dot for many years over in Fargo, Georgia. Talk about a small world!

See the old sign at Lem Griffis river launch on river left.

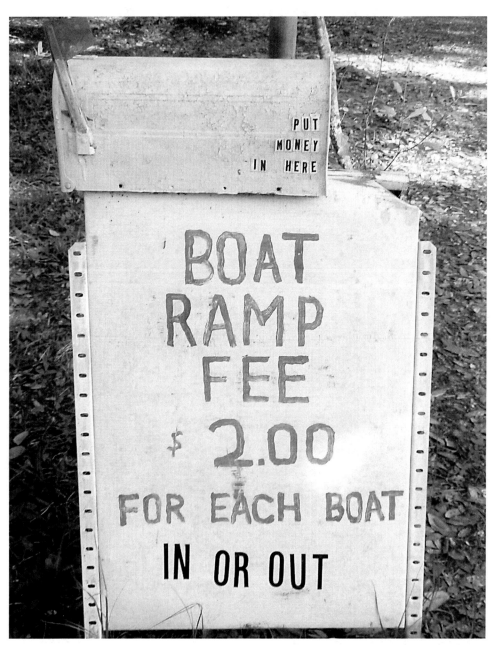
Self-service pay box.

Rustic camp room.

Al soon began telling us stories. The first one was about his own father, who before the 1930s often guided writers into the Okefenokee Swamp. One such man was A.H. Wright; he authored several books, including *Our Georgia Florida Frontier: The Okefenokee Swamp, Its History and Cartography*. Other writers for National Geographic Magazine found themselves drawn here as they recorded for the world the dark, hidden mysteries, stories, yarns, and legends of the mystical Okefenokee Swamp.

Al, a taxidermist, had displays of his handicraft around the quaint brown-paneled living room. Creatures big and small ominously stared down at us, including a white-tail deer, a mountain goat, and a black bear. Several wild ducks were suspended in flight, while a screech owl peered down from a small branch perch. When I inquired of Al about bass fishing in the swamp, he replied, "Bass fishing has not been good in recent years because of the acidity in the water. You see, the swamp usually burns about every twenty-five years, but there have been no significant fires here for fifty years. No burning means more acid in the water. Acidity keeps bass from spawning."

Al then relayed a brief history of the area for us. He said that up-river from the put-in at Lem Griffis launch, there was once a busy stagecoach crossing during the Georgia pioneering era. The crossing was ideal, for it provided one of the shallowest crossings on the river. Once called Lodeaver, the way to find the old pioneer crossing today is to look for the big sandbar up-river from Lem Griffis Fish Camp launch. Later, the Mixons, a family among Al's ancestors, built and operated the Mixon's Ferry. Here, stagecoaches loaded upon the small barge as a man would pole them across the Suwannee River. The horses would then swim the distance. Dot added that Al's grandmother Elizabeth once lived in a log cabin on the very spot. She would often feed and lodge passing travelers for the night. The lone, secluded forest of today was once a well-traveled place in the early days of pioneer Georgia.

Before we departed, Al got up and walked into another room. He brought back with him a stuffed snake, which he proudly set on the heavy oak coffee table before us. He called the object a "mutant diamond-back rattler." On the snake's back, there were no markings. Al allowed us to examine the strange reptile for a moment. Then he remarked, "Many people thought the snake was the offspring of a rattlesnake and a moccasin. No one I asked could figure it out! So I finally sent it to a herpetologist at Florida State University, and by identifying the jawbone, the scientist determined the thing was a diamond back rattler."[1]

Lem Griffis Fish Camp offers paddlers tent spaces and very rustic pole sheds. The sheds have cement floors. Also, there are picnic tables and the bathrooms are equipped with hot well-water showers. Launch at the Griffis place for a nominal honor-system fee. The put-in is where many paddlers begin extended journeys down the Suwannee River. Because the camp is adjacent to the Okefenokee Swamp, the topography looks much like the swamp itself.

At the boat ramp at Lem Griffis, the current flows swiftly amid low hanging tupelo, cypress, and maple branches. Be aware of fallen trees, sometimes imbedded in mud, which extend upward from the river's surface like ancient swords made for impaling. Such obstacles are strainers, and they can become a bit dangerous for some paddlers. A story from a camping trip will illustrate this point. Once, while on a guided trip with a family from Europe, Graham told a story of how a loaded canoe tipped in brisk-moving current. "My canoe party had not been in the dark water five minutes before the flowing river took a woman in her kayak straight into a strainer. As she struggled to maneuver her kayak back into the open water, her teenage son and her husband, in their fully loaded canoe, turned to look back at her as they attempted to assess her dilemma. When they glanced behind them, the current moved their craft directly into a century old bald cypress tree that was growing in the midst of the river. The woman was able to get out of the situation and away from the strainer; however, her husband and her son were not as lucky. They reacted by shifting their weight too fast. Both

A Paddler's Guide

Al Griffis recounts a strange tale about a "mutant" snake.

ended up in the water. While I gave instructions on how the two could best get the incoming water out of the canoe, I was grabbing bobbing cans, bags, and other supplies for our five-day camping trip on the Suwannee."

Seeing that they could not salvage the goods from their canoe, Graham bravely leapt into waist-deep river, scooping up supplies from the obscure, muddy bottom. Then all three men heaved the canoe to the river bank and dumped the water. Afterwards, they had to re-load all gear. Unfortunately, they discovered their eating utensils had been forever lost beneath dark currents. Graham used his resourcefulness, crafting makeshift spoons from twelve-ounce plastic bottles. Those plastic utensils served them well all week during campfire meals.

After the three men were situated back in their canoes and the party had paddled only a mere one hundred yards, a magnificent alligator appeared, slowly cruising across the river ahead of them. Graham remembers the woman had an expression of pure horror on her face. The reason for her ghastly expression was clear. Just a few moments ago, this gator had been swimming very close to her loved ones.[2]

In this unique section of the river, because it retains much of the characteristics of the Okefenokee Swamp, notice the large unusual pieces of driftwood which abound. No other stretch on the river offers such scenery.

Historical Note: There were many skirmishes in the Okefenokee Swamp between the Seminole Indians, the United States Army, and early pioneers. It was in the area of the Lem Griffis Fish Camp in 1836 that Captain William B. North attacked a group of Seminoles. During the conflict, known as "Battle Bay," fourteen Seminoles were killed.[3]

Notes

1. Griffis, Dot and Al. Personal Interview. March, 2008.
2. Schorb, Graham. Personal Interview. April 2008.
3. Folkerts, George W., and Lucian Niemeyer. *Okefenokee.* Jackson: University Press of Mississippi, 2002.

See Lem Giffis Fish Camp on river left.

A Paddler's Guide

Just before the Lem Griffis launch, paddlers may notice a sandy area called Lodeaver. Al Griffis' ancestors, the Mixons, built and operated a ferry at the location, once called Mixon's Ferry.

Rose Knox and Graham Schorb

Suwannee River Visitor's Center Interactive Display Revives Swamp/River History: Telling Stories of the Past

Chants from Native Americans linger in ravines . . . a song of yodeling echoes off cypress groves . . . musket blasts intrude on silence, as a wounded bear breathes a dying grunt; then shouts from hungry pioneers gather 'round . . . spirituals from weary slaves ring throughout rice plantations . . . the Okefenokee Swamp and the Suwannee River whisper tales of humanity's trial. The Suwannee River Visitor's Center in Fargo, Georgia, brings their stories to life.

The center features historical and topographical information about the diverse ecosystems, the wildlife, the cultural past, and the people of the Okefenokee Swamp. Exhibits include a ten-minute high-definition surround-sound nature film that reveals the wonders of the swamp. Visitors can view a re-created swamp scene, with mounted animals of otter, bobcat, black bear, and snakes. Other exhibits feature live frogs and carnivorous plants. In an interactive display, an engaging historical chronicle depicts how people once laboriously survived, making a back-breaking living in the Okefenokee Swamp and on the Suwannee River. Learn of the timber industry and other facts concerning unique local history. A collection of Florida books, including nature guidebooks, is available for purchase. The building of the Visitor's Center is constructed entirely from recycled materials. Many paddlers begin their journey at the Fargo launch

The ecosystem depicts wildlife of the Okefenokee Swamp.

A Paddler's Guide

because no permit is required. Graham starts many of his guided trips at the visitor center location. The center is a day use area and no camping is available.

To contact the Suwannee River Visitor's Center, call (912) 637-5156 or visit online at www.gastateparks.org

A guided party launches at Fargo, Georgia.

The Visitor's Center is constructed with recycled materials. Inside the center, browse a bookstore, view an informative Nature movie, take part in a fascinating interactive display, or marvel at a re-created ecosystem.

Rose Knox and Graham Schorb

The Legendary Suwannee River Whispers Echoes from History

The Suwannee River undulates approximately 242 miles from the Okefenokee Swamp in South Georgia, ending at the Gulf of Mexico in North Florida as it winds through various counties. Immortalized by famous nineteenth-century songwriter Stephen Collins Foster, the Suwannee boasts over 197 springs; 18 are first magnitude, and the only Class III rapid in the state of Florida is located at Big Shoals.[1] Habitat to a variety of wildlife, and undisturbed by dams, the river is one of the most spectacular waterways in America.[2] Once a sacred, bountiful place where Native American villages dotted her banks, today the Suwannee is used by modern people, mostly for recreational pleasure. The 1,100-mile Florida Trail, which parallels the Suwannee's high limestone bluffs for about fifty miles, is a superb hike for backpackers. Cave divers travel from across the globe to explore miles of snakelike watery caverns beneath her springs. Others traverse to the Suwannee River to paddle serene and peaceful currents in shades of spectacular hardwood forests.

The legendary river has served humanity over the ages, from Paleo-Indians who once hunted mastodons here over 10,000 years ago, to the steamboating era of the

A bald cypress tree is pictured here on the upper Suwannee.

A Paddler's Guide

Graham is dwarfed by an age-old cypress tree in the Suwannee River State Park.

1800s, when tons of cotton from area antebellum plantations were transported upon her currents, headed for the Gulf of Mexico. The river was once popular in the heyday of opulent hotels catering to the ultra affluent, and it played a prominent role during the War for Southern Independence, otherwise known as the American Civil War. The Suwannee whispers legends of a varied, compelling past, as her topographical wonders awe and inspire. While paddling tannic currents (the tealike hue is caused by tannic acid produced by cypress roots and decaying vegetation), catapult yourself back in time. Listen for the shrill whistle of a loaded steamship boldly announcing her arrival at a bustling 1800s river landing. Stand over graves at pioneer and Confederate cemeteries, or ponder the once-harried activity at old ferry crossings and river confluences. Imagine pioneer homesteads, escaped plantation slaves' encampments, Black Seminole villages, the transportation of logs and cotton, and turpentine camps upon her shores. Lend an ear for lively dance tunes emanating from a grand piano, or hear jubilant laughter from rich tourists, reverberating from once popular resort locations. Listen for brisk gunfire and strategic war commands, while Seminole braves raid the United States Army forts built on the Suwannee as Andrew Jackson attempts to willfully extract them from their lands, under the government's Indian Removal Act. At Charles Springs, walk the Spanish Trail, once called the Camino Real, where it is believed that Hernando de Soto and his party crossed the Suwannee in the 1500s. The innumerable lost stories of this land, this river, this basin, are now merely a shadow of the past. However, what little remains can give us a glimpse into how the river's significance helped mold the way human beings once lived upon the shores of the Suwannee River.

While paddling by limestone embankments, sand beaches, bubbling creeks, and springs within breathtaking forests, think of the people who once lived upon these shores.

As the Suwannee nears the Gulf of Mexico, the river widens and slows significantly. The high limestone embankments, so prevalent up river, are virtually nonexistent. Approximately twenty-six miles from the mouth, tidal flows influence the Suwannee's current; about five miles from the Gulf, the river turns brackish.[3] The Suwannee River has been called various names and has had numerous spellings. Several theories tell how the legendary river was originally named. One example is that Suwannee is the same name of a village in Gwinnett County, Georgia, which was once the location of a Cherokee Indian town, termed Suwani. The Cherokees claim that the village name has its origins from the Creek Indian word Suwani, which translates to echo.

Also named "River of Deer" by Hernando de Soto, historians and archaeologists believe de Soto and his army crossed over her waters in 1539, somewhere in the vicinity

The white-tailed deer was considered sacred to Native American tribes.

of Charles Springs. In the seventeenth century, the Franciscan mission, once located near Charles Springs, was called San Juan de Guacara, meaning Saint John of the water of many large springs. Later, the mission was destroyed by the British. Origins of the name are sketchy, too. Did the name derive from the Spanish or from the early native peoples? The debate is still unclear; it is unknown if the word Guacara is a Spanish word or if the name originates from the Apalachee or Timucua Indian languages.

In 1774, the Roman Catholics named the river the River Saint Juan Vignoles. Some scholars believe that the Saint Juan name was mispronounced by Indian blacks, calling it San Juan; and as the British heard the black Indians pronounce the word, they interpreted the sounds phonetically as Su-Wan-EE, from the word San Juan de. Yet another name for the Suwannee River comes from a 1769 Thomas Jeffrey map. Those maps name the river the Little Savana, or Carolinean River. Presently, the winding waterway is known all over the world as The Suwannee River, made famous by Stephen Collins Foster in his best remembered folk song, "Old Folks at Home." Some remember the song as "Way Down Upon de Suwanee Ribber."[4] No matter the name or the origin, the Suwannee River has a rich cultural and historical past, and people from all over the world descend upon her shores to enjoy her topographical wonders.

Notes

1. Ceryak, Ron, and David Hornsby. *Springs of the Suwannee River Basin in Florida, Water Resources Special Report 10-98*. Live Oak: Suwannee River Water Management, District Department of Water Resources, 1998.

2. e-movie National Geographic. http://news.nationalgeographic.com/news/2006/10/06 10 - 10suwanee-video.html

3. Ibid.

4. Holmes, Melton, Jr. *Lafayette County History and Heritage*. Mayo: 1973.

This picture reminds me of the song "The river is wide, I cannot get o're, and neither have I wings to fly."

White sand beaches are beautiful to behold and ideal for camping. Water levels of the Suwannee dictate beach availability.

Impressive limestone walls create a marvelous corridor on some sections of the Suwannee River. Many geologists believe the outcroppings may be 20 million years old.

Bob's Bear Encounter: Somewhere near Fargo, Georgia

While spending a day with Graham at the Suwannee Canoe Outpost, I was standing at the boat ramp one afternoon as he chatted with a paddler coming up from the river. The man had just finished an extended camping trip on the Suwannee. Bob, from Pennsylvania, told a remarkable story about an unusual black bear encounter down below Fargo, Georgia.

"One early morning, I heard a commotion in the thick palmettos, across the river from my camp. Minutes later, I saw a black bear. He charged from the woods and on to the beach. The smells from my breakfast fire apparently attracted it to swim across the river. Later, when I went back to the river's edge that morning, I turned around to walk back up to my camp, and that's when I saw a big bear standing by my tent!"

Recounting the story to Graham, Bob said the bear was as tall as Graham (who is six feet three inches tall) and was sniffing a pair of gloves Bob had hung to dry. Immedi-

Black bears were once widely hunted for sport. This 180-pound bear was killed in the Apalachicola National Forest in October 1965. The day before, a 300-plus-pound bear was hunted and killed. Courtesy of State Library and Archives of Florida

ately, Bob quietly slipped into his nearby canoe to marvel at the rare and fascinating animal from the river, where he hoped he was safe from the bear's possible attack. Bob said the bear knocked his tent down, dragged it several yards, and then marched away into the woods with one of Bob's brand new gloves! Though Bob's story sounds unnerving, seeing a black bear is a rare experience.

Bears in Florida are normally black with white markings, though some bears may be brown. Female bears can weigh up to 180 pounds, while males may weigh as much as 300 pounds. They are hardy, secretive, and solitary creatures and roam in densely vegetated areas. Black bears like to swim to keep cool in warmer months. Though they have poor eyesight, they possess a keen sense of smell and hearing. Black bears are rarely spotted in the wild, so Bob's encounter was unique. Finding food is a constant endeavor; they forage, feeding on berries, honey, insects, fruits, nuts, dead carcasses, and hearts of palmetto and cabbage palm. They are most active at night and in the early morning hours. Black bears were once hunted by Native Americans for food and clothing and worshiped as sacred by some Native American cultures.[1]

In recent history, black bears were hunted for sport in Florida National Forests, but are now listed as a threatened or endangered species in Florida. Some estimated 300,000 black bears are left in the United States, approximately 500 to 1000 in Florida.[2]

Black bears at Tallahassee Junior Museum. Courtesy of State Library and Archives of Florida.

A Paddler's Guide

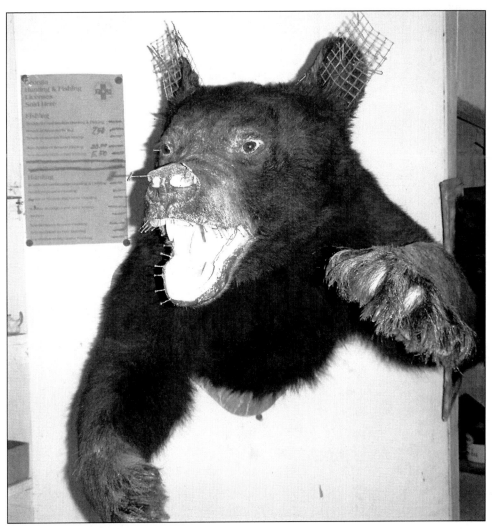

On a visit to Lem Griffis Fish Camp, Al Griffis took Graham on a tour of his taxidermy shop. Hunters of the black bear today must apply for special permits.

Notes

1. Gingerich, Jerry Lee. *Florida's Fabulous Mammals: Their Stories.* Tampa: World Publications, 1999.
2. Defenders of Wildlife. "Black Bear." http://www.defenders.org/

A Paddler's Guide

Section Two Map

Roline launch to Big Shoals launch
Mile 202.0 – 177.1

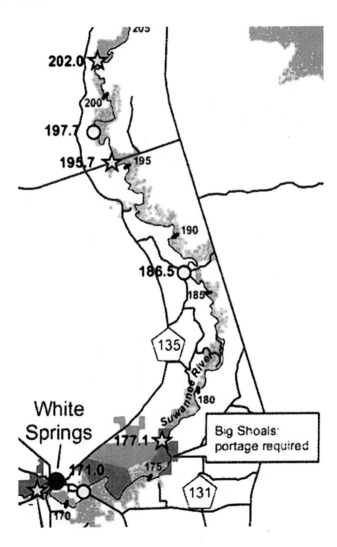

Navigation Warnings

Several small shoals are visible on Section Two during low water levels.

Camping Information

In medium to low water, beach sites can be found. Refer also to Suwannee River Water Management District (SRWMD) public land use information on the sectional map for designated camping areas.

Topography

Take note of unusual tupelo trees growing upon embankments. Tupelos are recognizable by their intricate, complex root systems. Their undulating and snakelike appearance makes the roots quite an anomalous sight. Many extend out on the top of the embankments, making superb subjects for nature photographs. Because of numerous tupelo trees on Section Two, listen for the collective chorus from buzzing bees, especially in late spring. Bees are attracted to the trees' sweet blossoms, and from the attraction they produce tupelo honey, a much sought-after southern delectable. The honey is known not to harden to sugar—as other types of honey do. Look, too, for a few lime-

Look for tupelo trees on Section Two.

stone outcroppings. They are visible in low water levels. Many bald cypress trees, with their roots and knees, line the embankments on both sides of the river. Some of the root systems are about four feet tall. From Tom's Creek to Cone Bridge, the river curves and twists with many dramatic bends.

Wildlife Spotted

Alligators may be spotted. Hunters often discard deer carcasses into the river near the Roline boat launch. For this reason, be on the lookout for numerous large alligators on the stretch of the river. On many occasions, while hosting guided trips or when he has been out for the day fishing on the river, Graham has spotted large alligators. He gives credence to the stories often told about animal carcasses; he calls this section of river "an alligator's buffet."

In June 2008, our canoe and kayak party spotted two alligators between the Roline launch and Highway 6 Bridge. One was approximately three feet long; the other was much larger and was swimming across the river. Also seen that day were five swallow-tail kites, two male pileated woodpeckers, one soft shell turtle, and several brown water snakes. Black bear, gopher tortoises, raccoons, wild hogs, barred owl, a variety of wading birds, white tail deer, and grey squirrels have also been identified.

The water level was low the day of our excursion, at 50.5 as recorded at White Springs. We took a break at the visible small shoals after the old Turner Bridge pilings.

Points of Interest

Tupelo trees, bald cypress, the American alligator, remnants of Turner and Cone Bridges, several creeks, unusual rock formations, many bird sightings, and a variety of wildlife.

Tupelo trees have intricate root systems.

Watch for cypress roots along embankments.

Remnants of Turner Bridge are visible as rusted pilings. They are located four miles downriver from the Roline launch.

A Paddler's Guide

Highway 6 Bridge crosses the Suwannee. The launch is just before the bridge on river right.

Monster Gator at Cone Bridge: About eleven miles downriver from Turner Bridge are remnants of Cone Bridge. On several occasions, Graham has witnessed a very large alligator approximately ten to twelve feet in length in these parts. He is not the only one who has seen such a large reptile here. Johnny Malloy, in his book *A Paddle Through Florida History: From the Swamp to the Keys* (University of Florida Press, 2003), relates sighting an unusually large alligator in the vicinity. His party had stopped for a break at the Cone Road Bridge site when he saw the rusted pilings of what was once the bridge. As he surveyed the area, he happened to look down-river. He then sighted a "monster" gator at least twelve feet in length. The reptile was calm, basking in the sun. Graham suspects he has witnessed the same creature slipping stealthily into the river from the white sand banks. William Bartram, in his work *Travels*, sketched the magnificent beasts as he journeyed through the southeast during the 1700s. Courtesy of State Library and Archives of Florida.

Gopher tortoises make their home in the Suwannee River Basin.

Rose Knox and Graham Schorb

Early Pioneers of the Okefenokee and the Suwannee River Basin

The early Georgia and Florida pioneers of the Okefenokee Swamp and the Suwannee River Basin were faced with daily hardships. In our modern times, we cannot imagine the life they bore, amid oppressive heat and humidity, in an era before air-conditioning; nor can we fathom the fight early settlers must have braved, with hoards of ravenous mosquitoes as these pioneers survived without repellent or screen windows and doors. Their lives, too, were dependent on the river and her rich soil basin.[1] They also often had violent clashes with Native Americans and with people from the North, vying for space and resources. And the wild frontier areas they inhabited were wrought with dangerous natural encounters. Hurricanes; tropical diseases, such as malaria; and life-

Early pioneer families often traveled in caravans using covered wagons. Courtesy of State Library and Archives of Florida.

Two generations of descendants from the Dan Lee family inhabited the Okefenokee Swamp beginning in the 1800s. Dan Lee was the first white settler to build a cabin on Billy's Island. There he farmed a piece of land that produced potatoes, corn, and sugar cane. Fishing, trapping, and hunting supplied additional food for his sixteen children. Of those sixteen, only fourteen survived. In 1913, the descendants posed for a family portrait; they are surrounded by the swamp's bounty. Notice skins of white-tailed deer, skunk, black bear, and raccoons. The Lee's sold the animal hides to supplement the family income.[3] Courtesy of The Robin Harper Family, and the Delma Eugene Presley Collection of South Georgia History and Culture, and Georgia Southern University's Zach S. Henderson Archival Library.

threatening confrontations with indigenous creatures—such as alligators, panthers, black bears, and poisonous snakes—were merely some obstacles indicative of what early white pioneers endured in forging and settling new untamed lands.[2]

Notes:
1. Ste. Claire, Dana. *Cracker: The Cracker Culture in Florida History*. Gainesville: University Press of Florida, 2006.
2. Russell, Franklin. *The Okefenokee Swamp*. The American Wilderness Time-Life Books. Alexandria: Time-Life Books Inc., 1973.
3. Ibid.

Turpentine Camps and the Longleaf Pine Forests

My mama, Lunita Parrish Knox, grew up playing in the wilds of South Georgia, not far from the Okefenokee Swamp. In her seventies before her death, she tape recorded some of her early memories as a keepsake and as a legacy for her children and grandchildren. Those stories chronicle a way of life that seems so foreign and old fashioned to us today. She spoke of attending a one-room schoolhouse and lamented the day her father had to slaughter her pet pig so the family could eat as they struggled to survive in the Great Depression. As a young girl of about six, she sauntered in sublime longleaf pine forests with her father. With only the sheer adoration a small child can have for a dad, mama loved to follow in his footsteps.

"Daddy had pine trees where he would go out in the woods and cut little Vs in them—put little troughs in them—and the sap would go down in a little clay pot, and then he would go out and gather those up and put them in a big barrel and take them to the processing plant, which was about fifteen miles away, over in Statenville. He had a little trailer he would hook up to the back of the car. I remember we had a model-A Ford. It was black, shiny—four doors. Not many people had cars. This was back in the Depression and we did not have a lot."

After church services on Sunday, the neighbors would often come over just to sit in the model-A Ford and marvel at such technology. Her daddy could not afford gasoline to take them on joy rides.

I can imagine her lanky, pencil-thin arms swinging back and forth behind his gangly figure as she played the child's game of stepping inside of his footprints. Often the two would take extended excursions, traipsing over sand pastures, forging through trickling creeks, and lingering in the deep shade of acres of piney woods near the Okefenokee Swamp. Though these splendid journeys seemed like a great adventure for my mama, her father was hard at work checking the longleaf pines for gum resin. He sold the tree's bounty to turpentine camps as a way to make extra money for his family, a wife and three daughters.

Five hundred years ago, the longleaf pines covered more than 90 million acres, flourishing along the southeastern coastal plain from Virginia to Texas and into Florida. Today, only several million acres remain. Most longleaf forests today grow in South Georgia and North Florida. Mama ran amongst the heavy shade and breathed the fresh pine air produced by trees of these incredible forests. She often reminisced about the clay cups that her father attached to the trees. "They called the markings cat faces, and that is just what they looked like." Metal gutters corralled the gum into each cup.

Because times were tough during the Great Depression, the collected resin was sold to naval stores to help her daddy, my grandfather, make ends meet.

Naval stores were a common sight along the Suwannee River and the Suwannee River Basin in the late 1800s to almost the mid 1900s. Often called turpentine camps, thousands of workers, including mostly African Americans, labored to make the turpentine and the by-products which came from the gum resin of the longleaf pines. The "Dipper" was a worker who removed the crude resin from the cup. Then resin was put into wooden barrels, and the barrels in wagons to be pulled by teams of mules and oxen to the turpentine still. There, the distilling process began. Huge kettles were heated over a wood fire, and the gum resin was emptied into the warm vessels. The process produced oil, called spirits of turpentine. The material produced in the still was used in shipbuilding and in the maintaining of ships. Turpentine had many other uses as well. The product was important in most American homes as a solvent for paint and varnish and as a thinner for paint, commonly known as mineral spirits. In the turpentine camps, spirits of turpentine were used in the wash to whiten clothes and as a cleaning agent for floors, silver, furniture, and porcelain. As a medicinal aid, it was used for bug bites, stings, burns, worms, boils, and sore throats.

The turpentine camp was a community in and of itself. Outside law enforcement rarely investigated criminal behavior. Rather, the camp owners settled disputes and

Clay cups were mounted on the longleaf pine in order to collect the gum the tree produced. The cutting on the tree resembled a cat's face. Courtesy State Library and Archives of Florida.

other unlawful events which might arise. The work in the camps was laborious, with the day beginning at four in the morning. Workers received their pay in tokens, and the tokens were then spent in the company store. Prices in the store, however, were intentionally set high, so workers found it virtually impossible to ever get out of debt.[1]

To see a longleaf pine forest today is rare, though some stands do exist in and around the Suwannee River Basin. When I occasionally seek one out, I think of my own mama and her daddy as I ponder the significance that the longleaf pine held for my South Georgia family, ancestors of early area settlers.

Notes
1. Cerulean, Susan, Laura Newton, and Janisse Ray, eds. *Between Two Rivers: Stories From the Red Hills to the Gulf.* Tallahassee: Heart of the Earth and the Red Hills Writer's Project, 2004.

Turpentine camps, also called naval stores, were prevalent in North Florida in the 1800s and early 1900s. Courtesy of State Library and Archives of Florida.

Fishing on the Suwannee

Fishing in lazy currents is a relaxing pastime, and the Suwannee is known by locals as the place to cast a line. Be reminded that Georgia and Florida laws require fishing licenses. Equipment varies according to the person fishing, but some people use a cane pole, while others prefer a rod and reel. With a little luck and patience, you might catch tonight's meal!

Many popular freshwater fish swim these waters. The rare Suwannee River bass, for instance, is a common choice for anglers, and fishing records have been made on the Suwannee River. In fact, the state record was 3.89 pounds and was pulled in from her tannic waters. Another state record was a red-breasted sunfish (red belly) that weighed in at 2.08 pounds; the spotted sunfish was also caught in the Suwannee. That weight holds the state record. Catfish are also a popular choice as the white catfish swims in abundance. On occasion, big channel catfish are caught.[1] Other fish which swim these waters are blue gill, black crappies, pickerel, and a variety of bass, including warmouth, largemouth, and small-mouth bass.

Here are the best methods for fishing in darker waters: Search out shallow flats and areas beside them; look also for shallow creek mouths, at medium to low water levels. Fish prefer places with overhanging scrubs or branches. When fishing for bass in fall months, try using artificial baits, such as Texas rigged worms and spinner baits. The color of bait and season of year are important factors in getting fish motivated to bite. In the Suwannee with its darker waters, experiment with colors of red bug, June bug, and blue or black lures.[2] There is nothing more satisfying than grilling fresh fish over the evening fire! Graham and his friend Randy have eaten many a fresh fish from the bounty provided by the river.

Sometimes fishing is surprising. While on a day trip to the Florida Sheriff's Boys Ranch, Graham and I came upon two young men fishing for catfish. They pulled the same freshwater eel in twice, in a matter of fifteen minutes.

Graham enjoys helping others fish; he is willing to maneuver the canoe for friends and family as he offers advice on places where fish may be hiding. His two nephews from Saint Petersburg, Florida, spend the summer months fishing on the Suwannee. One method they find successful is fishing with brim poles, using yellow or orange top water plugs. Parker and Robby cast the colorful plugs under low-hanging branches, or they search for limestone shelves, which are popular places for fish to hide. With a little patience and casting finesse, a day of fishing may render a scrumptious dinner! Bring heavy duty foil along, and plan to steam fish over hot coals. Fresh cut vegetables may simmer inside the fish packet. Lemon, olive oil, season salt, and butter will enhance flavors. Or pack a cast iron skillet, corn meal, potatoes, and oil to fry up a mess of fish, fried potatoes, and hush puppies.

Notes
1. Royal, Captain Ron. *Fresh It Is. Nature Coastlines.* Nov/Dec 2005.
2. Boning, Charles R. *Florida Rivers.* Sarasota: Pineapple Press, 2007

Randy Smith, lifelong resident of Hamilton County, catches a variety of fish in the Suwannee River.

A Paddler's Guide

Jerry Long catches a bass.

Ten-year-old Robby Schorb has grown up fishing on the Suwannee River. He tries his luck in the summer of 2008, near Roline.

The American Alligator:
Prehistoric Creatures on the Suwannee River

Hundreds of people canoe the Suwannee River every year. Many of those visitors are interested in seeing alligators. The deeper, darker waters of the Suwannee offer obscure visibility, especially in winding sections. People are innately afraid of "black water" and what might be lurking beneath opaque depths. Perhaps the fear stems from some long-nurtured ancestral memory that the human species cannot suppress. After all, the alligator has roamed the earth for at least 65 million years. The age-old reptiles, a direct link to the time of the dinosaur, maneuver gracefully in water, but are somewhat awkward on land; however, they can move at great speeds for short distances and can charge fiercely if threatened.[1] Never be lulled into false security by their size and bulk!

Graham recounts his most memorable alligator encounter. "Once, while paddling in a kayak on the Wakulla River, I came around a river bend and surprised a large mother alligator. I knew that she was most likely nesting, and I know mother alligators can be extremely aggressive if approached. She was not at all happy to see me so close to the beach, and she let me know it. Charging from the upper beach from her nest area (I could hear the sounds of baby alligators) she moved quickly towards my kayak, and plunged into the river, splashing me. The tip of her enormous tail hit the front of my kayak. I guess this was a warning to me; and believe me, I took it seriously! I paddled quickly away from the embankment to distance myself from her nest."

Sighting an American alligator on the Suwannee River is quite probable, especially in the sections from the Okefenokee Swamp to the White Spring area. There seems to be

We spotted an alligator on one of our many short paddling trips on the Suwannee. On this day, the river was high from tropical storm activity. We saw another alligator partly submerged just five minutes later.

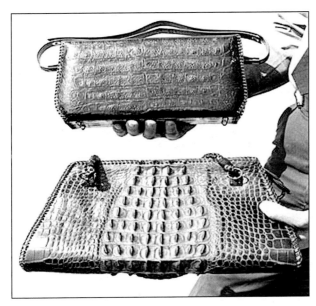

Handbags made from alligator skins. Courtesy of State Library and Archives of Florida.

an abundance of alligators (some very large) on these particular river sections. However, just because a paddler does not see any alligators does not mean that alligators do not see you! On our many river trips, we have seen alligators on all sections of the Suwannee. Some were tiny, while others were enormous!

Because people fear alligators so intensely, many of these reptiles are killed and left simply to rot upon riverbanks. Graham, in his many trips on North Florida rivers, has seen these unfortunate sights. "Once, on the Suwannee, up from the outpost," he recalls, "there was a dead alligator. He had been shot and was floating belly up. His body was completely white and severely bloated."

Such stories are all too common in the region's history. In fact, according to Tracy Revels in her work *Sunshine Paradise: A History of Florida Tourism*, guidebooks written in the late 1800s were intent on attracting rich hunters to Florida. In our day and age of conscious preservation, it is almost unfathomable that hunters sought alligators in lakes, lagoons, and rivers of Florida. Even steamboat passengers often took shots at alligators from atop decks of ships. One gory description describes how adventurous hunter-tourists would blast as many as a dozen alligators at one time. Another account describes how 162 alligators were killed in one afternoon.[2]

Although alligators were once on the endangered species list, Florida now allows limited alligator hunting, only by permit. The permits are necessary to keep numbers from burgeoning, but to also keep laws in place in protecting the alligator population. Man's fear and fascination almost decimated it. Sadly, by the 1940s the American alligator, valued for its meat and skin, was hunted almost to extinction. Today, there exists a varied alligator industry, including medical researchers from the University of Florida, who have discovered a molecular sameness in alligator eyes to that of human eyes. Other industries, such as jewelers, use the hide, bones, teeth, and claws to make necklaces, earrings, bracelets, pins and watchbands. Other products crafted from alligators are belt buckles, paper weights and back scratchers. The heads and feet are sold as souvenir trophies.[3]

Paddle quietly and watch intently to spot an ancient reptilian!

Notes

1. and 3. Strawn, Martha A. *Alligators: Prehistoric Presence in the American Landscape.* Maryland: The Johns Hopkins Press Ltd., 1997.
2. Revels, Tracy J. *Sunshine Paradise: A History of Florida Tourism.* Gainesville: University Press of Florida, 2011.

A LeMoyne lithograph of the Timucua hunting alligators. Le Moyne's depictions were often exaggerated. Courtesy of State Library and Archives of Florida.

Live Oaks

The live oak is a lush and beautiful tree and is visible along the Suwannee River. It is so named because, though it sheds leaves, the branches are never completely bare during fall and winter months. Known for having very hard wood, live oaks were once used to build ships. Some live oaks in the area are at least three hundred years old.[1]

Notes

1. Williams, Winston. *Florida's Fabulous Trees: Their Stories.* Tampa: Worldwide Publications, 1984.

"Live Oak on the Suwannee." Courtesy of Sue Knox.

Live oaks upon an embankment of the middle Suwannee River.

A Paddler's Guide

Bizarre, Unusual Wildlife Stories from Randy Smith, Avid North Florida Outdoorsman

Randy Smith, a third generation Floridian, was born and raised in Hamilton County. An avid outdoorsman, he has worked as a professional hunting guide, contracting his expertise to local quail plantations. He has also been employed for several years at the Suwannee Canoe Outpost on the Suwannee and area rivers. On the front porch of Graham's cabin, he told only a few of his river tales., sharing with us some of his most unusual experiences.

The first story took place in October 2001, when he was canoeing down by Dry Creek, near where the power line crosses over the Suwannee River. On that day, he sighted something very large and quite unusual swimming in dark water. To this day, he is still unsure of what the colossal creature was.

"I was in a canoe with a guy named Pepper John, and up ahead of us on the bend I saw a fish tail come out of the water. It was a forked tail, and I saw that it had a pink outline around the edge. And I'll tell you, I have never seen nothin' like it in my life! The fish came up to the surface, and I could only see about what I think was half of the fish—and half of it was four feet long. Whatever it was, it was huge!" I asked Randy if he thought the fish could have been a sturgeon. "No," was his immediate and definite reply. "It didn't have the armed back of a sturgeon; it had a slick, bluish grey body. Maybe it was a shark."

Sound unbelievable? Randy's bizarre account may ring a bit suspect to some, who vainly think rivers are somehow free from sharks. However, sharks have been known to swim up rivers as far as 100 miles. In an attempt to confirm the validity of Randy's account, I found no record of a shark in the Suwannee River; however, I ran across numerous stories of how people from all over the world have spotted sharks many miles up rivers. Randy's story does not seem unlikely, in view of the fact that when river levels rise, a large shark may very well swim up from the Gulf of Mexico and survive. When water levels recede, shallow waters might make it impossible for a large fish to swim over the sandbars and shoals, thus trapping large ones up-river.

Yet another of Randy's unusual experiences occurred when he was out for the day with Graham and Graham's family. The season was in early June of 2008; they were on the river, about halfway between the Boy's Ranch and Noble's Ferry. As Randy rounded a bend in the river, he spotted a mother deer giving birth to a fawn upon the riverbank. She was nestled under a large, downed live oak branch.

"She saw me," Randy recalls, "but she just laid there. She did not even try to move. When I got past her, she got up in the middle of birthing." Randy said that he thought the fawn was a breach birth and was born dead. The mother deer was fatigued, and that is why she was reluctant to move quickly when she saw Randy round the bend in his canoe.[1]

Notes
1. Smith, Randy. Personal Interview. 28 Aug. 2008.

Randy Smith is an avid outdoorsman. He shares several bizarre stories about the Suwannee River. Loyal river dogs Goldie and Jake are at his side. Randy is also featured in Tim Ohr's book *Florida's Fabulous Canoe and Kayak Trail*. Courtesy Anne Daniels of Denver, North Carolina.

A Paddler's Guide

Section Three Map

Mile 177.1 – Mile 150
Big Shoals Launch to Suwannee Spring Launch
Walking Tour of White Springs: Directions from the River

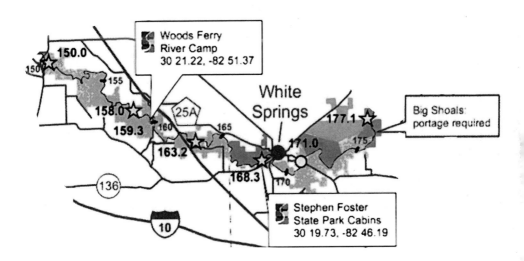

Navigation Warnings

A portage is necessary. Proceed with great caution!

At river mile 177.1, a wooden staircase is on river right. The location is Big Shoals State Park launch, a day-use facility. Less than one mile down-river is Big Shoals, Florida's only white water. Paddlers should begin moving to river left as they listen for the sound of rushing water. (You may not hear rushing water, but stay toward the left.) Before the shoals, look for a white (or possibly brown) round sign located on river left. It signals where to portage. The portage distance is approximately 150 yards. The put-in after the portage may be slick. Use caution when re-entering the river!

Camping Information

Camp areas are visible at the end of the 150-yard portage. Many desirable places to set up camp are there, some directly over the shoals. Campers seeking privacy may want to locate a site back away from the river because the area is well-traveled by nature lovers and paddlers in the fall and spring months.

The Florida Trail runs through the camp and is designated by orange blazes. Be sure to set tents away from the trail. There are also many other places to camp (in low to medium water levels) past White Springs, but few below Big Shoals.

At Big Shoals State Park on river right, and before the Big Shoals, there is no overnight camping. At river mile 168.3 in the Stephen Foster State Park, camping is available with a reservation and a fee. Below Interstate 75 at river mile 159.3 is a river camp at Woods Ferry, located on river left. Contact Suwannee River Water Management in advance to reserve a river camp.

Topography

See Deep Creek on river left above Big Shoals State Park. Later, paddlers will portage the Big Shoals, Florida's only whitewater. Notice swirling designs of frothy water immediately after the Big Shoals. Beyond the Big Shoals is Bell Springs on river left. Four miles down-river from Big Shoals, see Little Shoals. There is no portage required for Little Shoals, but proceed with caution. The Florida Trail crosses Swift Creek by suspension bridge. Below the Interstate 75 Bridges, on river right, is an area known as Camp Branch. There is a unique geological feature called Disappearing Creek. The creek may be accessed on river right, at (approximately) mile 156, where Disappearing

Creek enters the Suwannee River. The creek's obscure outflow is an undercurrent in the bank.

Wildlife Spotted

American alligator, white tail deer, Osceola turkey, beaver, grey fox, bobcat, white ibis, swallow tailed kite, cooper's hawk, great egret, wood stork, gopher tortoise, alligator snapping turtle, grey squirrel, sand hill crane, kingfisher, several species of reptiles, and a variety of birds.

Points of Interest

On river right just before the portage, see Big Shoals State Park, a day-use-only park. Big Shoals is the only Class III rapids in the state of Florida. Little Shoals is below the Big Shoals. Those who enjoy hiking may want to take a stroll on the Florida Trail as the trail runs through the Big Shoals camping area and is marked with orange blazes. Later the trail crosses the Suwannee to river right, at Stephen Foster Folk and Cultural Center. It then winds its way below Interstate 10, heading west.

Some paddlers take a break from the river at the Stephen Foster Folk and Cultural Center at White Springs, discovering the historical contributions of Stephen C. Foster. A walking tour of White Springs has much to offer visitors, including a building in White Springs, featuring nature paintings by Johnny Dame, The Nature and Heritage Tourism Center in White Springs, antique shops, the famous Telford Inn, the historical Bath House on the river, and more.

Restocking Supplies

Paddlers will approach the railroad track and the U.S. 41 Bridge at White Springs. Located at mile 171, on river right, is the Suwannee River Wayside Park ramp (White Springs). Proceed up the boat ramp and follow the sidewalk leading into town. Plan to walk three quarters of a mile one way. There are several stores in White Springs on the south end of town. They offer general supplies, ice, beer, food, and gas. A second place to restock is to go under the 136 Bridge; exit the river at the White Springs Bath House. A convenience store is located on U.S.41 to the left.

To Stephen Foster Folk and Cultural Center: On river right at the White Springs Bath House, exit the river and travel to the left (approximately 60 yards), following the trail up to the gravel parking lot. See the prominent sign for the entrance to the Stephen C.

Foster Folk and Cultural State Park. Follow the black-top road to the left to enter the park. An entrance fee is required. While there, discover the indelible contributions Foster made, including many historical exhibits.

To walk to the town of White Springs to explore the Nature and Heritage Tourism Center, Dame's Suwannee River mural, the Telford Inn, and more: From the White Springs Bath House, exit the river and travel to the right up the path. Go approximately one hundred yards and see the White Springs Nature and Heritage Tourism Center. There are many brochures, displays, and informational material there. To see the mural of the Suwannee River by noted artist Johnny Dame, look toward the flashing traffic light from the front porch of the visitor's center on the far side of U.S. 41; the building where the mural is displayed is behind the Adam's Store. To visit the Telford Inn, stand on the front porch of the visitor's center and look toward the flashing traffic light. Look back to the right about 90 degrees. The Telford Inn is just to the left of that point of reference on River Street. The walk to the Telford Inn is approximately two hundred yards from the front porch of the visitor's center.

Two paddlers tether their canoes together while camping at Big Shoals.

A Paddler's Guide

Graham set his camp up directly over the rushing water at Big Shoals. The river is in the background. On that night, the guided party had to weather a storm that produced four inches of rain!

While camping at the Big Shoals, the guide prepares a hearty beef stew for trip participants, in an effort to ward off the February chill.

Sandhill Cranes can sometimes be spied flying overhead as they migrate to Florida. Courtesy State Library and Archives of Florida and Dr. David E. LeHart.

Swift Creek meets the Suwannee River.

Spectacular wild azaleas grow along the banks of the Suwannee River during spring months.

Big Shoals: Only Class III Rapid in Florida

Big Shoals is a daunting rapid, and for this very reason, canoeists have been known to travel from all over the world to marvel at such rare beauty. The formation of the Class III rapid consists of several layers and multiple drops. The foam from swiftly rushing water churns and agitates after each geological drop, and the unique swirling designs from white foam in dark water might serve as marvelous inspiration for any artist.

Portaging on river left for safety is recommended. The portage distance is approximately 150 yards to the camp. Know that even for experienced paddlers, the geological makeup of the shoals, part of the Hawthorne formation of limestone, makes the shoals sharp and potentially dangerous. The Hawthorne layer consists of silt, mud, sand, and limestone.[1] The shoals, therefore, are not smooth and round like boulders in some rivers. Begin first listening for rushing water. Navigate early! Paddle to the left. Search out a sign on river left, indicating where to take out and portage. Proceed with caution. The former owner of the Suwannee Canoe Outpost, David Pharr, knows people who have

Camping at Big Shoals is exhilarating. Campers will hear a constant rush of water while relaxing high above the embankment.

chanced these rapids and paid with their lives. Only experienced white water paddlers should consider running the rapids at Big Shoals! Remember the old adage, "Better safe than sorry."

Notes
1. Price, Dennis. Phone Interview Concerning the Hawthorne Layer. May 2011.

Churning water creates magnificent swirls in the river at Big Shoals.

Members of a guided party are seen here portaging at Big Shoals. It is the only Class III rapid in Florida. Only very experienced white-water paddlers should attempt to run the dangerous rapid.

Rose Knox and Graham Schorb

White Springs: Ancient Gathering Place for Native Americans and Posh Resort Town in Late 1800s - Early 1900s

Historically much has happened in White Springs' unique location, for what lured humans to the area in the first place was the natural spring. Native inhabitants gravitated to mineral waters for healing power they believed the spring possessed. White Springs, as the place is called in 2011, is in Hamilton County; the spring itself is a second-magnitude spring located directly on the Suwannee River. The aquifer produces 32,420 gallons per minute, while maintaining a temperature of 72 degrees year round. Paddlers will see the spring house on river right.

Native Americans congregated thousands of years before the intrusion of the white man, who built many elaborate hotels in the 1800s and early 1900s. The hotels housed tourists intent on visiting the mineral spring known for its healing properties.[1] Seminole Indians frequented the spring when white settlers began to appear in the 1820s and 1830s. However, much earlier Indians, the Timucua and Apalachees (and their ancient ancestors the Paleo-Indians), were first to discover the medicinal qualities of the spring. History reveals that the early inhabitants revered the area of about seven miles surrounding the spring, and they deemed the waters and immediate land, sacred. So enchanted were these waters to early humans that the tribes mutually decreed no fighting would take place at the location. For this reason, varying tribes would gather together as the healing waters beckoned and became a Mecca for their sick.

In 1835, a man named Bryant Sheffield purchased one thousand acres for his plantation, and the spring was part of the tract purchase. Because he, like the Native Americans before him, believed the waters possessed healing powers, he decided to construct a double log hotel on the eastern side of the spring. Soon, visitors descended upon the area; a town was born. Later, the structure became an antebellum resort hotel, famous for its natural wonders and delicious food. During the War for Southern Independence, also known as the American Civil War, many plantation owners frequented the hotel, bringing their families and their slaves. As a result, the destination ultimately became a safe haven for Southerners and was known as "Rebel's Refuge.".

Many other ornate hotels were later built, including the especially elaborate "palatial Hamilton Hotel." The structure boasted open fireplaces, four thousand feet of piazzas, and electric bells. Other hotels such as the Horne House, the Colonial, the Oaks, the Paxton Hotel, the Hotel Jackson, and the Edgewood accommodated visitors looking for healing in the spring's waters. Unfortunately, some of the hotels burned in the fire of 1911, which consumed thirty-five buildings in all. The only remaining hotel from

People pose at the White Springs Bath House in the 1920s. Courtesy of State Library and Archives of Florida.

those days gone by is the Telford Inn.[2] Visit the historical building and take note of some of the famous names included in the guest book. Rooms are available for rent, and guests can enjoy a meal at the restaurant on site. White Springs was incorporated in 1885 and was a prominent steamboat landing. In 1997, the town was named in the National Register of Historic Places.

When Graham and I visited the famous Telford Inn, the rooms had just been newly renovated. After a hearty meal of authentic Southern fare in the hotel's restaurant, we decided to tour the building to see some of the rooms. With a grand invitation from one of the kind employees, we ventured upstairs to take a look around. Someone once told us the hotel had ghosts. Of course we do not believe in ghosts—or do we? As we arrived on the second floor and walked down the hallway, we stepped through the threshold of one of the finely decorated guest rooms. The heavy wooden door immediately slammed behind us, startling us both beyond belief. Standing there looking at each other, we were dumbfounded, for we were the only visitors up there, and no windows were open to create a draft in the room! To this day, we do not know what caused the door to slam.

Sometimes paddlers will stay in the Telford Inn for a night at the beginning of a canoe trip. There is a restaurant at the hotel, and other restaurants in White Springs offer delicious food too. Take a walking tour of White Springs; discover many interesting sights.

Notes
1. Hinton, Cora. *Early History of Hamilton County, Florida: A Bicentennial Project.* Jasper. The Jasper News.
2. Chance, Martha. *Early History of Hamilton County, Florida.* Jasper: The Jasper News.

Bathing beauties pose at the Bath House in 1925. Courtesy of State Library and Archives of Florida.

A Paddler's Guide

The Colonial Hotel and the Hotel Jackson were both popular White Springs destinations for wealthy tourists in the early 1900s, drawing out-of-state guests as well as some prominent local residents to Florida springs. The spa retreats once advertized benefits that provided not only relaxation but medicinal miracle cures. Courtesy of State Library and Archives of Florida.

The Hotel Jackson was one of several opulent hotels that catered to affluent visitors. Courtesy of State Library and Archives of Florida.

The famous Telford Inn as pictured in 2008. The inn is the only remaining hotel from the early-1900s tourist era, which brought thousands of tourists to White Springs for relaxation and healing. Many other resort hotels burned in the fire of 1911. Take a break from the river and visit the Telford. It houses a restaurant and can provide lodging. Remember to stroll through the lobby to read about local history. Also see the Telford Inn guest book to learn about the prominent visitors who once lodged in her rooms.

Paddlers will see the famous White Springs Bath House on river right. Take a break from the river here. Follow the directions provided in Section Three for a walking tour of White Springs. Be sure to see the Stephen Foster Folk and Cultural Center, and also visit an area shop that houses paintings by the locally known Suwannee River artist Johnny Dame.

Rose Knox and Graham Schorb

Stephen Collins Foster Folk Culture Center: Songwriter's Historical Contributions Honored

No name associated with the Suwannee River is more iconic than that of the American composer Stephen Collins Foster. His songwriting presented the South's antebellum culture and the Suwannee River to the world, as his romanticized songs painted indelible images of hundreds of laboring black field hands happily singing hopeful spirituals. In those depictions, the river steamship whistles and blows, billowing steam as cotton is loaded from river landings. Because of such idealistic songs, he became world famous; "Way Down Upon the Suwannee River" is one of the most recognizable song lyrics in the entire world. "Old Folks at Home," as it is often called too, was made famous by Foster, who lived from 1826 to 1864. Born July 4 in Lawrenceville, Pennsylvania, Foster died January 13 in New York, New York. Though he had little formal training in composing, he nevertheless became known for his tunes about the antebellum South. Though he is most remembered for his "Swannee River" (historical spelling) he never laid eyes upon her tannic currents himself.

During the composition, the song initially included several southern rivers; after he saw the Suwannee on a map and realized "Swannee" sounded better, he changed the name. A story is often told in a detailed account from Morrison, Foster's brother, who remembers the day in 1851 when Stephen asked Morrison to help conjure ideas of a two-syllable southern river. According to Morrison, Foster needed the name for use in a new version of a song he had written earlier, "Old Folks at Home." Morrison suggested the Yazoo River; Stephen rejected the idea, for the name had already been used by other writers. Morrison then offered the Pee Dee River, which flows through North and South Carolina. Foster at first wrote the line "Way down upon the Pedee River" in the composition process, but he was not satisfied with the ring of that line. Morrison opened an atlas in quest of another river's name. When he came across the Suwannee and read it to Stephen, Foster delightedly cried, "That's it!" At that moment, according to Morrison, Stephen jotted the name down; the song was complete.[1]

At that time period, the sale of five thousand copies of a song was considered a monumental success. "Old Folks" sold 150,000 copies in just two years.[2]

Some of the grandest years of Foster's life were 1850 and 1851. During that time, he was relishing the proliferation of his songwriting career. He fell in love and got married, and his daughter Marion was born. Perhaps such pinnacle moments in his life are what spurred him to compose one of the world's best-loved melodies, "Old Folks at Home." Through his romanticized view of the antebellum South, the Suwannee River has become legendary. Fletcher Hodges Jr., a former curator of the Foster Hall collection and an expert on Foster, comments on how Foster's songs were forever seared into the American consciousness. He writes of the Suwannee River's significance: "It has become a half-legendary stream, encircling the earth. It flows through the soul of humanity. It has become the symbol of all mankind's vague, lost, wordless dreams, of joys that have vanished, of unattainable longings, of homesickness and timesickness." Some of Foster's other popular songs, including "My Old Kentucky Home" and "Old Black Joe," also reflect a romanticized view of the Old South. In his career, Foster wrote over 200 songs; 150 were parlor songs, 30 were for minstrel shows. He also published religious hymns.[3]

The Stephen C. Foster Folk Culture Center State Park in White Springs, Florida, honors Foster's contributions to American history and songwriting. Located directly on the banks of the legendary Suwannee River in White Springs visitors can learn about how the Seminole Indians once crafted dugout canoes, or they may relive the hardships endured by early pioneers of the Suwannee River Basin. As visitors stroll through the museum, they will discover the intricate and artistic antebellum dioramas all depicting North Florida history. While at the museum, see the authentic notes of Stephen Foster and view paintings that were inspired by Foster's songs. When walking in the park (or paddling on the river), listen for the ninety-seven-bell carillon tower, which plays the many famous Foster melodies. Visitors will also enjoy Craft Square, where they may witness the arts of stained glassmaking, quilting, blacksmithing, and other various crafting skills. The park is located directly on the river, and the canoe launch is on river right at mile marker 168.3. For information on Stephen Foster Folk Culture Center State Park, call 386-397-2733 or visit online at www.floridastateparks.org/stephenfoster/[4]

Notes
1. and 3. Hodges, Fletcher, Jr. *The Swanee River and A Biography of Stephen C. Foster.* White Springs: The Stephen Foster Memorial Association, Inc., 1958.
2. Garrison, Webb. *A Treasury of Florida Tales.* Nashville: Rutledge Hill Press, 1989.
4. Florida State Parks. "Stephen Foster Folk and Culture Center State Park." http://www.floridastateparks.org/stephenfoster/

My Old Kentucky Home and *Way Down Upon de Swanee Ribber* are just two of the many dioramas depicting the antebellum South, which was a prominent theme in Foster's songs. These intricately crafted dioramas are displayed at Stephen Foster Folk and Cultural Center. See directions in Section Three on how to walk to the park from the river. Courtesy of State Library and Archives of Florida.

Diorama of Stephen Foster's Famous Song
"Way Down Upon de Swanee Ribber"
at the Stephen Foster Memorial on the Suwannee River
White Springs, Florida   W-7

A Paddler's Guide

Several large paintings are housed in the antebellum-style Foster museum. They commemorate his inspirational songs.

The Belle of the Suwannee was a famous tourist paddleboat. (It should not be confused with the famous steamer of the same name.) In the foreground, women dress as southern belles in an effort to re-create the antebellum South of Foster's songs. The photograph was taken around 1937 on the Suwannee River at the Stephen Foster Folk and Cultural Center. Photograph and caption text courtesy of State Library and Archives of Florida.

Wall Murals: Johnny Dame's Nature Depictions

When I visited the Suwannee River Diner in White Springs, Florida, years ago, I marveled and was deeply moved by nature paintings on four walls. The mysterious essence of the Suwannee River, with its wild and diverse topography, had been distinctly and colorfully captured. My memory of night scenes, portrayed in varying layers of lavender, had been meticulously implemented to depict oncoming darkness and full moonlit scenes. The serenity of night renditions touched me to the core. If artists are Shamans of a culture as Joseph Campbell once declared, then Johnny Dame is a Shaman.

On the banks of the middle Suwannee in early June of 2008, I sat and talked with Johnny Dame, a North Florida artist who takes a spiritual naturalist approach to painting the Suwannee River; he is the creator of the magnificent river depictions. Below is our interview that illuminates how he gets his inspiration, and how through his paintings he is able to educate and to preserve natural areas. Johnny is not only a talented artist, but also a musician and an environmental activist.

Note: Suwannee River Diner is now closed; however, Dame's images are still painted inside the building. At the time of publication, the building serves as a antique shop.

Question: Tell me a little about yourself.

Johnny: I grew up in Polk County Florida in Lake Alfred. I am a seventh-generation Floridian. My father and my paternal grandmother were both artists. My parents recognized early that not only was I going to be an artist, but I would also be really involved in Nature.

Question: Does where you are from influence what you paint?

Johnny: I have a strong cosmic sense of place and easily find myself in love with various Nature places as I encounter them. Discovering the connectivity of life forms in an ecosystem is most exhilarating! Sharing this excitement with others is best!

Question: In what ways do you get your creative inspiration?
Johnny: The cyclic movements of Nature.

Question: What is a Spiritual Naturalist?
Johnny: I read stories in college in the Naturalism genre. I realized early that this mode of writing embodied the idea of Man conquering Nature or Nature conquering Man. I was baffled by this. For what were people like Henry David Thoreau, John Muir, or William Bartram? I knew that there had to be a way to combine them both; so I came up with the term Spiritual Naturalist, which is what those authors were and what

I am. This is one who sees the connectivity and interdependence of both Man and Nature—not one ruling over the other.

Question: In what ways do you think your paintings change the way people think and feel about the Suwannee River?

Johnny: Our culture has handled the management of natural resources in a completely fragmented way. This is a result of a combination of factors, which include political boundaries that do not conform to Nature and isolationist scientific procedure. Hence I saw the need to portray the connectivity and holistic reality of the world. This is my number-one goal, to help people at whatever level of consciousness they find themselves and to help them see the connectivity to Nature. "A picture is worth a thousand words" is an understatement—it should be worth a million.

Question: Do you think your paintings will inspire people to help save and preserve the river?

Johnny: One way I attempt to get people to see that the entirety of natural systems encompasses a multi-faceted approach, which includes artwork, maps, music, poetry, and storytelling. I have determined that there has to be an entirely new way of looking at our natural resources. My solution is called Holistic Resource Conservation Plan. I named it so because we have to have an entirely new way of teaching, managing, and functioning with our natural resources. By establishing and re-establishing a sense of place on all levels, there becomes the potential, both personally and collectively, to redefine our relationship with Nature that is all inclusive. I have taken artistic and poetic license and labeled the land in realistic and comprehensible ways. I have done this by proclaiming the entirety of land that is underlain of the Florida aquifer. I want to show that the Florida aquifer is one eco-province constituted with various eco-regions woven together, and each eco-region makes up various eco-systems—all of which is characterized by unique physiographic land forms.

Question: What do you want people to know about you and about your paintings through the creative process?

Johnny: I want people to know that I am committed to healing the division between humanity, Nature, and spirituality.

Question: In what ways has spending time on or near the Suwannee River changed you?

Johnny: Spending time on the Suwannee has given me both a sense of timelessness and the perception of ancient time. It is a living, flowing encyclopedia. The river gives me a sense of my place in this wondrous mosaic of life.

Question: If you had to choose your two favorite paintings of the Suwannee Wilderness areas, what two would you choose and why?

Johnny: Definitely the diner mural in White Springs, which is a continual image of the whole river. That mural has a twenty-four-hour cycle and all twelve months of the year depicted. It is floristically, botanically, zoologically and geologically precise. And then there is a little painting that is an impressionistic painting of the Suwannee River in the early spring—with golden green leaves, pink and white native azaleas, light of the open forest, and the classic tea-colored Suwannee. The reason I like this one so much is it captures the essence of the river. When I see it, I want to be nowhere else in the world but here.

Question: If you had to choose one painting that you think represents and embodies all of your Suwannee River Wilderness paintings, which one would it be?

Johnny: The Suwannee Wildflower Wheel. It has a nice view of the Suwannee, but it also has the twelve wildflowers that bloom in each sign of the Zodiac. This work gives a sense of wholeness which incorporates land, water, and sky. It portrays the beauty and uniqueness of each month of the year as flowers bloom with each sign of the Zodiac.

Question: Tell the story of how you ended up painting the walls at the Suwannee River Diner in White Springs, Florida.

Johnny: In 1998, Steve Williams approached me about putting some artwork in The River Gallery (no longer in business) in White Springs. In 2000, Steve heard through the grapevine that a local six-generation Florida family (Wayne and Rose Stormant) had bought a restaurant in White Springs. Wayne's father had always wanted to see a mural of the Suwannee River done in White Springs. Steve heard about that and connected me with Wayne and Rose.

Question: I looked you up on the Internet and saw the paintings of your work online. Also, I marveled at the mural painted on the walls of the Suwannee River Diner. Has your artwork and environmental activism received any attention?

Johnny: Yes. Janisse Ray, the famous Southern [anthologized] author who wrote *Ecology of a Cracker Childhood* and *Wildcard Quilt*, contacted me after seeing the mural in White Springs. She has just finished a book called *Pinhook Swamp,* all about the connectivity to the land. I drew the art for the cover of that book.

Question: What artistic endeavor are you involved in right now?

Johnny: I am working on several books that incorporate all of the aforementioned concepts. I feel like it is imperative in this time to provide various means of instruction—an entire myriad of ways to help people integrate harmlessly with the natural world. These books embody the multi-faceted process mentioned before.[1]

So take a break from the river and come to 16538 Spring Street to see Dame's paintings in the Suwannee River Diner (the diner is no longer in business). Also in White Springs, within walking distance of the building with the mural, are other notable attractions. See the visitor's center, which has historical and cultural exhibits, or visit restaurants. (The famous Telford Inn has a restaurant.) See also several antique shops.

Notes
1. Dame, Johnny. Personal Interview. March, 2008.

During our interview, Johnny presents his latest work. We are standing in what is called an oxbow—a place where the Suwanee River flows around us on three sides. In the background palmetto thickets and a hardwood forest shade the embankment.

A Paddler's Guide

Beginning in the back of the room, Dame takes the observer through a visual tour of the topography of the river. Starting in the Okefenokee Swamp, Dame's "pre-historic night scene" is painted in blues and lavenders. Notice the mastodon in the background. See the mural in White Springs. Courtesy of Johnny Dame Jr.

A Florida panther rests on an overhanging perch. Courtesy of Johnny Dame Jr.

A sunset on the Suwannee River is a spiritual experience. Courtesy of Johnny Dame Jr.

The tea-colored Suwannee flows past the limestone wall at the once-posh resort of Suwannee Spring. See the mural in the S.O.S Café in Spirit of Suwannee Music Park in Live Oak, Florida. Courtesy of Johnny Dame Jr.

Running Spring flows into the Suwannee River. Courtesy of Johnny Dame Jr.

A first-magnitude spring gives life and nourishment to many wild creatures. Visit Dame's mural in the Spirit of Suwannee Music Park. Specific directions to the location are given in the river Section Four. Courtesy of Johnny Dame Jr.

Dame portrays the Big Shoals at low water. He says of the entire mural that it is a twenty-four-hour cycle; all twelve months of the year are depicted. The painting is floristically, botanically, zoologically, and geologically precise. Visit the mural in White Springs. Courtesy of Johnny Dame Jr.

The Alligator-Snapping Turtle: "Dinosaur of the Turtle World" Makes the Suwannee Home

The alligator-snapping turtle lives on the Suwannee River and makes its home in canals, lakes, and rivers of the southeastern United States. It has a prehistoric appearance, with beak-like jaws, sharp spiked shell, and scaly tail. For this reason, the species is often called the "dinosaur of the turtle world." The alligator-snapping turtle is the largest freshwater turtle in North America. Males average 26 inches in shell length and weigh around 175 pounds. Some males have exceeded 220 pounds. Females are much smaller and can weigh as much as 50 pounds.[1] To attract prey, the alligator-snapper lures fish into its mouth by displaying the bright-red worm shaped flesh, which is attached to its tongue. Unsuspecting fish are lured to the turtle's mouth. Alligator-snappers can live beyond a hundred years old.[2]

Stories have been told of turtles much older than a hundred years, though. Al Redmond, an old-time trapper, has told some of those stories. He once captured the reptile to provide turtle for the canned soup industry, which almost drove the species to the brink of extinction. During the butchering process of the giant turtles taken from the Flint River in Georgia, Redmond found strange artifacts. Some of the turtle shells were damaged and had indentations. Redmond also found relics of spearheads and arrowhead where the turtles had been shot. Also pulled from the turtles, according to Redmond, were musket balls—50-caliber sharps, possibly from the American Civil War of the 1860s.

In his later years Redmond tried to save the turtles, trapping them for breeding purposes only. Every year he set free tiny snappers into the wild. Estimating the age of the alligator-snapping turtle, Redmond once said a 316-pound turtle could easily be five hundred years old, because they grow less than a pound a year in the wild.

Once, while fishing in the river, a fisherman caught a large snapper. He brought it to the Suwannee Canoe Outpost, where the turtle remained in the back of his truck. Later, after all of the curiosity seekers had taken a look, the fisherman released the snapper back into the Suwannee.

Notes

1. *National Geographic.* "Alligator Snapping Turtle." http://animals.nationalgeographic.com/animals/reptiles/alligator-snapping-turtle.html
2. Orenstein, Ronald. *Turtles, Tortoises & Terrapins: Survivors in Armor.* Buffalo: Firefly Books Inc., 2001

In mid-September 2009, down-river from Suwannee Spring, a local fisherman caught a 40-pound alligator-snapping turtle in the Suwannee River. The turtle was later released.

The alligator-snapping turtle can exceed 220 pounds. Drawing by Joe Akerman.

Section Four Map

A Paddler's Guide

Suwannee Spring to Interstate 10 Bridges
Mile 150 – Mile 125

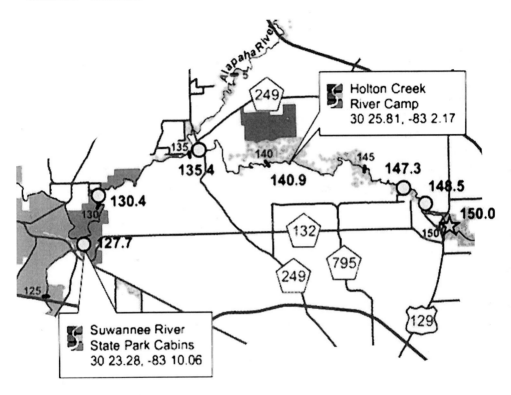

Navigation Warnings

Located approximately one mile below Suwannee River State Park is Ellaville Shoals. Proceed with caution!

Camping Information

Campsites on the river are abundant in low to medium river levels. There are campsites at the Suwannee Canoe Outpost located at Spirit of Suwannee Music Park for a fee. Warning: During festivals and music events, the music may be loud. Such events attract thousands of people annually; however, some months are quiet and serene. Check park schedule for event calendar.

Holton Creek river camp is located at mile 140.9. An advance reservation is required. Contact Suwannee River Water Management for information. Refer to the phone number under the Preparation chapter. Gibson Park, also called Noble's Ferry, and Suwannee River State Park both have camping sites for a fee, too.

Topography

Take note of sublime limestone walls visible at low to medium water levels. Creeks and tributaries on this section include sugar creek, mill creek, Mitchell Creek, Holton Creek, the Alapaha rise, Alapaha River, lime sink run, and the Withlacoochee River. At low to medium water levels, explore sugar creek on river right, about a quarter of a mile down from Suwannee Spring. The place is a good spot to have a picnic and to explore. At the confluence of the Alapaha River, realize that in summer months the Alapaha riverbed is often dry, for the river is fed by an underwater aquifer that recedes in summer months. Lime sink run at the Suwannee River State Park, in medium water levels, is an excellent run for paddlers to enjoy; see breathtaking natural sights. On river right, the confluence of the Withalacoochee vigorously joins the Suwannee River. Florida Power plant intake and outflow ditches are visible on river left just before the Ellaville Shoals. After Ellaville Shoals, on river left are the rusted remnants of an old steamship. The wooden planks are still visible but only in low water level. The Ellaville Shoals are breathtaking, but proceed with caution. People crash here and lose gear. Remember, like Big Shoals, the shoals at Ellaville are very sharp. There are numerous springs, including Suwannee, Holton Creek, five holes, lime, Suwannacoochee (located about a hundred yards up the Withalacoochee River), Ellaville, and many unnamed springs.

Wildlife Spotted

Florida panther (extremely rare), grey fox (rare), brown water snake, Osceola turkey, grey squirrel, American alligator. While on a series of day trips, Graham and I encountered a variety of birds, including the great blue heron, a green heron, several red tail hawks, two pileated woodpeckers in flight (one was a male and the other a female), an osprey, numerous turkey vultures, beaver and beaver nests, red earred sliders, a mother raccoon and babies, a fresh water eel, and one Gulf sturgeon that flipped his forked tail to the surface on a deep river bend. The sound of cicadas in October 2008 was almost deafening. Also seen in this section are the gopher frog, Suwannee cooter, gopher tortoise, cooper's hawk, great egret, barred owl, and peregrine falcon.

Points of Interest

There is a man-made limestone wall that was once part of a posh resort with bath house and bottling plant. See wall on river left. Also, near the location there was once a United States Army fort, at Suwannee Spring. In addition, see the historical kiosk and out-buildings at Suwannee Spring. The old Highway 129 Bridge crosses over the Suwannee below Suwannee Spring. See the wood carvings, floating barge building, and flood pole at Suwannee Canoe Outpost. Spirit of Suwannee Music Park at the Suwannee Canoe Outpost location features some of Johnny Dame's nature murals inside of the S.O.S Café. Also view Dame's work at a kiosk in the café parking lot. On this section is Florida Boys' Ranch. Gibson Park is located on river right, just beyond County Road 249 Bridge. Be sure to visit the old ferry barge and crossing, the Confederate earthworks, and Town of Columbus site and cemetery at Suwannee River State Park. Trek to the Drew Mansion site and historical marker, kiosk, and old Drew Cemetery at the confluence of the Suwannee and the Withlacoochee Rivers.

Restocking Supplies

There is a general store located in Spirit of Suwannee Music Park. To get to the store, exit at the Spirit of Suwannee Music Park (Suwannee Canoe Outpost) boat ramp. Travel up the boat ramp and take a right. Follow the blacktop road for approximately three quarters of a mile. The general store offers general supplies, ice, and beer; it is located to the right of the S.O.S. Café in the Craft Village. Gas is available on Hwy 129.

The old rail trestle of the Live Oak, Perry, and Gulf Railroad is visible down-river from the Suwannee Canoe Outpost.

Limestone walls, as high as thirty-five feet, tower above the river on this spectacular, peaceful section of the Suwannee River.

Along Section Four at certain times of the year, beaver slides and beaver dens are visible to the keen observer.

A Paddler's Guide

Deese-Howard Ramp is located on river left, 1.8 miles from the Suwannee Canoe Outpost. Locals call it the "pole ramp."

On river left, just before the Suwannee River State Park boat launch, is the famous limestone outcropping called Balancing Rock. It is not visible in high water.

Graham's kayak party takes a break to picnic at Devil's Elbow near Holton Creek.

Three bridges are visible at the confluence of the Withlacoochee and Suwannee Rivers. The first is the railroad bridge, the second is the old Highway 90 Bridge, and the third is the current Highway 90 Bridge.

Gabe Baxter poses by planks of an old steamer (the Izard) near the confluence.

Two paddlers take a break.

Section Four is one of my favorite places to paddle with dogs Marley and River.

Remnants of an old steamer.

Rose Knox and Graham Schorb

An Experimental Dam at Suwannee Spring: Pilings Still Visible

The Suwannee River is one of the most undeveloped rivers in America. Paddlers may navigate the Suwannee with no artificial impediments such as man-made dams. However, there was once a proposal to change and develop the Suwannee River. In July 1964 a letter requested to build a series of low-level dams on the Suwannee River between White Springs and Branford. The information was documented in the minutes of the Board of Commissioners of Suwannee County. Boat lifts around each dam were also proposed. To accomplish the construction, the blasting of rock shoals was approved. The purpose of the changes, according to the letter, was to allow river levels to remain high enough at all times to promote fishing and boating. The counsel surmised that the predictable water levels would also benefit nearby farming areas during dry level periods. As a result of the proposal, the first experimental dam was constructed at Suwannee Spring. The idea of building these dams proved a failure, for at a later date in September 1967 the minutes of the board meeting revealed a motion that the board write the Suwannee River Authority to request that the experimental dam at Suwannee Spring be removed from the river, in order to make the Suwannee River more easily navigable.[1]

Paddlers can still see the remnants of the experimental dam in low river levels. On river left, before the bend and before the Suwannee Spring beach, several pilings remain visible. The embankments on both sides of the river at the bend reveal unnatural evidence of Man's interference. From the park's parking lot, the remnants may be seen by walking down the wide stairway. On the bend at the beach, sand bags and metal remain.

Notes
1. United States. County Commissioner's Meeting. *Proposal to Construct a Dam at Suwannee Springs: 1964.* Live Oak: 1964.

A Paddler's Guide

A dam at Suwannee Spring was built in the 1960s; however, the structure was later removed in the same decade. Courtesy of State Library and Archives of Florida.

Rose Knox and Graham Schorb

Suwannee Spring: War Fort, Popular Resort Location—Limestone Walls Remain

Suwannee Spring has served as an important historical location over the centuries, and it is a favorite place for many locals. When paddling by the limestone walls, I sometimes paddle over to the spring. I get my kayak in the outflow, just outside of the man-made walls. Dangling my feet in cold water, I listen to rushing streams. Sulphur mineral water coming from cavernous depths brings an acrid smell. I wonder what the spring and spring area must have been before the land was touched and changed by the hands of the United States Army and the early pioneers. Was this, like White Springs, a sacred Native American gathering ground, where mineral waters healed and invigorated nearby tribal communities? What more recent history does tell is that during the early 1800s the site was used by pioneers as a safe haven from Native American retaliations. A fort at the spring provided protection for white families as they endured ever-increasing resistance from the natives, who saw their way of life being overtaken by ever-encroaching white settlers. For instance, during the period of the Second Seminole Indian War, records of native retaliations against white settlers reveal that the Clemons family moved from the fort at Suwannee Spring, with intentions to homestead approximately five miles southeast of today's Live Oak. However, during his relocation effort, Mr. Clemons was on his way back to the fort to secure the last of his family items when he was killed by Native Americans, intent on keeping outsiders off of their homeland.[1] Also, during the span from 1836-1837, steamships delivered much needed supplies to the fort at Suwannee Spring, after the safe haven was land isolated by extreme flooding of the Suwannee River.[2]

Later, from 1890 to 1925, Suwannee Spring was a popular tourist resort. Visitors from across the United States traveled to the "infallible mineral waters," as wealthy tourists believed that the sulphur contained medicinal powers, which could heal such ailments as indigestion, gout, malaria, rheumatism, nervous dyspepsia, constipation, nervous prostration, loss of appetite, skin diseases, liver diseases, female troubles, jaundice, eczema and all blood disorders.[3] Basic facilities for bathers had been constructed by 1845, and local newspapers began advertising the new amenities that could accommodate up to one hundred people.[4] There stood several grand hotels and eighteen private residences on the site. So significant was Suwannee Spring that the Atlantic Coastline Railroad made frequent stops at Suwannee Station, which was located one mile west of the spring. A spur line ran directly to the resort hotels, delivering weary passengers to the front door of the hotel.[5]

The first of the magnificent hotels had twenty-two guest rooms, with adjacent bath cottages, a horse stable, and a large one-story frame house for the servants' quarters, an annex of twenty rooms, a bottling shipment plant, and a bath house; however, the bath house was first used as a bowling alley. Guests also enjoyed hot sulphur baths and body massages. Meals served at one of the hotel restaurants during this period were acclaimed as some of the most outstanding in the region. In fact, in 1851 a visitor to Suwannee Spring, Clement Claiborne Clay, son of a former Alabama governor, said that the gopher gumbo he had been served was "excellent."[6] All of the amusements came to an abrupt halt when the hotel burned to the ground. Soon after, a second resort was built in its place; to entertain guests, shows were brought in from New York and Chicago. In addition, guests enjoyed other entertainment, including music from a Steinway grand piano, a billiard room, and a clay-pigeon shooting area. The second hotel was also destroyed by fire.[7]

The last hotel was consumed by fire in 1925, and the end of the romantic resort hotel era at Suwannee Spring came to a close. Visitors can see the remnants of the still-standing, magnificent limestone wall, with its visually appealing, architecturally crafted arched windows. Sulphur water, clear and cool, still bubbles from an aquifer below ground; cool waters today make it a popular swimming hole for local residents during sultry summer months. On the beach, the old bridge pylons remain visible. Several small, decrepit cottages are shrouded by scrubs, vines, and thick foliage. A kiosk at the park reminds visitors of what the hotels looked like and gives a brief history of the spring.

In her book *Tales from the Suwannee River Country*, Emily B. Curtis, who grew up in North Florida during the Great Depression, has vivid memories of tragedy at Suwannee Spring. She recalls how the spring flows into the river through arched windows. She and her playmates would often climb in and out of these windows and end up frolicking on the white sandy beach beside the dark river. Parents were always greatly concerned about their children playing too closely to the water's edge, for the current was strong and at times could be treacherous. She remembers several stories of people being carried away by the river and finally drowning.

On one occasion, her family had planned an afternoon picnic. The time was late in the day, and they had set up their food on the beach. Rescue workers suddenly appeared, because a young girl had been taken by the current. The child's mother was in the parking lot in a car, and Curtis remembers the lamentations echoing down to the river. She knew the situation was hopeless.[8]

Paddlers may want to stop and explore the beach, the park, the kiosk, the out buildings, and take a cool dip in the medicinal spring waters that drew so many to these welcoming waters in the distant past. While dipping in the cool currents, think on those people who once traversed to these sulfuric healing mineral waters.

Notes
1. Musgrove, Eric. *Reflections of Suwannee County: 150 Anniversary Edition 1858-2008*. Live Oak: North Florida Printing Co., Inc., 2008.
2. Ibid.
3. and 5. Historical Kiosk at Suwannee Springs, Live Oak.
4. and 6. Revels, Tracy J. *Sunshine Paradise: A History of Florida Tourism*. Gainesville: University Press of Florida, 2011.
7. *Echoes of the Past: A History of Suwannee County 1858 -2000*. Saint Petersburg: Southern Heritage Press, 2000.
8. Curtis, Emily B. *Tales from the Suwannee River Country*. New York, New York: Writer's Club Press, 2002.

The photograph of Suwannee Spring limestone wall with arched windows was taken in April 2008 at high water. The river is in the background. Paddlers will see the famous wall on river left. A group of concerned citizens has rallied support to try to restore the crumbling wall.

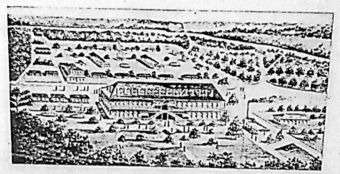

Advertisements like this one once attracted thousands of guests to healing waters. The photograph of the kiosk at Suwannee Spring reveals an artist's rendering of the large resort hotel and cottages that once attracted affluent tourists to the spring. Photograph taken at kiosk at Suwannee Spring.

Two kayakers, Lauren and Meghan, stop to swim in the refreshing water at Suwannee Spring in the summer of 2008. Courtesy of Susan Maultsby of Madison, Florida.

The outflow at Suwanee Spring.

A Paddler's Guide

Taken at the kiosk at Suwannee Spring, this picture portrays an opulent hotel once located on the river. Notice the car on the spur line of the Atlantic Coastline Railroad, which brought wealthy visitors directly from the rail station to the front steps of the hotel. It was drawn by horses. There were several grand hotels at the location at various times, bringing in musical acts from places like Chicago and New York. All of the hotels burned to the ground. The last was destroyed in 1925. Courtesy of Suwannee Valley Genealogical Society.

Swimmers sit atop the limestone wall at Suwannee Spring in 1922. Just as it did decades ago, the wall at Suwannee Spring remains a popular place for locals and visitors to congregate while enjoying the cool sulpher waters of the spring. Paddlers can see the rusted pilings of the original bridge (on river left and right), where horse-drawn carriages once crossed the river. The first bridge was built in 1893 by B.F. Boon and Nathaniel Bryan. It cost $208.89 to construct. Later, the steel bridge seen in the background here was built in 1901.[4] Courtesy of State Library and Archives of Florida.

In the 1920s a row of cottages was part of the resort area at Suwannee Spring. The now-dilapidated cottages (as they still stand) are a reminder of the once-opulent resorts that entertained wealthy guests at the turn of the century. The structures are not visible from the river.

Directions to the Cottages: To visit the old buildings, walk up from the river at Suwannee Spring through the day park; travel through the parking lot. Take a right on the blacktop road-entrance to the spring. Walk approximately one hundred yards to the intersection. Turn right at the intersection and walk about fifteen yards. Take a right into the woods. See the old cottages back among a wooded area. Intact row of cottages photograph courtesy of Suwannee Genealogical Society Library and Bivian Howell.

Ruins of an old service station near the cottages.

Exterior of a cottage.

Interior of a cottage.

Just after the limestone wall at Suwannee Spring, paddlers will move under a picturesque bridge, now abandoned. The much-used 129 Bridge is just beyond the old one. If paddlers wish to take a photograph of Suwannee Spring from a "bird's eye view," they may go up on the old abandoned 129 Bridge and look back up-river.

Brown water snakes are non-venomous. Paddlers sometimes see the non-aggressive reptile sunning on limestone outcroppings, often mistaking them for poisonous water moccasins.

Suwannee Canoe Outpost: Floating Barge

The Suwannee Canoe Outpost, located 19.8 miles from the Stephen Foster Cultural Center, has an unusual appearance and an intriguing story. Intentionally built as a floating barge, the former owner, David Pharr, designed and constructed the anomalous outpost. The building is made from a variety of resources, originating from unlikely, diverse places. To illustrate, the structure is equipped with several cubic feet of Styrofoam, enough to float 19,600 pounds. In addition, pines and black cherry trees were harvested from the nearby Pharr property. Also, the window frames were cut from a virgin cypress tree. In 1947, the frames were originally part of a locomotive stop near Buford, Georgia. The red cedar posts were cut in the 1970s, near Suwannee Station; others were brought in from forests near Ocala. The cedar posts are featured as porch columns, and they are a sight most eccentric. Paddlers often will stop for a break to marvel and take photographs of the distinctly different and artistically conceived outpost construction.

With nature and a Native American theme in mind, an artist named Phil Longo was contracted by Pharr in 1992, to carve images into the wooden posts. Featured upon the posts is a mother bird feeding her young, while a stealthy snake slithers up to get a closer look. Other depictions include Chief Red Deer and Riverman. A bronze plaque below each serious expression reads, "Chief Red Deer and Riverman, Guiding and Guarding." David Pharr once told me that he thinks the image of the Riverman resembles Randy Smith, who was once a Suwannee Canoe Outpost employee. Smith is a native Floridian and an avid outdoorsman who tells several fascinating stories in this guidebook. Other detailed carvings portray an owl, a brown eagle clutching a fish in its talons, and a great blue heron. The inscription on the plaque below them reads "The Predators."

Also see displayed at the outpost the large wheel salvaged from the Suwannee River, which was once used for harvesting timber in the 1800s. Don't forget to look for the shy black cat. He is the outpost mascot appropriately named "Eddy."[1]

While visiting the location, walk up the blacktop road about one mile to the S.O.S Café. Here you can view the breathtaking murals of artist Johnny Dame.

Notes
1. Pharr, David. Personal Interview. 10 May, 2008.

Visit the Suwannee Canoe Outpost building, which was built as a floating barge. The outpost is safe from flooding, for it rises at high river levels. See the unique wood carvings on the outpost columns. Pictured above are "Riverman Ever Guiding and Guarding" and "Chief Red Deer looks on." Other interesting carvings include a variety of birds and a snake.

A Paddler's Guide

Eddy serves as outpost mascot. The shy cat loves swimming in the Suwannee River!

The Suwannee Canoe Outpost is a floating barge. Notice the bold color sycamore leaves. The trees were tiny saplings when David Pharr planted them in the year 1996. Look to the far left from the outpost and notice the high pole with painted bands. The bands indicate that the river has risen greatly in times past. The shot was taken by Daphney Hobbs in the outpost parking lot during the flood of 2004. Courtesy of Daphney Hobbs of Panama City, Florida.

A water-level pole chronicles depths of record floods.

The Florida Panther: History and Local Sightings

> The animal envoys of the Unseen Power no longer serve, as in primeval times, to teach and to guide mankind. Bears, lions . . . are in cages in our zoos. Man is no longer the newcomer in a world of unexplored plains and forests, and our immediate neighbors are not wild beasts but other human beings, contending for goods and space on a planet that is whirling without end around the fireball of a star. Neither in body nor in mind do we inhabit the world of those hunting races of the Paleolithic millennia, to whose lives and life ways we nevertheless owe the very forms of our bodies and structures of our minds. Memories of their animal envoys still must sleep, somehow, within us; for they wake a little and stir when we venture into wilderness.[1]
>
> —Joseph Campbell

In wilderness areas of the Suwannee River Basin, panthers live and forage for food. The majestic cat is known by a variety of names, including puma, mountain lion, catamount, and cougar. The Florida panther, the official animal of Florida, is a sub-species of the cougar; the great cat is also one of the most endangered mammals in the world, with approximately eighty to one hundred of them surviving today. They were hunted almost to extinction by early cowmen, who needed to protect their herds, and overly enthusiastic hunters who sought them for their hefty bounty.

Panthers roam a wide range in forests, piney woods, and hardwood hammocks. They can travel fifteen to twenty miles in a day, moving both day and evening hours in summer months.[1] The great cats do not shy from water and will swim wide stretches of lakes, rivers or wetlands. Though usually quiet, they can make many sounds and on occasion will scream.[2] Some say the cry of a panther sounds like the wail of a woman in distress.

Early records from Florida pioneers indicate they often had disastrous encounters with Florida panthers, according to Joe and Mark Akerman in their book *Jacob Summerlin: King of the Crackers*. One account tells of a cattleman who was brutally attacked by a panther. Though he clubbed the panther to death and escaped, the man was crippled for life.[3] Other accounts of humans and panthers come from the book *The Ben Lilly Legend*. Lilly was born in 1856 and became one of the foremost hunters of pumas on the continent, killing thousands of bears and pumas in his lifetime. The book by J. Frank Dobie chronicles the interaction of man and beast and gives an early account of the dangers to early settlers in America.[4]

As paddlers pass from the Suwannee Canoe Outpost to the Suwannee River State Park, they should be aware that several Florida panther sightings have occurred in this particular area of Suwannee County. Though sighting one is extremely rare, a woman coming off of Section Four of the river recounted an intriguing story to Graham. She said she had seen a large animal with a long tail and a small head, pacing back and forth on a low-hanging live oak branch. She asked Graham, "Are there big cats—like, say—panthers around here?" After Graham confirmed that such a sighting was possible, she was convinced she had indeed seen one of the sleek climbing cats.

Other area sightings have been claimed by reliable sources. For instance, one local man by the name of James Meeks was born and raised in Suwannee County. Meeks, a retired park ranger, saw a panther walk across Warner Road in the year 2008. Warner Road is approximately two to two and a half miles from this particular section of the river. Meeks said he had previously sighted two panthers in South Florida, while serving in the military, so he knew what they looked like.

Graham has spent much time on Section Four of the river. On occasion in the last several decades, he has heard reoccurring strange sounds emanating from the thick hardwood forests. The cries seem much like that of a woman. He too believes the call is the cry of a panther. So look and listen. There may be a Florida panther stealthy traversing the wild areas within the Suwannee River Basin. Rarely are the noble cats sighted, but they have been spotted in these parts. Section Four is one of my favorite places to paddle, but I have never had the honor to spy the cat that the Native Americans once revered.

Notes
1. Joseph Campbell, The Power of Myth with Bill Moyers. Edited by Betty Sue Flowers. New York: Doubleday, 1988.
2. info@bigcatrescu.org
3. Gingerich, Jerry Lee. *Florida's Fabulous Mammals: Their Stories.* Tampa: World Publications.
4. Akerman, Joe A. and Mark J. Akerman. *Jacob Summerlin: King of the Crackers.* Cocoa: The Florida Historical Society Press, 2004.
5. Fergus, Charles. *Swamp Screamer: At Large With the Florida Panther.* Gainesville: University Press of Florida. 1998.

A Paddler's Guide

The Florida panther is the state animal of Florida. Though shy and extremely elusive, several panther sightings have occurred in the Suwannee River Basin. When Florida was still a frontier, early pioneers and cowmen encountered the big cats, often with tragic results. Courtesy of State Library and Archives of Florida.

Rose Knox and Graham Schorb

The Florida Sheriff's Boys Ranch Located Directly on the Suwannee: A Good Place to Fill Water Bottles

The Florida Sheriff's Boys Ranch is approximately seven miles down-river from the Suwannee Canoe Outpost. Construction began in 1958, and development eventually became a 2,537-acre, self-contained facility. The ranch houses boys to the age of eighteen; over the decades, thousands of boys have benefitted from services offered by Florida Sheriff's Boys Ranches in the state.[1]

When paddling Section Four, look for the well-manicured grass acreage on river left. The small, alluring Guinea Creek converges with the Suwannee River just before the beach on river left. In medium to low river levels, a white sand beach with a shady area is a welcoming sight to paddlers. Sometimes in searing summer months, I paddle up the creek as towering embankments loom over me. The winding tributary passage has served as my much needed refuge in lightning storms; though I do not recommend such methods of retreat! Here in Guinea Creek, I swim and float in the chilling waters to refresh my body. The enchanting place is filled with bird song, dashing squirrels, and towering oaks. Such sights invigorate my spirit as does the cold spring water. Sweet innocent secrets are found here, too; for once I surprised a tiny spotted newborn fawn as it rested beside the creek's edge. Enjoy the peace Nature brings at Guinea Creek.

Refill Water Bottles: Walk up the beach, go about thirty yards from the river to the grassy area, and look for the water spigot on the right.

Notes

1. *Echoes of the Past: A History of Suwannee County 1858 -2000*. Saint Petersburg, FL: Southern Heritage Press, 2000.

A Paddler's Guide

Guinea Creek winds through a high, lush bluff on the Florida Sheriff's Boys Ranch property. See the creek on river left, just before the Boys Ranch boat launch. Look on river left for the manicured grassy area that signals the launch. The location is a good place to fill water bottles.

After a day trip, Graham and I loaded the truck at the Boys Ranch launch.

The Alapaha River: A Tributary to the Suwannee

The Alapaha River is 190 miles in length and originates in southeast Dooly County. The small tributary winds through eleven Georgia counties, eventually emptying into the Suwannee River in Hamilton County, Florida. The Alapaha Rise is a spring located half a mile upriver from the confluence of the Suwannee and Alapaha Rivers, and the aquifer produces six thousand gallons of water per second. The outflow eventually gushes into the Suwannee River, making the Alapaha a major tributary.

The narrow, undulating river is remote and unspoiled. Along the shores are scenic natural wonders, such as twenty-foot limestone walls, small waterfalls, and numerous class II rapids. Evidence of Native American presence has been discovered in many areas of the river and river basin. The Alapaha River has known many names, including the Alabaha, Alapa Haw, Lop Haw, Lopahatchy, to name only a few. In 1891, the "stream" became known officially as the Alapaha River.

In the 1930s, sand was mined on the banks of the Alapaha. Today the river basin is vital to commercial farmers growing blueberries. During summer months and in times of extreme drought, the water recedes back into the aquifer; all that remains is a dry riverbed.

When paddling past the Gibson Park boat ramp, also known as Noble's Ferry launch, look for the outflow on river right. The location is where the Alapaha joins the Suwannee River. Many locals like to fish at the confluence. Some area residents claim there was once a Native American trading post near the confluence.[1]

Notes
1. Schorb, Graham. Personal Interview. April 2008.

A Paddler's Guide

Gibson Park, also known as Noble's Ferry, is located on river right, just beyond County Road 249 Bridge. Camping is available for a fee. Down-river from Gibson Park, the Alapaha joins the Suwannee.

A ferry once transported passengers across the river at the confluence of the Alapaha and the Suwannee Rivers. The old road that led to the ferry is still visible on Suwannee River right. The Alapaha tributary is pictured on the right and the Suwannee on the left.

Small waterfalls flow from springs along the winding and remote Alapaha River. Impressive limestone walls rise forty feet high on some sections. The Alapaha is a major tributary to the Suwannee River; when the aquifer is low, the Alapaha riverbed is dry.

Jessica Arnaudin paddles near the confluence of the Alapaha in 2008.

Mark "Manitou Cruiser," a noted canoe racer, paddled over 1200 miles in a Florida race—which he later won! Mark stayed in Graham's Suwannee River camp and was spotted again and photographed near the high embankments at the confluence of the Alapaha River as he made his way to the Gulf of Mexico.

The Suwannee River Experience: A Solo Journey at High Water

The rains have arrived. After almost a year of drought, sheets of water hurry earthward as the river welcomes a deluge. The month is late February, and the Suwannee River has been thirsty for a while. There are places I've walked on the middle Suwannee in past months that are too shallow. I've found myself plodding across her expanse without ever getting my ankles wet. Dragging a kayak across a sandbar is never any fun. (Dragging a fully loaded canoe is a nightmare!) Today I need not worry. As I put my surf and rescue kayak in at Noble's Ferry in Suwannee County, the river is moving like an unrestrained dancer. The water is thirteen feet higher than the last time I was here, just two weeks ago. The rain in these weeks has lifted the river like a resurrection. People here are glad for rain. The folks in North Florida in the past several years have witnessed ponds dry up and creeks disappear. Animals, depending on water holes, have had to move on. But today there is an excitement in the air like hope with baptism.

The parking lot at Noble's Ferry is overrun with pickup trucks. I realize that today is the first time in months that boaters, using small engines, have had the chance to run the river, uninhibited. I notice a familiar face at the ramp. We speak. He says he's waiting on friends. They are searching the river for a houseboat. Several men are moving the craft today off of the river. As I load my dog and my day gear, I notice the swirling movement of black water. A year of low water has harbored debris among ancient banks. I see an entire man-made deck lodged on the side of the river, uprooted from its intended place. Two blue barrels bob like overgrown fishing floats as they cruise by me. Intact root systems are swept away in the current like gargantuan brown spiders looking for a place to light. I marvel at what the river offers up, almost like an unworthy sacrifice. Graham says he thinks an overindustrious person could survive out here on just what is found on the river. I believe him as I see the bounty in the Suwannee today.

The winter season is perfect for paddling! The sky is an alluring blue—the kind of sky you think about only in dreams. The blue is surreal. Not a cloud is visible. There is a brisk breeze today, too. As I paddle out into the Suwannee, the river takes my craft, moving me swiftly though tannic waters. About a quarter of a mile down from Noble's Ferry boat launch is the Alapaha River. Often her riverbed is dry. Today, however, the winding Alapaha is full to the brim. Her strong currents merge with the Suwannee, pushing me even more deliberately down-river. Liquid power pulses under me. Transmogrified circles and figure eights of froth design gather around my kayak. There is a white insignia left on black water in agitated froth.

People dot the embankment above me. There is a boy of about nine standing beside a white five-gallon bucket. Beside him are fishing poles lined side by side like obedient soldiers.

"Catch anything?" I say.

"Yep, one two-foot catfish and five bream," he says proudly.

I smile and reply, "I guess ya'll are gonna have a fish fry tonight, huh?"

He has a look of astonishment. How can a passing stranger be so right about his dinner plans?

"Yeah, that's what we're doin' tonight." He responds tentatively, now a bit unsure of himself.

After years of drought the rains have finally come, resurrecting water levels as high as thirteen feet. Rose and river companion Marley ride the swift, strong currents of the Suwannee River, from Noble's Ferry to the Suwannee River State Park, April 2008.

My attention moves from the boy to sounds of splashing water ahead. I see a white hound on top of limestone. The outcropping juts up from the Alapaha. The large dog is leaping off of a mostly submerged limestone projection. He then climbs back on his tiny dog island. At first I am alarmed; I yell back to the boy. "Is that your dog?" A man suddenly steps from the woods and stands silently beside the child. His face reveals exasperation and perhaps a little fear. He is obviously put out with his pet, but his tone is not one of panic—not yet, anyhow. The hound, it is now evident, loves the water and is playing, much to the dismay of his owners, who would like to have him back safely on land. Large alligators swim these waters. No one wants to see his pet taken by one. This is the innate fear of those who love their dogs. I am only imagining. But I think this is true as I reach down to pet my own little dog, Marley, my lone passenger on the voyage.

As I paddle down the Suwannee, I breathe in frosty air. I am aware of how coolness tickles my face; I feel intensely alive! This is what Henry David Thoreau must have meant when he said something about "sucking the marrow" out of life. I am living! My senses are filled with green foliage, dark and light. I notice grey-trunked live oaks hovering over the river as I, too, take note of sprightly palm fronds dancing in the breeze. I hear the call of a red-shouldered hawk just above me in the bow of the big oak. The call pierces my consciousness like the frigid air.

Later, about two-and-a-half miles down-river from Noble's Ferry launch, I paddle up on three small motor boats. I see two men in one boat. They are involved in a tedious task; they are trying to maneuver a houseboat in dangerous current. The house is a light brown, cedar-shingled structure with sliding doors on each end. There are other men walking on both porches. They yell curt directions to each other because they have lodged the boat unintentionally (I gather) and are trying to move the boat into open current. But the river has a mind of her own. She always has. She always will. That is the power, the legend of rivers. The men must use their wits and their know-how to work the boat in order get the house to move with the current. I have a feeling that they know these woods, and they too have an understanding of the river. The houseboat will soon be moved off the river.

I paddle past, hurrying out of their way. On the right, just ahead about fifty yards, I watch as a great blue heron takes flight. The moment seems frozen in time. Later, two wood ducks fly overhead. They scold me for disturbing them. Further down-river, I notice two black crows and two turkey vultures perching on an overhanging oak branch. I marvel at how the branch lifts itself above the river. My imagination soars. Perhaps this is as good a place as any for a Florida panther to creep gracefully along a low-hanging extension such as this one.

I notice only a dozen or so houses upon the embankments of the eight-mile stretch to the Suwannee River State Park boat ramp. The homes are situated on twenty-five-foot-high bluffs. Graham and I have a friend named Ray. He has a house on one of the highest pinnacles and tells of an old Native American trading post that was once located near the confluence. The area served as a significant place, for the high topography of the banks and the merging of two waterways were ideal settings for trade and for sentinel perches and settlements. The oral story of the trading post has been passed down by his family. I ponder the historical fact, thinking of those ancient peoples who have traversed here before me, and I am thankful also for the unpredictable rise and fall of such a magnificent river. Her currents, with their unrelenting rising and falling, keep Man's intrusion and overdevelopment at a minimum.

Lime Sink Run: Breathtaking Excursion at Suwannee River State Park

Many historical, topographical, and wildlife opportunities await visitors at the Suwannee River State Park. After arriving at the boat launch on river left, notice directly to the left, running somewhat perpendicular to the ramp, a small tributary flowing into the Suwannee. The outflow is referred to as Lime Sink Run and has been touted as the world's smallest river. In spring months depending on water levels, the creek flows, sometimes swiftly, into the Suwannee River. Cold waters surge from beneath an aquifer, amid natural limestone walls, and the run undulates back about a quarter of a mile within the park.

Standing resolutely in the run is one of the most impressive cypress trees we have ever seen. Getting to the tree, however, will take some effort. If water levels permit, paddle over the tiny rushing waterfall while immersing your senses in relaxing sounds

Look for the boat ramp at Suwannee River State Park on river left. Just beside it (to the left) is the beautiful Lime Sink Run, a fascinating natural place to explore.

A Paddler's Guide

Though the tree was growing upon the Ichetucknee River embankments, beavers have been spotted in the Lime Sink Run area. Historians believe that Hernando de Soto and his army followed a Native American path on the Ichetucknee River as his expedition explored regions of North Florida.

of moving water. Within the run, discover the age old bald cypress trees and their four-foot root systems. Shade from prodigious live oaks and other hardwoods will blanket the way. Wild ducks, grey squirrels, a variety of song birds, white-tailed deer, and beavers have all been sighted frequently in the tiny tributary. Scant remnants of early pioneer mills are evident there as well. Be on the lookout for such man-made structures.

If the water level is not high enough to paddle the run, hiking the trail to experience the forest and run is the next option. First walk up the boat ramp, taking a left at the top of the launch. Follow the foot trail that extends out into the park woods. (This is not the path that directly parallels the Suwannee River.) Along the scenic trail, enjoy many serene views. The footpath will lead eventually to a stand of large cypress trees. Walking the trail reminds me of my childhood fantasy. How I longed to live like the child in the book *My Side of the Mountain,* as he climbed inside his very own hollow tree for the night! My fourth grade teacher, Mrs. Sanders, introduced me to the title, and I am forever searching in forests for just the right tree that might make suitable housing. Since I do not have the luxury of actually spending the night in a tree, Graham snapped a photograph of me posing inside a hollowed-out one here along the Lime Sink run path. Remember the two ways to get to these sights, for sometimes the sink runs completely dry, so paddling the tributary is impossible; however, the surrounding hardwood forest is nonetheless breathtaking from land's perspective.

Once, in the spring months when hiking the trail, I saw hundreds of Atamasco lilies. There is a walking bridge in the run area too, so have a camera ready to snap unique photographs of wildlife and of the natural topography, including the limestone outcroppings, spring flowers, age-old cypress trees, lush scenery, diverse wildlife and hollowed-out trees.

See the ancient limestone outcroppings of Lime Sink Run.

A Paddler's Guide

When the aquifer is full, the spring runs fluidly; however, sometimes the run is dry.

Enjoy a peaceful stroll on a secluded hiking path along the run. It is one of many excellent hiking trails within the park.

Ferry Crossings, Cotton Gin Wheel, Old Stagecoach Road: Visit Them in Suwannee River State Park

Directions to Historical Areas: When visiting the Suwannee River State Park, travel up the boat ramp, following the paved road to the right, toward the general parking lot. Up ahead, on the far side of the main parking lot, is a small building with bathrooms and a shelter. (It was the original office of the park.) Go past the building to the grassy area near the Suwannee River and search out a wooden walkway. The walkway is located past the cotton gin wheel and is close to the river, at the confluence of the Withlacoochee and the Suwannee Rivers. Stroll up to the walkway.

While there, notice the geological depression. The large indent in the Earth was once the Confederate earthworks. Old Stagecoach Road ran through here; the old passage made travel possible for horse and animal-drawn wagons to access the river ferry, which was in operation in the 1800s. The site was the major east to west road that spanned Florida, crossing the Suwannee River at this location. During the 1800s, wagons were ferried to various places on both sides of the Withlacoochee River.[1] Though the confluence was an important and busy crossing, many ferries traversed the Suwannee at numerous locations all along the banks and shores of the river.

Edwin LaMasure's 1907 portrait depicts how people and animals were once ferried across the Suwannee River. The portrayal is of a crossing near Branford, Florida. Courtesy of State Library and Archives of Florida.

The iron chassis of an old rail tram, once used in the logging industry, is displayed in the Suwannee River State Park near the confluence.

One important ferry was operated by Charles Dean, who lived in a home on the Suwannee River near the confluence of the Withlacoochee. Near there he ran a busy ferry, and in the late 1800s he charged fifty cents for a crossing. Eric Musgrove, in his historic fictional novel *There Let Me Live and Die*, portrays a realistic picture of a river crossing in that period:

> Richard jumped back on the wagon and ushered the horse down the sloped landing to the wooden ferry tied up at the river's edge. The ferry was about ten feet wide and thirty feet long, large enough to hold a six-team wagon with ease . . . moving to the center of the ferry . . . Mr. Dean untied the ferry and pushed off using the long pole he had. Dean . . . attached his pole to the long rope spanning the Suwannee River . . . using the current to propel them along, the ferry soon reached the Ellaville side of the river.

In a family cemetery, a small gravestone with the name Charles Dean is visible from Highway 90, approximately two hundred yards east of the agricultural inspection station. The CSA inscription reveals he fought for the Confederate States of America during the American Civil War. The cemetery is a fairly long and difficult trek from the river.

Later, when automobiles became popular, they too were ferried across the Suwannee River.

Notes
1. Historical Kiosk at Suwannee River State Park. Live Oak.

One important ferry was operated by Charles Dean near this location. Dean lived in a home on the Suwannee River near the confluence of the Withlacoochee. His grave is located in a small cemetery adjacent to Highway 90 (go east), approximately a half mile from the old Highway 90 Bridge, approximately two hundred yards beyond the Agricultural Inspection Station. The CSA inscription on his tombstone stands for Confederate States of America.

A Paddler's Guide

The Town of Columbus was once a thriving settlement of five hundred people. A sawmill was operating there; the old wheel of a steam-powered cotton gin is on display in the Suwannee River State Park, near the confluence of the Withlacoochee and Suwannee Rivers.

Confederate Railroad Bridge and Confederate Earthworks: Men Died Protecting the Crossing

The voices of singing Confederate soldiers destined for battle told stories of hope and obliteration. Those tales may still linger at the Suwannee River Railroad Bridge and Earthworks. So, too, screams mixed with regretful prayers may have seeped into limestone walls as mortally wounded Confederate rebels were brought back from the battle at Ocean Pond to their final destination: Madison, Florida. Some died in the Wardlaw mansion. They are buried in Oak Ridge Cemetery.

Located within the Suwannee River State Park, near the confluence of the Withlacoochee and the Suwannee Rivers, is what is left of the Confederate Earthworks. The Earthworks were constructed and manned by Southern sentinels as the area was equipped to defend the all-important railroad bridge against Union troops. Fifteen thousand Florida men fought for the Southern cause in the American Civil War, the

The covered railroad bridge played a significant role in the Civil War. The 1870 photograph depicts the bridge as it existed when Confederate sentinels guarded the crossing. Courtesy of State Library and Archives of Florida.

A Paddler's Guide

George Drew, before he was elected governor of Florida in 1877, rallied support from locals of the area when he learned that Federal Marshals (prompted by angry Republicans) from Jacksonville were headed via railway to his mansion to arrest him. In an embellished account by Eric Musgrove in his novel *There Let Me Live and Die,* the people of the vicinity assisted Drew in prying up the rail tracks and in burning the covered bridge, thus halting Drew's arrest. For a more definitive historical account, refer to Clothilde O'Hara Mainer's *Yesterday in Old Columbus,* written in 1972. A cement remnant is all that remains of the old covered bridge located in the Suwannee River State Park at the confluence of the Suwannee and Withlacoochee Rivers.

war that Southerners at the time called The War of Northern Aggression. The state's soldiers comprised just 2 percent of the Confederate Army.[1]

Another Florida contribution to the Southern war effort was thousands of head of cattle, which Florida provided to keep the Confederate Army from starving; the Confederacy relied heavily upon the bridge to deliver cattle in order to nourish men and ready them for war. Many of the cows were herded to Madison, Florida, the county just across the Suwannee River from the bridge location. All totaled, Florida offered seventy-five thousand cows, and the beeves assisted in feeding the Confederate Army. The bridge at the Suwannee River was merely one bridge that was heavily guarded during war time as soldiers manned them to protect the flow of much-needed supplies.[2]

The Earthworks built at the site were located in a strategic position, for the bluff was also a pinnacle place to guard the head of navigation on the Suwannee River. The Northern strategy was to take the railroad bridge in the year 1864; they wanted to have control of such significant passage of troops and supplies, which aided the enemy's cause. Union forces were unsuccessful, however, in their attempts to capture the bridge. When they arrived on one cold February day at Olustee (near Ocean Pond), fifty miles east of the confluence, they were defeated by Confederates. The North retreated. The bridge was secured. Losing the bridge at the Suwannee River and Withlacoochee's confluence to Union forces might have proven disastrous for the South, because so much needed food in the form of Florida beef was transported by railway in order to feed Southern troops.³

Local historians in Madison County, my own home town, recall several prominent citizens who stood guard at the Suwannee River Bridge during wartime. Judge Enoch Van J. Vann, President of the Confederate Senate and a well-known attorney, once recalled that he and Chandler Holmes Smith, a Confederate planter who lived in a magnificent Greek revival antebellum home in the heart of the town of Madison, were standing guard at the western section of the Suwannee Railway bridge when a train filled with Confederate troops sped past them as the locomotive hurled toward Jacksonville in order to merge with General Joseph Finegan. The strategy was to send fighting men to Ocean Pond in an attempt to halt the Union troops under General Truman A. Seymour. Vann recalls the lively soldiers were singing songs and shouting cheers as they passed over the Suwannee River.⁴

Men wounded at the Battle of Olustee (Ocean Pond as the battle is sometimes called) were transported from the battlefield by train to Madison County, where they succumbed to gruesome injuries. Dying to save the Suwannee River Bridge, they now are

Florida's Cattle Guard or Cow Cavalry was a Confederate militia unit. The group was organized to combat Union troops in their attempts to steal beef intended for the Confederate Army.³ Courtesy of Joe Akerman

only nameless, voiceless men, some hastily buried in the Oak Ridge Cemetery in Madison, Florida. Once brave soldiers, today they repose in a regimental row, sleeping eternally under shades of century oaks. Their tombs are inscribed with only the letters C. S. A., acronym for Confederate States of America. When I stand on bluffs at the Suwannee River, or when my shadow looms over the graves at Oak Ridge Cemetery, chills run through me. I wonder which ones might have been singing in the days before the cold February battle in 1864. Listen for soldiers' songs and be attentive to wrenching cosmic appeals as you paddle under the bridge—the bridge for which men were willing to die.

Notes
1. Clark, James C. *200 Quick Looks at Florida History*. Sarasota: Pineapple Press Inc., 2000.
2. Historical Kiosk at Suwannee River State Park. Live Oak.
3. Akerman, Joe. *Florida Cowman: A History of Florida Cattle Ranching*. Kissimmee: Florida Cattleman's Association, 1976.
4. Browning, Edwin, Junior. "Ellaville Stood by Confederacy." *The Tallahassee Democrat*, 25 June 1970.

Suggested Reading
Nulty, William H. *Confederate Florida*. Tuscaloosa: The University of Alabama Press, 1990.

Rose Knox and Graham Schorb

Bustling Trade Center: Cemetery Marks History in the Suwannee River State Park

The Town of Columbus was a trading site located on the Suwannee River during the mid 1800s. The once thriving settlement of five hundred people offered a stage coach stop, a railway stop, and a steamboat landing. A ferry and sawmill were also important to the town and many commodities were traded there. Several large plantations in the area delivered cotton via wagon to the Town of Columbus, and thousands of pounds of cotton were shipped by steamboat down the Suwannee River to the Gulf of Mexico.[1]

While walking in the Suwannee River State Park, look for the Confederate Earthworks site, which is where the town once existed. Be sure to visit the old cemetery known as one of the oldest grave sites in the state of Florida, and read the historical markers throughout the park.

Directions to Columbus Cemetery Located in the Suwannee River State Park
1. Walk up the boat ramp and follow the blacktop road.
2. Take the third left which is directly across from the children's playground (approximately one hundred yards from the boat ramp—no GPS used for directions).
3. After taking this third left, follow the blacktop to the right. The road cuts through the campground.
4. Walk about twenty-five yards to where the blacktop begins to curve and parallels a limestone road.
5. Walk off of the blacktop road to the limestone road, which is also the gas line easement through the park.
6. Turn right (south) on the limestone road. Go under the power lines, which have orange colored balls attached.
7. At the power line, cross over Old Stagecoach Road. The dirt road is unmarked.
8. Continue walking south approximately one hundred yards.
9. Look to the left; the old Columbus Cemetery is back in a pine stand.
10. The trek is approximately four hundred yards from the Suwannee River boat ramp.

Notes
1. Mueller, Edward A. *Suwannee River Steamboating*. Florida Historical Quarterly, Vol.45, No. 3, January 1967, pp. 269-288,.

A Paddler's Guide

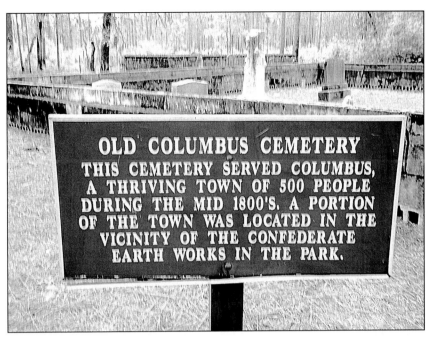

The cemetery of the Town of Columbus is a reminder of the once bustling trade center on the Suwannee River during the 1800s.

Many pioneer gravestones dot the Columbus Cemetery.

Thomas E. Swift's gravestone bears the sad lament:
Sleep husband sleep thy toils are o'er;
Sweet be thy rest so oft needed before;
Well have we loved you but God loved you more;
He has called thee away to that bright happy shore.

The cemetery reminded me of a verse from Robert Frost's "Disused Graveyard." Frost writes about how the graveyard is full, and no person is ever buried there anymore; but people still visit the cemetery to look at the graves. The poem begins, "The living come with grassy tread to read the gravestones on the hill,/The graveyard draws the living still,/But never anymore the dead. . . ."

In the 1800s, North Florida plantations produced tons of cotton. The all-important crop was hauled by oxen, mules, and horses to the Town of Columbus, located directly on the Suwannee River.
Courtesy of State Library and Archives of Florida.

A Paddler's Guide

Once the cotton was picked by plantation slaves, the crop was baled and later transported via steamboat to the Gulf of Mexico. Cotton was king in North Florida! Courtesy of State Library and Archives of Florida.

Steamboats Navigate the Suwannee

Last night I dreamed about steamboats. My mind's eye saw them as they navigated the Suwannee River. Some were elegant crafts as long as 136 feet in length, boasting lavish staterooms. I was reminded of the romantic picture painted by Mark Twain in his descriptions of steamboats on the Mississippi. However, my dreams were not mere fiction, for back in the 1830s the legendary waterway of the Suwannee River was a veritable highway for such magnificent vessels. Beginning in the 1830s, steamboats aided in maritime operations during the Second Seminole War, from 1835 to 1842. In addition, they were used to restock supplies and were owned or chartered by the United States government.

Steamboats traveled up-river from the mouth, beginning at the Gulf of Mexico.[1] According to the Saint Augustine News of 1845, the first commercial steamer, the *Orpheus*, constructed in New Orleans, was routed to carry mail from Cedar Key to the town of Santa Fe on the Santa Fe River. The ship was to also travel up the Suwannee River to the thriving Town of Columbus. The place was bustling in the 1840s, as the cotton trade, provided by large plantations in the immediate area, supplied cotton for transport. At Columbus, wagons loaded with cotton came. In fact, in the fall of 1843, over three thousand bales were shipped from the trading post. Steamboats on the Suwannee were significant, because roads and railroads were still scarce, and there was a need for a great amount of supplies to maintain the many sawmills and turpentine camps in and on the Suwannee River Basin.[2]

Yet another important vessel, which oft traversed the waters, was the *Madison*. Built for specific use on the Suwannee River, the ship was named after the small Florida town. It was 120 feet long, 22 feet wide, and 4 feet deep. Her captain was James Tucker, a prominent river man. Tucker was also known for his association with steamboats on the Ohio and on the Mississippi rivers. The *Madison* was utilized as a United States Mail steamer, making bimonthly runs up to the Town of Columbus. Not only did the *Madison* deliver mail, but the steamer also transported general merchandise such as "venison, hams, cow hides, deer skins, tallow, beeswax, honey, chickens, eggs, hogs, and beeves" for trade along the banks of the Suwannee.[3]

Known for her shrill whistle, the steamer could be heard from ten miles away and the captain made sure the whistle was sounded intermittently to give townspeople time to arrive at river landings. There, nearby villagers would engage in trade. Often when I am hiking trails in the vicinity, I imagine what excitement must have accompanied the sound of the whistle as the shrill announcement drew residents from their homes and to the riverside.

At the start of the American Civil War, Captain Tucker rallied a company of Confederate soldiers and formed Company H or the 8th Florida Infantry. The season was around September of 1863. Because of impeding war, his steamboat, the *Madison*, was abandoned by Tucker. His plans were to submerge her at Old Troy Spring with future plans to resurrect her at the conclusion of the Civil War. He sent a much needed supply of corn to Troy, and after the grain was delivered, he gave specific directions to three men to scuttle the *Madison*. Remaining true to their word, E.J. Davis, John M. Caldwell, and Joab Ward took the *Madison* from Troy landing to the spring. Following their orders precisely, they scuttled her there. Captain Tucker's dream of bringing her up after the war, however, was destroyed. In an unpublished manuscript, "The Steamboat *Madison*," John M. Caldwell reveals what happened to her during that tumultuous period:

> Her boilers were removed, split lengthwise, carried to the sea coast and used in the manufacture of salt. Her smokestacks were cut up . . . and used by farmers as funnels for their sugar furnaces. The cabins were torn up and the lumber used by whomever wanted it, and when the war ended, all that remained of the *Madison* was her hull resting on the rocks under the crystal waters of Old Troy spring."[4]

Driven by need under lean times of wartime, area residents had utilized the sunken steamer for utilitarian purposes of survival.

Anyone visiting Troy Spring today can still see remnants of a vessel resting there. A historical mystery also remains: Caldwell describes a much smaller craft than these remnants indicate. Perhaps there were two ships named *Madison*, the second constructed to ride the fame of the first. Such information may never surface.

A famous double-decked steamboat was the *Belle of the Suwanee* (spelled with one n), built by Captain Robert Absolom Ivey at Branford. Construction was completed in 1889, and she was named in honor of Ivey's daughter, Bertha. Weighing 180 net tons, the craft was touted as "a legend in her own time."[5] One of her most attractive features, which may have made her quite popular, was her bridal chambers. Those accommodations became all the rave for wealthy honeymooners in Florida during the 1890s.[6]

Imagine how she must have appeared at night, against the dark tannic currents of the Suwannee, her kerosene lamps reflecting a lucid image as laughter of reveling passengers echoed from her double decks. Fine cuisine was served to hungry guests, and the highlight of the menu was fresh Suwannee River catfish! The ship cruised the Suwan-

Captain James Tucker. Courtesy of State Library and Archives of Florida.

nee until 1896, when some accounts reveal she went under during a hurricane. However, other sources indicate the ship endured the hurricane of 1896, though it suffered damage. Those accounts suggest that the steamer continued navigation until 1900, when her seams ripped asunder, not far from the mouth of the Suwannee River, relenting to violent waves, as she succumbed to liquid depths in only eight feet of water. However, other stories portray that her majestic days came to an abrupt end in September 1900, when she was destroyed by heavy seas, about twenty-five miles north of the mouth of the Suwannee River, at a place called Horseshoe Bay. Ironically, she was lost in only eight feet of water. Dan McQueen, a famous pilot of African heritage, captained the *Belle of the Suwanee* among many other steamboats of the era.[7]

The heyday of steamboats on the Suwannee River came to an end around 1896, with the exception of a few vessels, which continued to navigate the waterway. There were many other steamboats maneuvering river, and they had names such as the *Orpheus*, the *Minerva*, the *Glasgow*, the *Colonel Cottrell*, the *Wawenock*, the *Erie*, the *Caddo Belle*, the *Suwanee* (Thomas Edison was her passenger), the *Eva*, the *Bertha Lee*, the *Yulee*, and the *Izard*. The *Yulee* and the *Izard* lie at the bottom of the Suwannee; the *Izard* rests down from the confluence of the Withlacoochee and the Suwannee near Suwannee River State Park. Some remnants of the *Yulee* may still remain at the mouth of the Suwannee; the *Madison* remains at Old Troy Spring.[8] When river levels are low, there is evidence of an old steamship on embankments of the Suwannee River.

When paddling the Suwannee's waters, listen closely for a faint ghost whistle announcing the arrival of a loaded steamboat. At night, while camping under velvet skies, imagine a vessel filled with excited passengers—an elegant ship illumined in the glow of kerosene lamps. Watch her slowly pass by. Then sleep in a tent on white sand beaches and dream with me of steamboats.

Notes

1, 2, 3, 4, 6, and 8. Mueller, Edward A. "Suwannee River Steamboating." *Florida Historical Quarterly*, Vol. 45, no. 3, January 1967, pp 269-288.

5 and 7. Musgrove, Eric. *Reflections of Suwannee County: 150 Anniversary Edition 1858-2008*. Live Oak: North Florida Printing Co., Inc., 2008.

An artist's depiction of the *Madison* docked at White Springs. Courtesy of State Library and Archives of Florida.

Belle of the Suwanee. Courtesy of State Library and Archives of Florida.

A Paddler's Guide

The *Three States* captained by Captain Ivey. Courtesy of State Library and Archives of Florida.

The *Louisa* in her heyday. Courtesy of State Library and Archives of Florida.

The *City of Hawkinsville* at Branford. Courtesy of State Library and Archives of Florida.

The *Louisa*. Courtesy of State Library and Archives of Florida.

A Paddler's Guide

Drew Mansion at Ellaville: Famous Logging Location

Governor Franklin Drew was an influential figure in the South, especially on the Suwannee River. He was a Northerner, born in New Hampshire, but he established himself in the South as a successful lumber and salt industry figure. When the American Civil War began, he harbored mixed loyalties. He sided with Northern political views, yet he was married to a Southern woman; this union tied him closely with Southern ways and traditions. The Confederacy benefitted from his marital loyalties as he aided their cause, providing them with much needed troop supplies of lumber and salt. It was not until the last remaining months of the war that he joined the Union army. When he later ran for governor, many Southerners were unaware of his past loyalties with the North. He served as governor of Florida during the difficult era of Reconstruction from 1877 to 1881.[1] The railway system there allowed Drew to board the train destined for Tallahassee. But much of Drew's official government business was conducted from his mansion.[2]

At the conclusion of the war, his successful lumber business at the Town of Columbus (once located at the site of the present day Suwannee River State Park) was now out of operation. He relocated, crossing the Suwannee River to the Madison County side, and there he established a new steam-sawmill industry that was destined to grow to the largest in the state of Florida.

The place became a thriving mill town that Drew named Ellaville. According to some stories, the name was derived to honor an elderly black woman who had worked for his family for many years. Ellaville burgeoned into a vital town of over one thousand residents. Residents and visitors had access to two churches, a post office, an express office, a telegraph unit, a Masonic Lodge, and two schools. No saloons were allowed. Lumbermen and trappers often visited the town in search of jobs or to trade goods.

Drew constructed a home for his family at Ellaville in 1868. The home became known as the Drew Mansion and was a two-story dwelling with ten rooms. Inside was an impressive staircase constructed of imported mahogany and finely crafted fireplaces with elaborate facings and marble mantles. From the high plaster etched ceilings, were sparking chandeliers. The mansion estate was known for manicured and formal gardens.[3] Some historians claim the home was the first residence in the state with electricity, telephone, and indoor plumbing.[4]

In 1883 Drew sold his Ellaville sawmill to Mr. Louis Bucki from New York City; Bucki ran the mill for several years and made the mansion his home. Others operated

Governor Drew. Courtesy of State Library and Archives of Florida.

the mill after Bucki; however, as yellow pine became scarce, the mill shut down, and the town died, officially commencing in 1942, when the post office closed its doors.

By the 1930s, the Drew Mansion had been abandoned according to a Madison County resident L.A. Bailey. Bailey visited the site in 1930 on a school field trip. His tale depicts a much dilapidated mansion: "A family of gentle negro sharecroppers lived in the downstairs area of the former governor's house. They had nailed the cellar door shut to keep the haints from coming up and had boarded off the upstairs areas of the house to keep them from coming down." In the 1970s, the Drew Mansion was completely destroyed by fire.[5]

The property was later acquired by the state of Florida and today is part of the Suwannee River State Park on the Madison side.

The once-glorious mansion was built in 1868 by two of Franklin Drew's brothers. In its heyday, guests strolled through the famous manicured gardens. Posing are Louis Bucki and his wife of New York. Bucki was a business partner with the governor. Later, the mansion was purchased by Robert L. Milinor in 1893; the Milinor family lived there until 1911, until flood waters forced them to abandon the home. Courtesy of State Library and Archives of Florida.

Much later, the home fell into disrepair. Years of abandonment took its toll on the once-opulent mansion. Cloaked in shadows of neglect, the structure existed until the 1970s. A fire consumed and destroyed the home completely. Courtesy of State Library and Archives of Florida.

Directions to Historical Site: After paddlers leave the boat ramp at the Suwannee River State Park, they will travel less than a quarter of a mile before coming upon a wide place in the river where the Withlacoochee River vigorously joins the Suwannee. The confluence is located before the railroad bridge and the Highway 90 Bridges (old and current). Look ahead for the Withlacoochee River on river right when paddling down the Suwannee. To visit the historical marker and a kiosk, and the Drew Mansion site, paddle about 150 yards up the Withlacoochee River. Still visible is the stone spring house on river left. The spring house is called Suwannacoochee Spring. The area was used in times past for logging. Walk up beyond the stone spring house into the park. Approximately 150 yards from the river (straight ahead) is a historical marker. The remembrance sign chronicles the history of Civil War Reconstruction era and provides details of the Drew Mansion. Also in the area is the kiosk that has information on the Drew site and the location of the old cemetery.

Directions to the Park and Kiosk: Walk up from the stone spring house on a well-traveled path. See a parking lot. Follow the path to the kiosk, which is located on the site and offers directions on how to locate the old mansion estate. Walking to the overgrown and ill-maintained Drew Mansion location, a visitor will find evidence of the once palatial home. There are still brick remnants from the foundation. The root cellar and cistern remain too. Northeast of the old home site is a small cemetery where Drew buried his wife, several infant children, and one teenage son. Some accounts suggest that the son was drowned in the Withlacoochee River. Often when I am on the Withlacoochee enjoying a day at Melvin Shoals, I think of Drew's son. Some believe he lost his life somewhere on the river near the shoals.

Directions to the Drew Mansion Site and Cemetery: *Warning*—Only adamant and in-shape folks may be interested in hiking the distance to the Drew Cemetery site. From Suwanneecoochee Spring, follow the path leading away from the spring. Go under the railroad trestle through the parking area to old Highway 90. See an old building that was once a popular seafood restaurant. Go right on old Highway 90 to the road, Ellaville Central. Turn to the right, crossing the railroad tracks, and look for a path on the left. The mansion site is approximately seventy-five yards from the road back in the woods. The spot is not well maintained. The place is known today as a famous ghost town that Governor Franklin Drew called Ellaville. The property of the old estate and old home site is located in Madison County.

Notes

1, 3, and 5. Sims, Elizabeth et al. *A History of Madison County, Florida.* Madison: Jimbob Printing Inc., 1986.

2 and 4. Musgrove, Eric. *Reflections of Suwannee County: 150 Anniversary Edition 1858-2008.* Live Oak: North Florida Printing Co., Inc., 2008.

Suggested Reading

The book *From Zero to Ninety* by Charles R. Noegel chronicles life and times in Ellaville during the early 1900s. Noegel tells about the stores, the train depot, and life on the river at the turn of the last century, and he includes photographs from that period. His book offers interesting reading about the Ellaville area.

Explorers of the historical site may run across the old cistern. *Note:* The place is not maintained, and walking to the old homestead and through the area may prove somewhat difficult. Courtesy of State Library and Archives of Florida.

Drew Sawmill at Ellaville in the 1800s. Courtesy of State Library and Archives of Florida.

Drew and Bucki Company Store, Ellaville. Courtesy of State Library and Archives of Florida.

The Drew Cemetery has had its share of vandals. The headstone was missing for a long time. In recent years, however, someone anonymously returned it to the steps of the Suwannee Valley Genealogical Society. The Society mounted the stone in cement, restoring it to its proper place. According to Drew papers in the Suwannee Valley Genealogical Society records, the child named Mary Amelia was the granddaughter of Governor Franklin Drew.

The graves within the Drew Cemetery once cradled American Civil War soldiers. However, each grave has been looted; what remains are merely slight indentions in the ground. The stones visible here are all that is left of the base of each head and footstone. The markers have all been stolen. Some locals believe the thieves were in search of brass buttons from military uniforms. Others surmise that perhaps someone wanted a macabre souvenir.

The old Drew logging spring house is located at Suwannacoochee Spring, just up the Withlacoochee River, about one hundred fifty yards on the left. The outflow is a place where we pause to cool down during spring and summer months. The adventurous hiker may choose to find the old mansion site, historical kiosk, and Drew Cemetery.

Paddlers May Encounter Various Snakes on the Suwannee: Story of Rattlesnake in Suwannee River State Park

O.B Sasser was once a park ranger in the Suwannee River State Park during the early 1990s. There he killed a five-foot rattlesnake after campers reported sighting one on a well-traveled hiking path. Because the snake was a potential threat to park hikers and campers, Sasser made the difficult decision to kill the snake in order to protect tourists. Graham tells the story about that day.

"I was with O.B. as he climbed in his truck to figure out the situation. He had a small hatchet. My first thought was, 'What's he planning on doing to a five-foot rattler with such a short handled hatchet?'" Yet O.B was an outdoorsman. He was well familiar with the dangers in hardwood forests, and had a know-how about him, as men of Nature tend to do. He exited the truck and used the hatchet to cut a small sapling. After stripping the sapling of branches, O.B. began vigorously rubbing the tip of the sapling. Next, in one swift movement, he came down with the sapling, striking the diamondback rattler directly upon the head. He killed the snake with one stroke!

Graham asked O.B. why he had rubbed the tip of the sapling with his hands. He replied, "Rubbing the stick makes the wood warm. The snake will strike at a warm object. This makes killing a poisonous snake easier and less hazardous." Graham took the snake back to his cabin, where he skinned the reptile. The five-foot snakeskin is displayed on an interior doorway.

Warning: Do not try this method on your own! When hiking in hardwood forests, be mindful that rattlesnakes live on the river and in the basin. Graham and I do not endorse the killing of a snake. However, sometimes in tourist areas park rangers have to make serious decisions concerning wildlife. Graham was told as a child by a famed herpetologist, Ross Allen, that when encountering a rattlesnake the proper thing to do is to tip your hat and walk seven feet around and away from the snake. Graham saved the skin in order to honor the snake's legacy, giving the meat to friends. Rattlesnakes were revered among indigenous peoples.

Paddlers often come up off the river asking about the large, docile snakes (though some guidebooks say they are feisty) that can be seen sunning on downed logs or lounging upon limestone outcroppings along the Suwannee River. Often, what paddlers are sighting is not a poisonous snake at all, but a common reptilian inhabitant, the brown water snake. Though they have markings similar to those of venomous rattlers, the brown water snakes are non-poisonous.[1]

A Paddler's Guide

Snakeskin in Graham's cabin.

Occasionally someone will see a moccasin. Please note that the moccasin is a very aggressive, poisonous snake and should be avoided at all costs!

A variety of other poisonous snakes inhabit the wilderness areas of the Suwannee River and Suwannee River Basin too. One story we have heard told comes from river guide Greg Pflug. He relates that once one of his fellow paddlers encountered a coral snake resting underneath a tarp. The tarp had been set down on the river's beach, and the coral snake crawled under it.

When camping on beaches and hardwood forests of the Suwannee River Basin, beware of snakes. Know, too, that Graham has been on the river and in the woods for twenty-five years. He frequently camps on beaches and embankments of area North Florida rivers. Rarely does he encounter a coral snake; he has only come in contact with a moccasin a few times while in the wild. Using a guidebook with information on Florida snakes might be helpful in identification. The best advice regarding snakes is to steer clear of them.

Notes
1. Bartlett, R.D. and Patricia. *Florida's Snakes: A Guide to Their Identification and Habits*. Gainesville: University Press of Florida, 2003.

Brown water snakes sometimes rest under beached canoes. David Pharr holds one he encountered at the Suwannee Canoe Outpost.

Paddlers may encounter brown water snakes resting in dead trees or lounging upon limestone embankments. Graham and I saw one basking in an overhanging tree across from the Dowling Park boat launch. People often confuse brown water snakes with the cottonmouth moccasin because of similar markings. The brown water snake, however, is non-venomous. It is the second largest water snake in Florida and is exceeded in size only by the Florida green water snake. An adult female can grow to five-and-a-half feet in length, but the male is usually smaller. Brown water snakes feed on fish and amphibians, and although some nature guidebooks say they are feisty, Graham and I have never encountered an aggressive one. These snakes are found along the Suwannee River and within the Suwannee River Basin.

A Paddler's Guide

Black snake.

A Paddler's Guide

Section Five Map

Interstate 10 Bridges to the Hal W. Adams Bridge Ramp
Mile 125 – Mile 98.2

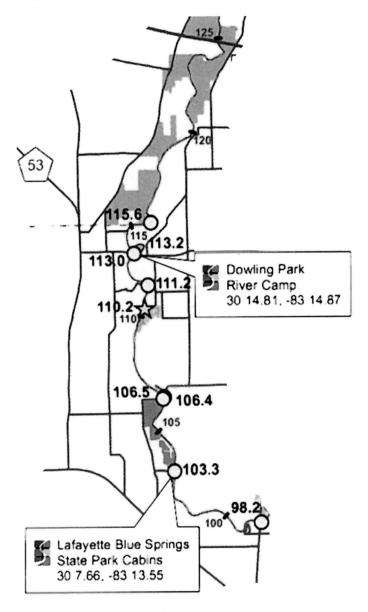

Navigation Warnings

There are several shoals in low water.

Camping Information

Numerous camp areas are available in low-to-medium water levels. Specifically look for suitable beach sites down from Anderson Spring on river right. Dowling Park river camp and Lafayette Blue Springs State Park have campsites, but paddlers should make a reservation and pay a fee.

Topography

Anderson Spring is a popular swimming hole for locals. Limestone walls take on a flat, rounded appearance on this section, and the river begins to widen significantly after the two bridges (first bridge is the Highway 250 Bridge and the other is the old Southern Railway Bridge) past the Dowling Park boat launch. Embankments begin to flatten. There is evidence of civilization, such as docks, river camps, and homes. Charles Spring and Charles Cemetery are historically significant places to visit, because they have impressive cultural tales of clashes between pioneers and Native Americans. Several creeks are fun for exploration if river levels permit. Explore Lafayette Blue Springs State Park too.

Wildlife Spotted

In April of 2008, Graham and I spotted a plethora of wildlife, including footprints of wild boars at Allen Mill Pond, a six-foot American alligator sunning on the riverbank, many red-eared sliders, one brown water snake, several great blue heron, a pileated woodpecker, an American bald eagle overhead, and a school of mullet swimming out of Lafayette Blue Spring as they entered the Suwannee River.

Points of Interest

Anderson Spring and Charles Spring are day-use facilities. They both offer places to explore. See the historical marker and Old Bellamy Trail (originally the Old Spanish Trail) approximately one hundred yards from the boat launch at Charles Spring. Visit the pioneer cemetery of the Charles Family. At the Charles Spring location there was once a Christian mission set up to convert Native Americans; afterwards a ferry crossing made the site a bustling trade center in pioneer Florida.

Restocking Supplies

Restock supplies at Dowling Park Landing (dock) on river left. Exit the river. There is a grocery store up from the landing at the Advent Christian Village. Also available is a laundromat, a barbershop, a restaurant, and a bank. The bank houses an ATM machine. Some campers have told Graham that they have made reservations there. They said they enjoyed staying in a comfortable room. No alcohol is available for sale in Dowling Park.

Restocking Information at Dowling Park: First option is Dowling Park Landing.
1. See the sign for Dowling Park Landing at the floating dock on river left.
2. Up from the landing is a grocery store at the Advent Christian Village. No alcohol is available at the location.
3. Also located at the Advent Christian Village are many amenities, including a post office, a restaurant, a barber shop, a laundry mat, and a bank with ATM machine.
4. General supplies and ice

Restocking Supplies Down-River from Dowling Park Landing: Highway 250 – Mile 113.0.
1. Beyond the Dowling Park Landing is the Highway 250 boat ramp on river left.
2. The ramp is located approximately a half mile down-river from the Dowling Park Landing.
3. Exit the river; walk up the boat ramp to Highway 250.
4. At Highway 250, proceed to the left-east.
5. Within sight of the boat ramp is a convenience store. Beer, snacks, general supplies, ice, and gas are available at the location.
6. The store is approximately three hundred yards from the river.

Paddlers will see the Dowling Park Landing on river left. The Advent Christian Village is located up from the floating landing. Many amenities are available at the Advent Christian Village, including a grocery store, a restaurant, and a bank. Some paddlers have relayed to us that they have rented accommodations there for the night.

A guided party of high school students from Colorado enjoyed a week of camping on the river. Before their trip, each one had to conduct specific research on one aspect of the river's history, topography, or wildlife. Papers were written and documented. Their academic understanding of the river gave them great insight concerning her legendary status and her abundance of natural wonders. Graham added to their knowledge by telling stories as they gathered around a campfire.

See Lafayette Blue on river right. The park is designated by signs and a boardwalk. Schools of mullet often dart in and out of the spring run.

Rose Knox and Graham Schorb

Native Americans on the Suwannee River: Ancient Indians and the Later Confederations

Imagine the cooing of a baby as his smiling mother hums quiet lullabies. The scene takes place not too far from a gentle river's edge. The mother is adorned in exquisite jewelry, carefully crafted from wood or bone. Perhaps she dangles the artful object to pacify her child.

Or imagine erratic sparks flying as strong hands of great hunters forge sharp stone projectiles made for killing big game like the mastodon or giant sloth. Think of a quiet paddle stroke as sleek warriors stand in supply-packed dugout canoes, steadily meandering down the Suwannee on a trade journey to the Gulf of Mexico.

Archaeological evidence of once great native nations offers mere hints of highly intact, sophisticated cultures of Native American tribes, once thriving and worshiping upon the Suwannee River and within the basin. Official archaeological investigations have upturned varied relics and mounds. Those age-old inanimate objects retell a fascinating cultural story of the first peoples concerning their mores and their societal lives. The ancient Native Americans were the first peoples to inhabit what is now known as the state of Florida. Some scholars believe they may have lived in the region as many as thirteen thousand years ago, but maybe even before then. These were people who traversed to the North American continent from eastern Asia during the Pleistocene or Great Ice Age. Some historians surmise they came by way of the land bridge, which joined Siberia with Alaska. The issue of their migration and presence, however, is still under debate.

The ancient Indians, often named Paleo-Indians, lived on what is today the Florida Peninsula. At that time, sea levels were approximately three hundred feet lower than present levels, making Florida's land surface twice as large. As glaciers of the Great Ice Age began to melt around eleven thousand years ago, water levels of oceans rose to today's levels. Since water levels were much lower then, and Florida's topography differed with less springs, lakes, and rivers, the ancient Indians sought out water sources such as indentions in limestone outcroppings and deep springs. In such places, hunters would dismember their kill. Consumption of the downed game came afterward.[1] As a result, Paleo-Indian relics have been recovered underwater or in and around deep natural spring areas all along the Suwannee River and Suwannee River Basin.

The later tribes emerged as distinct cultures with religious rites and conceptual knowledge of language and symbols. One confederation that lived in the basin was the Timucua Tribe. These Native Americans, today called the lost tribes of Florida, had a complex, intact culture complete with religious ceremonies, farming techniques, and

A Paddler's Guide

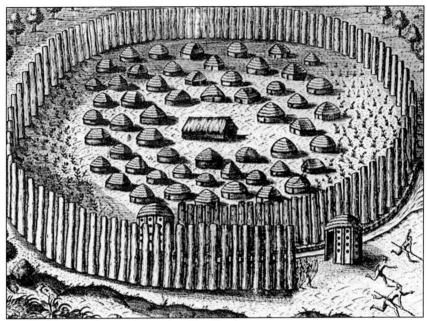

The image portrays a Timucua village engraving by Theodore De Bry, which came from a drawing by Jacques Le Moyne from 1564, and was first published in 1591. It should be noted that De Bry created many depictions of Florida Indians that were not always historically correct. He took creative license as he adapted his images from ideas he derived from Brazilian Indian cultures. His works of Florida Indians are nevertheless intriguing and fascinating. Courtesy of State Library and Archives of Florida.

economic systems. When the European explorers initially arrived on the Florida peninsula, there existed thirteen major Native American confederations. They have been named the Guale, Apalachee, Timucua, Pensacola, Potano, Ocale, Tobobaga, Mayaimi, Ais Jeaga, Calusa, Tequesta, and Matecumbe.

The largest of the confederations was the Timucua. They occupied the northeastern portion of the Florida panhandle, and their population is estimated at around two hundred thousand. They inhabited areas from west of the Aucilla River to the Gulf coast, near present-day Tampa Bay. Eastward they ranged to Cape Canaveral and northward into South Georgia. The Timucua survived by farming and hunting. Their major crops consisted of beans, maize, tubers, with added vegetables and fruit. The people also harvested tobacco, using the plant as an herb in their rituals. The men of the tribe hunted alligator, deer, bear, and bison; they also relied on trapping small game for survival. The Timucua adorned themselves with paint and tattoos, often decorating themselves in ornaments made from shell and bone, and the men were known to wear earrings made from fish bladders. Animal hides were used to make their clothing, and they constructed cloth from fibers of plants, such as moss. As Europeans encroached, the Timucua were systematically Christianized but were eventually wiped out by epidemics. By 1763, there was only one Timucuan living.[2]

The Timucua Confederation was part of the Mississipian Mound-Builder societies, and such ceremonial mounds from these cultures are prevalent in Central and North Florida today, though many were bulldozed over in Florida to make way for modern development.[3] One such mound is located within the Suwannee River Basin. It rises twenty-eight feet above sea level near Cedar Key. For a more comprehensive study on aboriginal sites, refer to Mac Perry's book *Indian Mounds You Can Visit: 165 Aboriginal Sites on Florida's West Coast.*

The Apalachee Confederation also resided in the panhandle of Florida, and like the Timucua, farmed and hunted. They have been described as a peaceful nation and were the first of the Florida tribes to suffer almost utter annihilation.[4] Spanish accounts of the early 1600s reveal that, though disease had ravished the population, there remained 107 Apalachee towns. A 1650 account says there were eight thousand Apalachee. They, too, were Christianized, but often resisted fiercely as they yearned to hold to the ways of their own peoples. One historical account describes the gory scene of how Christian

Theodore De Bry shows native Florida Indians as they dry food over an open flame. Notice the snake, the alligator, and the fish; all were abundant in the Suwannee River Basin and were used as a food source for native tribes. *Courtesy of State Library and Archives of Florida.*

natives at the Apalachee missions were set afire to be burned alive. Others were flayed alive. The Apalachee were also sold by the thousands as slaves to labor in the plantations of the Caribbean and the Carolinas. They, like the Timucua, were a highly communal, religious, and self-sufficient culture before the arrival of the Spaniards.[5] Their crops yielded beans, maize, pumpkins, and a variety of fruit; they supplemented their food crop with bear, turkey, deer, and bison, making snares to entrap small game. Fish and shellfish in area rivers, lakes, streams, and ponds provided meat for the tribe too.[6]

Some historians and archaeologists believe that as many as twelve million Native Americans lived, thrived, and worshipped on the North American continent as far back as 14,000 years ago.[7] However, in merely 350 years of the white man's intrusion, through war, famine, disease, and forced deportation, only 250,000 remained by the year 1850.[8]

Other books of interest on Native Americans include *Indian Art of Ancient Florida* by Barbara Purdy, *Florida Indians and the Invasion from Europe,* and *Florida's Indians from Ancient Times to the Present* by Jerald T. Milanich.

Notes

1, 2, 4, and 7. Morris, Theodore. *Florida's Lost Tribes.* Gainesville: University Press of Florida, 2004.

3, 6, and 8. Ervin, William R. *Let Us Alone.* W and S Ervin Publishing Company. 1983.

4. Covington, James W. *The Seminoles of Florida.* Gainesville: University Press of Florida, 1993.

Other Suggested Reading

Harvey, Miles. *Painter in a Savage Land.* New York: Random House, 2008.

Theodore Morris depicts a Paleo-Indian hunting a Florida mammoth. According to Florida archaeologists, several skeletal mammoth remains have been recovered from area North Florida rivers. Courtesy of Theodore Morris.

A Paddler's Guide

A panther warrior of the Timucua tribe wears a headdress representing high military rank. Courtesy of Theodore Morris

Theodore Morris depicts an Apalachee tribe member bundled in the hide of a Florida black bear. Courtesy of Theodore Morris.

A Paddler's Guide

These Native American relics were discovered in North Florida. Some are Paleo-Indian artifacts, while others are later points. The two large center artifacts in the frame on the right were tools. All points were found on private property. Private Collection.

Watch for Wild Boar: Ancestors of Hernando de Soto

As a small child I often stared, horrified, right into the vicious jaws of a maddened boar! Bristles stood erect upon its neck, while two-inch razor-sharp fangs threatened my disembowelment. Before I could allow my imagination to carry me to deathly places, I heard Mama's falsetto song calling us to dinner. "Rosie! Charles! Come and get it!" A feast was being laid out on a family table in the back woods of South Georgia.

Back in the late 1960s and early 1970s, Mama travelled lone woods through pine forests as she made her way from North Florida, with my twin brother and me, to our Parrish Thanksgiving celebration. We spent the day at the remote hamlet known as Haylow, Georgia. Mother's sister, our Aunt Gladys, would magically conjure her own unique southern seasonings as she prepared her delectable turkey and dressing, known throughout the region as "the best." My uncle was a hunter of wild boar, among other game. As a trophy, he had displayed an especially ferocious boar's head over the sofa in the family room, an irresistible lure for curious visiting children.

After wolfing down our choices of turkey, dressing in giblet gravy, fried chicken, fried okra, fried liver, smothered venison steak, green beans, butter beans, acre peas, corn on the cob, mashed potatoes, creamed corn, deviled eggs, yams, red-sliced tomatoes, Vidalia onions, collard greens, macaroni and cheese, homemade biscuits drowning in butter and drizzled in tupelo honey, corn and cracklin' bread, pickled beets, radishes and cucumbers, and then our choices of desserts—homemade South Georgia pound cake, seven layer chocolate cake, pineapple upside-down cake, and a variety of flavored puddings and home-made jellies from may haw, blackberries, and plums—Charles and I would run back to Uncle Louis's family room. Balancing ourselves on the sofa, we stuck our heads as close as we could to the gaping mouth of that razor-toothed black monster. No amount of discouragement from Mama or Uncle Louis—who ranted when we walked with dirty feet on his furniture—could keep us from the terrible jaws of such a beast!

From the Okefenokee Swamp to the Gulf of Mexico, wild boar forage for food in hardwood forests along the river's edge. They are descended from breeds that Hernando de Soto introduced during the 1500s as he marched through the southeast in quest of riches. Much later in the late 1800s and early 1900s, when popular resort hotels upon the Suwannee River were desirable destinations for wealthy tourists and hunters, the boar were deliberately stocked as game in order to provide for successful hunts. Guidebooks advertising to affluent hunters guaranteed them a beastly trophy when they hunted in the wilds of Florida. The advertisements attracted many rich tourists to

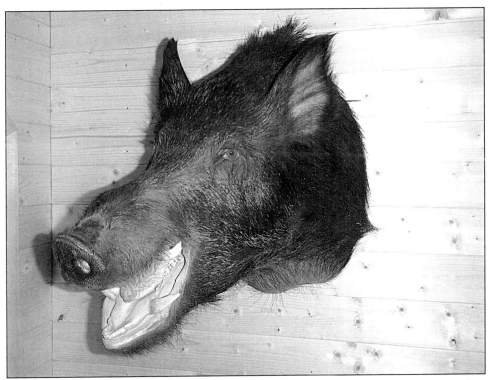

Danny Breedlove of Franklin N.C. killed a wild boar in Georgia. Boars were brought in by Hernando de Soto's army in the 1500s. Danny has the boar head mounted on his living room wall.

the Suwannee River Basin. Two such hunting preserves along the Suwannee River were located at Suwannee Spring and another near Dowling Park.

Wild boar also played an important role to early settlers. During the pioneering days of Florida, when the state remained a wild place, settlers often allowed their cattle and the wild boar's ancestors, hogs, to traverse freely, marking them with special identification methods to specify ownership. Often called piney-woods rooters, the feral hogs in Florida can be aggressive beasts, famous for their bad temperament and violent, unprovoked attacks. They have been known to charge people, rattlesnakes, and bears. In pioneer Florida their meat was also an important food staple for early settlers.[1]

Guidebooks describe wild boars as mostly black (some are brown) and spotted. All should be considered aggressive. Wild hogs may charge if provoked. With razor sharp, two-inch-long teeth, they can disembowel a hunting dog or other aggressor with a mere movement of the head.[2] In Patrick D. Smith's historically based fictional account of pioneer Florida, *A Land Remembered*, one of his characters vehemently warns his son of wild boar: "You see where I shot him . . . Right in the head. You gut shoot a wild boar, he'll run a hundred yards after he's hit, and tear your leg off with them tusks."[3] Smith's story reminds paddlers not to approach these animals.

Evidence of wild boar is found in muddy banks along the Suwannee River where they leave ample footprints. Look for deep indentions in mud or sand where they have visited the river for a drink of water and are foraging for food there in the soft embankments. Wild boar prints were visible along muddy shores on a day we passed Allen Mill Pond. Keep a vigilant eye out for the beasts de Soto brought, and for the ones wealthy Suwannee River tourists once hunted in days gone by. Perhaps you will see one of the wild beasts along the banks of the Suwannee River. Hunters today still hunt the boar.

Notes

1. Ste. Claire, Dana. *Cracker: The Cracker Culture in Florida History*. Gainesville: University of Florida Press. 2006.
2. Gingerich, Jerry Lee. *Fabulous Mammals: Their Stories*. Tampa: World Publications.
3. Smith, Patrick D. *A Land Remembered*. Sarasota: Pineapple Press. Sarasota. 1984.

Wild boar on a beach near Fargo, Georgia.

Dowling Park History: Lumber Town, Tourist Attraction, and Christian Retirement Community

In the late 1800s through the early 1900s, prominent American men began envisioning riches to be had in the natural resources of North Florida. One such man was Thomas Dowling who realized the potential promise of vast, virgin acres of longleaf pine forests, growing near the Suwannee River and the river's basin. In 1903 he constructed a mill on the Suwannee River, using the Live Oak, Perry, and Gulf Railroad to transport his lumber. Mr. Dowling, too, longed to build a resort hotel that would attract wealthy tourists to Florida. Other men, like Henry Flagler and Henry Plant, had previously constructed hotels in Florida locations such as Saint Augustine, Palm Beach, Miami, and Tampa. Both had been greatly successful catering to the ultra rich; in fact, Flagler's 1887 Ponce de Leon in St. Augustine revitalized the town's economy. Fulfilling his own vision, Dowling constructed an extravagant hotel, naming it The Park Hotel. As planned, affluent tourists flooded to the Suwannee River from many locations to enjoy such advertised amenities as a bowling alley, billiards, two swimming pools, and landscaped grounds.

Others flocked to The Park Hotel to hunt, fish, and horseback ride.[1] Before the Park Hotel was ever constructed, rich northern marksmen made their way to other Florida destinations during the Reconstruction era earlier, when guidebooks advertised to Yankee hunters the bounty of Florida's wild lands. Many Reconstruction-era marksmen, mounted on horseback, hunted along Florida Rivers in pursuit of raccoon, opossum, wild turkey, geese, ducks, snipe, quail, woodcock, partridge, curlew, deer, bear, and wildcat. Guidebooks of the day guaranteed even the most inexperienced hunter a trophy of antlers, but an avid marksman like A.J. Alexander of Kentucky could down sixty deer in a three-week span. The advertisements portrayed wild Florida as a mysterious hunting wonderland for big-game seekers; Florida panthers were touted to be as great as royal Bengal tigers. In shades of lavender moonlight, bear hunts on Florida beaches were orchestrated around buried turtle eggs as voracious bears emerged from winter slumber. On other Florida rivers such as the St. John's, advertisements lured "gator" hunters. Standing on the decks of steamships, sportsmen took shots at swimming and sunning alligators, and one party killed 162 alligators in one afternoon alone.[2]

Similar hunting scenarios throughout Florida found their way to the banks of the Suwannee in North Florida, as posh resorts offered organized hunts for boar and other wild game on the river's basin for wealthy tourists.

Once known as "Hudson on the Suwannee," Dowling Park was renamed for the Dowling family and grew into a thriving community by 1910, with a railroad depot, several stores, a hotel, seventy-three tenant houses occupied by sawmill laborers, and an administrative construct for the lumber company operations. Several family dwellings on the Suwannee River, built for prominent people in the vicinity, were there too. The Park Hotel was positioned directly across the river from the sawmill.[3]

Like many other grand resorts in Florida such as the hotels up river at White Springs and Suwannee Spring, The Park Hotel targeted prominent northerners through advertisements as a new getaway on the "romantic Suwannee River." People were drawn to the area to bathe and swim in "healing" sulfur waters. In 1925, however, fire consumed and destroyed The Park Hotel. No architectural evidence remains on the Suwannee River to indicate that The Park Hotel ever existed.

At around the same time in 1910, the founder of Sears and Roebuck Company, Richard Sears, purchased several thousand acres of Florida timberland. He also acquired The Dowling Lumber Company, the mill at Dowling Park, and the Live Oak, Perry, and Gulf Railroad. With these holdings, he began new businesses such as the Suwannee River Land Belt Company. Richard Sears' own Sears catalog advertised land tracts by mail order for eleven dollars per acre; over ten thousand customers bought razed timberland before they ever even visited their properties. Many purchased the land on time, paying five dollars down and five dollars a month.[4]

The Advent Christian Village was conceived in 1913, when Thomas Dowling's minister, Burr Bixler, convinced Dowling to contribute an expansive portion of land upon the Suwannee River so Bixler might establish an orphanage and home for "old and worn out ministers and missionaries." Bixler had created a campground there previously on the same land donated by Dowling in 1911.[5]

After the heyday of the lumber industry in Dowling Park, Thomas Dowling and Richard Sears donated four hundred acres to The Conference of Advent Christian Churches. By 1914, the place had become a facility to house orphans and was a Mecca for retired ministers and their wives. Today, Dowling Park is a Christian retirement community.[6]

Paddlers often stop at Dowling Park Landing to restock supplies at a small grocery store located at the Advent Christian Village, just up from the Dowling Park Landing.

Notes

1, 4, and 6. Echoes of the Past: A History of Suwannee County 1855-2000. Saint Petersburg: Southern Heritage Press, 2000.

2. Revels, Tracy J. Sunshine Paradise: A History of Florida Tourism. Gainesville: University Press of Florida, 2011.

3 and 5. Musgrove, Eric. Reflections of Suwannee County: 150 Anniversary Edition 1858-2008. Live Oak: North Florida Printing Co., Inc., 2008

In Florida during the late 1800s, it was not uncommon for resort hotels to advertise to big game hunters. Some of the ads recruited those sportsmen looking to kill bears, panthers, and alligators. Courtesy State Library and Archives of Florida.

Live Oak, Perry, and Gulf Railroad was a logging rail line in the late 1800s; it remained in operation until 1949. Photograph taken in August 1933. Courtesy of State Library and Archives of Florida.

The Park Hotel at Dowling Park was once a grand resort attracting rich visitors from the North; however, it burned in 1925. Later, the land was donated to the Convent of Advent Christian Churches. No evidence on the Suwannee River hints at the former location. Paddlers may find the Advent Christian Village an ideal stop to restock supplies. Courtesy of State Library and Archives of Florida.

Ivey-McIntosh Cemetery

The Ivey Cemetery, also known as Ivey-McIntosh Cemetery, is situated upon the high banks of the Suwannee River and tells a silent story of early settlers in Florida. The final resting place, marked by white, eroded stones surrounded by iron grated fencing, cradles the relatives of the Ivey and McIntosh pioneers (among other family names). Located on river left, approximately four miles down from Charles Spring, the river front acreage, there between the Suwannee, and the cemetery is on a high embankment of private property lots. Therefore, getting to the site from the river may prove harrowing and illegal.

According to Bivian Grady Howell, cemetery researcher, seventy-two grave plots have been recorded there.[1] In the late 1800s, Robert (Bob) Ivey and his brothers, Jesse N. and F.C. Ivey, along with several other relatives, moved into Suwannee County from Georgia, following the years after the American Civil War. Robert Ivey began purchasing acres of land in the southern portion of the county. Not long afterwards, he began building and captaining steamboats, and one of his most popular was the *Belle of the*

The Ivey-McIntosh Cemetery cradles seventy-two graves.

Suwanee.[2] Though many Iveys are interred there, Captain Robert Absolom Ivey is buried in Oak Grove Cemetery, one mile east of Branford off of U.S. 27. Bob Ivey not only became a famous steamship captain, but also served as a private in the 8th Florida Infantry during the American Civil War. One of his riverboat pilots was a famous mulatto named Dan McQueen. The often dire experiences of people on and near the river basin are brought to vivid life in the local fictionalized history book *There Let Me Die* by Eric Musgrove. Musgrove is a seventh-generation Suwannee County native.

Graham and his nephew Parker visited the site via roadway on an especially hot, humid day in June 2011. Graham called me from his cell phone the day of his visit. As he explored the elevated bluff, he described the terrain as that of a Florida scrub. Walking in the graveyard made him consider the way of life of the early Florida pioneers.

Some of the grave markers read:

1. John Rice 1833-1911. He was a judge in the Civil War era.

2. Colonel Washington Lafayette Irvine 1832-1882. He was the operator of Irvine's Ferry.

3. Lura V. Irvine 1873-1888. She was the daughter of Colonel Washington Lafayette Irvine. He named the town of Luraville for her.

4. Perry A. McIntosh 1853-1936. He was a Luraville physician. His two-story house still stands today just off Highway 51.

Notes

1. Howell, Bivian Grady. "Questions Concerning Location of Ivey Cemetery," e-mail to cemetery researcher of Suwannee Valley Genealogy Society Library. 08 May 2011.
2. Musgrove, Eric, "Questions Concerning Captain Robert Ivey," e-mail to local historian and author. 10 May 2011.

Suggested Reading

Musgrove, Eric. *Reflections of Suwannee County.* Live Oak: North Florida Printing, 2008.

A Paddler's Guide

Parker Schorb explores numerous pioneer grave plots.

Rose Knox and Graham Schorb

Charles Spring: A Native American Christian Mission Site and Bustling Crossing in Pioneer Florida

With some six hundred men, two hundred horses, and several hundred boar, Hernando de Soto's army came ashore at Tampa Bay, forging northward in quest of riches. Following a Native American trail upon the Ichetuckee River, de Soto's secretary, Rodrigo Ranjel, presents a detailed account of Native American presence and culture as he also describes a river with embankments twenty-eight feet tall. The Suwannee River is the only waterway in the region that matches Ranjel's description.

Upon entering what is today Suwannee County, the Timucua chief of Napituca informed de Soto's recruited Native American scouts that he planned to destroy the Spanish with numerous methods of torture: poisoning, boiling, roasting, burying some up to the head, or dangling others by their feet from trees. Undaunted by such ominous threats, de Soto's men confronted hundreds of battle-ready Timucua warriors. The Spanish cavalry soon drove the warriors into several nearby ponds in what is current-day Live Oak, drowning many. The Timucua, who survived the initial Spanish onslaught, fired arrows from the surface water, while fellow warriors heaved them upward from the pond's depths. Ultimately, the Timucua were forced to succumb to Spanish forces as they were no match for cavalry soldiers or superior Spanish weaponry. At first, de Soto planned to take the surrendered as captives, but soon realized the mighty Timucua, though in chains, would never bend to Spanish domination. So he ordered his soldiers to kill all but the youngest. Those he saved were used as camp slaves. Rodrigo Ranjel's account recorded nine village chiefs and several hundred warriors were slaughtered in battle or during brief captivity. The conflict is often called Battle of the Lakes or Battle of the Ponds.[1]

Many historians believe that Hernando de Soto and his men came through the area of Charles Spring around 1539, and according to his secretary, his party camped in the ancient town called Napituca, located today somewhere between the towns of Houston and Live Oak, though the site has never been discovered. Weaponry used by both sides included bows, arrows, lances, and crossbows. The conflict is remembered as one of the initial, significant conflicts ever to be fought in the inner borders of the United States. Historians believe that de Soto's party departed Suwannee County in the area of Charles Spring as he journeyed westward.[2]

At Charles Spring beyond the boat ramp, see the historical marker noting the Bellamy Trail, once called the Old Spanish Trail. Because of conflicts with Seminole Indians in the early 1800s, the United States Congress passed a bill which would contribute to bet-

A Paddler's Guide

Charles Spring was once a bustling place in pioneer Florida. Reuben Charles operated a ferry and a trading post there. Family tragedy struck him, however, as one child was accidentally killed by Native Americans and other family members succumbed to perilous deaths as well.

ter communications with the cities of Tallahassee, St. Augustine, and Pensacola. The bill approved a connecting road, and a Leon County plantation owner, John Bellamy, was hired to construct the all-important route. Built from the labor of slaves, the corridor is remembered as the Bellamy Trail.

Charles Spring acquired the name from the man named Reuben Charles. He and his wife Rebecca are thought to be the first permanent pioneers of the area. The Territorial Council of Florida, in 1824, allowed Charles a charter to operate a ferry on the Suwannee River. At the site he built his family home, a trading post, and an inn on a prominent embankment, high above the Suwannee River. Reuben and Rebecca Charles had four children named Andrew, Drucilla, Mary, and Reuben Henry. It was common during the period of Native American conflicts for pioneers to wear red aprons or scarves whenever they departed into the area woods. Those pioneers who donned the colorful accessories were spared by the Native Americans. Struggles between the settlers and pioneers made North Florida a dangerous place indeed. So the wearing of red was a sure signal for area Native Americans to steer clear of certain protected individuals. Yet conflicts still ensued, and often settlers were caught in the crossfire or killed by mistake.

There are several conflicting accounts regarding the death of Reuben Charles. According to one story, in 1836 Reuben was walking on the banks of the Suwannee River and was attacked and killed by Native Americans.[3] However, Dan Coleman, a descendent of the Charles family, reveals a much different story. He communicated the information through Bivian Grady Howell, the cemetery researcher for the Suwannee Valley Genealogy Society Library, and Howell relayed the details of the event to me. Coleman believes that Reuben was killed during the Second Seminole Indian War, probably between 1836 and 1840. The family has a document, signed by Reuben, that reveals he was alive as late as 1836; however, he was not listed in the 1840 Florida Census with his wife and three children. Who killed him is unknown; since his death happened during the Seminole Indian War period, however, he may have been killed by

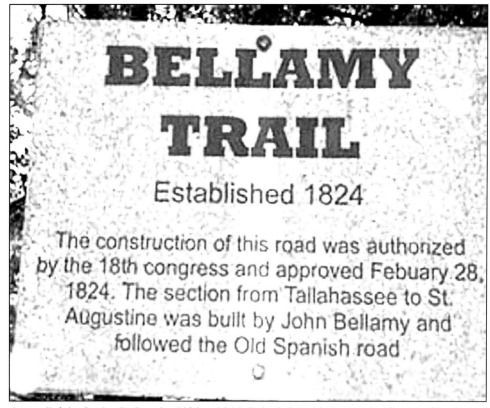

Once called the Camino Real, or the Old Spanish Trail, the Bellamy Trail was a significant road in pioneer Florida, connecting Tallahassee to Saint Augustine. The trail was built by slaves.

In the Charles Cemetery are grave markers of Reuben, Rebecca, and their children. The Charles family operated a ferry, a trading post, and an inn at Charles Spring in the 1800s. Reuben and his daughter Mary (it is believed) were killed by Native Americans near the Suwannee River. Rebecca, his wife, died of wounds inflicted by a mysterious gunshot as she walked upon her front porch.

Native Americans, because at that time white settlers and Indians were regularly at odds and often killed one another. Coleman has not heard exactly where Reuben was killed, but he says that north of the Charles Spring area is one guess. [4]

A story that holds more certainty reveals that a daughter of Reuben Charles, Mary, was accidentally killed by Native Americans as she was preparing to meet an early stagecoach. She dashed from the house, but in her rush, she forgot to don her red apron, the telling signal to local Native Americans that she should be spared. The natives of the tribe were reportedly shocked by the mistake. Yet another tragedy struck the family when Reuben's wife, Rebecca, died in 1852 by wounds inflicted by a mysterious gunshot while she was on her front porch. Approximately two hundred yards from Charles Spring, a marble grave marker memorializes Rebecca. Reuben Charles, and his daughter Mary, and other siblings are also buried in the Charles Cemetery. [5]

Directions to Charles Cemetery

1. Exit the boat ramp at Charles Spring on river left.
2. Walk approximately fifty yards to the top of the ramp.
3. Look for the Bellamy Trail sign to the right.
4. Follow the famous trail approximately two hundred yards, crossing the dirt road.
5. Go past the fenced area.
6. Continue to follow the trail to the Charles Cemetery where Reuben, Rebecca, and their children are buried.
7. Be sure to read the inscriptions on Rebecca's grave, and notice the two large cracks on the stone slab that were caused by vandals. The large postal box is where visitors sign a guest book. They sometimes record supernatural happenings they have encountered at the site. Read those ghostly tales.

Notes

1, 3. Musgrove, Eric. *Reflections of Suwannee County: 150 Anniversary Edition 1858-2008.* Live Oak: North Florida Printing Co., Inc., 2008.

2. Burch, Betsy C. et al. *Echoes of the Past: A History of Suwannee County 1855 – 2000.* Saint Petersburg: Southern Heritage Press, 2000.

4. Howell, Bivian Grady. "Questions Concerning Conflicting Accounts of Rueben Charles' Death," e-mail to cemetery researcher of Suwannee Valley Genealogy Society Library. 10, Sept. 2008.

5. Cerulean, Susan, Laura Newton, Janisse Ray, eds. *Between Two Rivers: Stories From the Red Hills to the Gulf.* Tallahassee: Heart of the Earth and the Red Hills Writers Project, 2004.

When the Spanish marched into North Florida, they discovered miles of cultivated fields and orchards farmed for as far as the eye could see. Within these planted acres were rows of fruit trees, and planted in those rows were crops of grains, corn, and beans, enough to sustain tens of thousands of people. The Native Americans of Florida lived in close-knit large communities with complex spiritual and social rituals. Contact with the Europeans through war, disease, and slavery decimated these peoples and their culture. Many historians believe that Hernando de Soto and hundreds of his Spanish soldiers marched through the area known today as Charles Spring in 1539. Courtesy of State Library and Archives of Florida.[5]

Hernando de Soto. Courtesy of State Library and Archives of Florida.

Converting the Timucua: Christian Missions on the Suwannee River

The Franciscan missionaries initially arrived in Florida in 1573 and began what they considered the sacred task of converting the Timucua to a "new" religion called Christianity. As a result, sixteen thousand Timucua were converted. The religious conversions happened between 1609 and 1612, near the Suwannee River, at a spring named Baptizing Spring. (Note that Baptizing Spring is not directly located on the Suwannee River.) It was there that the Spanish Franciscan missionaries established a mission for the Timucua of the region. Baptizing Spring was also called San Juan de Guacara—the word Guacara derived from the Timucua word for Suwannee.

In 1656 the small mission experienced an unexpected Native uprising. As a result, many Franciscan missionaries as well as natives perished during the revolt. The following year, the mission was moved about seven miles to what is now Charles Spring, located directly on the Suwannee River. The purpose of the relocation was to re-establish the mission at the place where the "Camino Real" crossed the Suwannee River. The "Camino Real" was also named the "Royal Road" and was a Spanish road that traversed westward to Saint Augustine. Today the road is known as the Bellamy Trail. The governor's intent was to use Timucua labor to ferry settlers and trappers across the Suwannee River via canoe. Because of the unrelenting demand and workload put upon them, many Timucua abandoned the mission and their newly found faith of Christianity.

Later, in 1691, the mission at Charles Spring was attacked by Apalachicola Indians and destroyed. [1] No evidence of the mission exists today. Archaeological remnants, however, were excavated near Baptizing Spring, and some of the items recovered were mission period stone projectile points, as well as abundant evidence of shattered flakes. A Franciscan religious medallion was also excavated in the vicinity.[2]

Yet another convent was established before 1611. It was a little-known Timucuan village named Cofa, located at the mouth of the Suwannee River, not far from the Gulf of Mexico. In that same year, seventeen "Christian" Indians were murdered on the Suwannee River (called Cofa River) as they transported supplies to the Franciscan friars living there. [3]

Notes

1. "San Juan Catholic Mission History." www.sanjuanmission.org/missionhistory.html
2. Weisman, Brent Richards, *Excavations on the Franciscan Frontier*. Gainesville: University of Florida Press, 1992.
3. Worth, John E. *Timucuan Chiefdoms of Spanish Florida: Volume 1 Assimilation*. Gainesville: University Press of Florida, 1998.

The native Timucua lived in close-knit communal villages and worshipped their own deities before the Spanish arrived in the 1500s. Upon the arrival of the Spanish Christians, the Timucua were converted, often forcibly, into the Christian faith. Le Moyne took creative license when depicting the Native Americans. Lithograph from Le Moyne, 1500s, courtesy State Library and Archives of Florida.

Modern-Day Baptisms

> As I went down to the river to pray,
> Studyin' about that good ole way,
> And who shall wear a starry crown,
> Good Lord, show me the way,
> Oh sisters, lets go down,
> Let's go down, come on down,
> Oh sisters, lets go down,
> Down in the river to pray
>
> —Alison Kraus

I can hear Alison Kraus's angelic voice singing the hymn-like song. All the while I can still see Graham's description of white-clad believers as they flock to the riverside.

As in the iconic baptismal episode from the movie *Brother Where Art Thou*, Graham happened upon a congregation of approximately thirty Christian followers at the river's edge one day while he was hiking trails near the Suwannee River State Park. Donned in long-sleeved cotton shirts, the alabaster cloud of disciples seemingly drifted to the Suwannee's edge. Arriving upon her shores, they stood attentively. A skinny, youthful preacher stood in waist-deep tannic currents. He clutched a black King James Bible as swirls milled around him. Graham stood upon a high embankment as he observed the speaker read from the New Testament, conveying ideas in Matthew 28:

> Then Jesus came to them and said, "All authority in heaven and on earth has been given to me. Therefore go and make disciples of all nations, baptizing them in the name of the Father, and of the Son, and of the Holy Spirit, and teaching them to obey everything I have commanded you."

After his voice subsided, one by one, each solemn believer filed into several long lines, awaiting immersion in the metaphorical cleansing blood of the lamb -the depths of the Suwannee River. While the line of devotees inched ever closer to the welcoming preacher, a collective voice in three part harmony drifted over the river, a song of hope and of rebirth.

Shall we gather at the river,
Where bright angel feet have trod?
With its crystal tide forever,
Flowing by the throne of God
Ere we reach the shining river,
Lay we every burden down,
Grace our spirits will deliver,
And provide a robe and crown . . .

The Suwannee River and her bubbling springs have long been used to baptize people into the Christian faith. The Spanish first Christianized the Timucua at a place called Baptizing Spring and later near Charles Spring. Depicted here is a group of modern believers being immersed in a southern river. Courtesy of State Library and Archives of Florida.

A Paddler's Guide

Section Six Map

Hal W. Adams Bridge Ramp to Ivey Memorial Park Ramp in Branford
Mile 98.2 – Mile 76

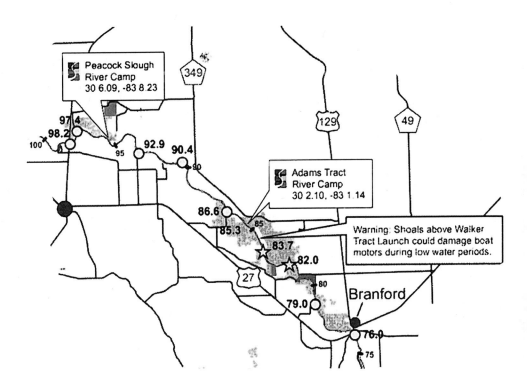

Navigation Warnings

There are several shoals. Proceed with caution.

Camping Information

Camping may be more difficult on Section Six. Dotted along each side of the river are numerous private residences and private property signs. See Suwannee River Water Management sites such as the Walker Tract and the Little River Tract. There are also state river camps such as the Peacock Slough River Camp and the Adams Tract River Camp. Contact Suwannee River Water Management for information, fees, and reservations. See the number in the beginning of this guidebook.

Topography

There are many prominent springs and some smaller springs on this section, including the historically famous Troy Spring. Other springs are Telford, Peacock, Running, Bathtub, Convict, Royal, Owen, Mearson, Ruth, and Little River Spring State Park (day use only). There are several islands on this section. (Note: The Peacock Springs park was renamed Wes Skiles Park in 2010. Skiles was a noted worldwide cave diver.)

Wildlife Spotted

On a trip in 2008, Graham and I encountered a variety of wildlife, including six jumping Gulf sturgeon, numerous king fishers, two great blue heron, two red-shouldered hawks, a flock of wood ducks, numerous turkey vultures, one American bald eagle in flight, and a twelve-foot American alligator—to this day the largest alligator I have seen on the Suwannee River. Other sightings included barred owl, osprey, sandhill cranes and a plethora of wading birds and sunning turtles. (The 2008 trip is recounted in "Canoe Camping on the Legendary Suwanee River: A Narrative" under Map Section One of this book.)

Points of Interest

The sky-blue Hal Adams Bridge; the Drew Swing Bridge, often called the Ghost Bridge; an island that was once the site of Fort Macolm, built by the United States army to combat Indian retaliations during the Seminole Indian Wars; and many prominent springs, including Peacock Springs and Royal Spring, which are both known worldwide for cave diving opportunities. Somewhere on this section, between Peacock Springs and Royal Spring, a Spanish silver coin was found in 1981. It was analyzed by a specialist in Spanish colonial coins at a local Florida university. The coin expert reported that the silver piece was minted in Mexico, and he dated the coin from the 1500s to 1600s. The piece was most likely lost during the Spanish missions of the later part of the seventeenth century.[1] At Troy Spring see remnants of the old steamer *Madison,* which rests at the bottom of the spring run. Little River Spring is landscaped in limestone walls. It is a beautiful spring with a variety of trees in the park, including bald cypress trees.

Restocking Supplies

Mayo and Luraville, which are nearby towns, are located north and south on Highway 51, but they are miles from the river. At the Ivey Memorial Park ramp at Branford, go up the ramp to the parking area. Head north through the parking lot to Highway 27 and travel right—east; there are convenient stores with supplies, ice, beer, and gas. Restaurants are in sight.

A stealthy twelve-foot alligator slips into the tannic waters of the Suwannee River between Royal Spring and Owen Spring. He was sunning on the embankment; at our approach, however, he slid beneath dark waters.

The small island was visible at medium water level. See it just down-river from the Old Drew Bridge.

Several small springs gush forth from the aquifer.

A Paddler's Guide

River Rendezvous is a Mecca for outdoor enthusiasts, such as campers and divers. Convict Springs is located on river right at the same location. Made to look like a modern-day swimming pool, the once pristine, natural spring has been altered by human hands.[2]

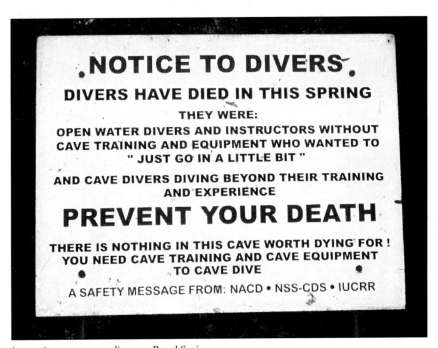

An ominous sign warns cave divers at Royal Spring.

Notes

1. Council, Clyde C. *Suwannee Country: A Canoeing, Boating, and Recreational Guide to Florida's Immortal Suwannee River.* Sarasota: J and G Printing Inc., 1988.
2. Stamm, Doug. *The Springs of Florida.* Sarasota: Pineapple Press, Inc., 1994.

Hal Adams Bridge: First Suspension Bridge in Florida

The Hal Adams Bridge is named for the man from Thayer, Missouri. Born in 1884, Adams came to Mayo, serving as a county judge of Lafayette County from 1907 to 1961. The bridge was constructed in 1947 and at the time of completion was the only suspension bridge in Florida. Before the bridge was built, another river crossing was built in 1902, approximately a mile down-river. In the flood of 1928, however, that bridge was destroyed. Before either of the bridges was erected, a ferry crossed the Suwannee, near the location at Luraville, and was operated by Washington L. Irvine.[1]

Notes
1. Moses, Grace Emerick. *Footprints Along the Suwannee*. North Florida Printing, 1981.

Paddlers will see the sky-blue bridge spanning the Suwannee River. Called the Hal Adams Bridge, it was named after a prominent county judge of Lafayette County. He served from 1907 to 1961. When constructed, the crossing was the only suspension bridge in Florida.

Hal Adams attended the dedication ceremony of the bridge. He is the elderly man in the middle of the group. Courtesy of State Library and Archives of Florida.

A Paddler's Guide

Irvine Ferry

Taken some time before 1880, the image depicts the Irvine Ferry crossing at Luraville. Located approximately 200 feet down-river, where the old Luraville Bridge was later built at Telford Spring, the ferry served to transport passengers over the Suwannee River. Notice the gentleman, fourth from the left, dressed in full military attire of a Confederate soldier.[1] Courtesy of State Library and Archives of Florida.

Old Drew Bridge (Some Call the Ghost Bridge): Abandoned in 1920s

Standing like a forlorn shadow of the past, a ghost bridge remains positioned in mid-river, near mile marker 95. Referred to as the Drew Bridge, the span remains turned parallel with the river in the open position, just the way it was left during the 1920s. Resting upon a magnificent steel and concrete pillar, with kingpin in the center, the moving bridge required muscled efforts of two men. The task was accomplished by manually operating a huge handle.

Built in the 1900s, the crossing was vital to railroad transportation, for the structure was part of Frank Drew's Florida Railroad. Frank Drew was the son of George Franklin Drew, the first Democratic governor after the American Civil War. The governor was an important figure in Suwannee River history in the late 1800s, specifically for his involvement in trade in the Town of Columbus and in the town of Ellaville, both sites are located up-river.[1]

Notes
1. Holmes, Melton Jr. *Lafayette County History and Heritage.* Mayo, 1974.

A Paddler's Guide

Often called the Ghost Bridge, the old railroad Drew Bridge was abandoned in the 1920s and remains in the open position. The mysterious essence of the span was ever more evident on a dreary, misty day in September 2008.

Rose Knox and Graham Schorb

Peacock Springs: Where Native American Cultures, Pioneer Families, and Cave Divers Congregated

Note: In 2010, the spring was renamed for Wes Skiles.

Every place on Earth has a story to tell. If Peacock Springs could speak, perhaps it would offer tales about human lives in celebration and in suffering. One story might be about a village of native peoples, their voices drifting over a mighty tea-hued river. Collective laughter in ritualistic song might rise up to honor, perhaps, a successful hunt for alligator, bear, or great panther. Or, the spring may tell of how human hands molded decorative vases as artisans painted intricate colors of legends, using brushes made from animal bristles and feathers. Other secrets the spring might recount are how rich southern plantation soil was hastily dug, and valuables of gold were hidden there. Threatening warnings, perhaps, reached agitated ears of wealthy men; those southern land owners who stood to lose all if invading northern forces marched over miles of cotton fields. Another song sung might be of inviting caves, luring divers to watery graves. Peacock Springs tells stories of such a history.

Though a place where people today swim and scuba dive, Peacock Springs was once home to ancient natives. Fragments of their lives have been discovered as archaeologists have recovered intricately designed pottery in around the spring, revealing that Paleo-Indians, Weeden Island Indians, and post-AD cultures inhabited the spring area. Delicate imprinting and brushing methods painted on broken pottery pieces indicate art designs from the Weeden Island civilization, those peoples living in villages in the basin approximately 1200 to 1700 years ago. One such village was discovered nearby.

Much later in history, Peacock Springs and Slough were named after Dr. John Calvin Peacock. Peacock moved to Luraville around 1857, and records indicate the family relocated from Troy, North Carolina. The Peacock family settled and established a town they first called New Troy, later named Luraville, after Lura V. Irvine, the daughter of Colonel Lafayette Irvine. During the American Civil War, Dr. Peacock caught wind of intentions of Union forces to take the railway bridge located at the northwestern edge of the county. If the North captured the site, supplies to the Confederacy would be severed—and, he suspected, much of his own wealth would be plundered by invading Federal forces. History reveals Federal commanders often had in their possession government census maps, making them privy to estates where prominent citizens lived. Therefore, Union commanders planned their routes meticulously, according to the census map, around such wealthy landholders.

In preparation for a potential Union onslaught, Peacock harvested, baled, and then buried cotton and other valuables beneath a field, cleverly disguising recently disturbed land with seeds that grew into tall corn stalks. Peacock also planned to scuttle his own boat in the slough to protect his property from Federal invaders. Ultimately, the Union troops were turned back, and at the war's conclusion, Dr. Peacock dug up his hidden treasures, and later sold the cotton for a good price. Consequently, he remained a wealthy man, unlike other prominent Southerners who suffered tremendous personal financial loss.[1]

According to cemetery records of Suwannee County, the doctor is buried in the Peacock family cemetery, located in the Peacock Hideaway subdivision, in a limestone eroded grave that today bears no name.[2] Little trace of the Peacock home and cotton gin remain. Finding his boat in the slough proved difficult for us, but park rangers have relayed that there are, indeed, remnants of an old wooden craft just outside the mouth of the slough where it joins the Suwannee River. Might this be Peacock's boat?[3]

In more recent times, the spring has called divers to her caves. Back in the 1970s, *Skin Diver Magazine* and other guidebooks advertised the spring, making the area a Mecca for cave divers. Hundreds of scuba divers from all over the globe as far as Japan and Germany gathered and stood in long lines, just to get the chance to explore the intricate caverns. The famous caverns boast 28,000 feet of underwater passages and house critical habitats for twenty-five species of endangered cave-adapted animals, including a cave shrimp, eighteen crayfish species, and a blind salamander.

Diving in the caverns has proven hazardous over the decades as many divers have tragically lost their lives. Only divers showing proof of scuba certification are allowed to explore the underwater spectacle. The diver Sheck Exley was known for contributing to painstakingly mapping miles of underwater caves at Peacock Springs and other caves around the world; a memorial stone honoring Exley is located at Peacock Springs. He died in a cave-dive accident in Mexico before the publication of his partially completed manuscript *"The Conquering of Peacock Slough."* The manuscript was later re-visited and edited by Sandra Poucher, then renamed *Taming of the Slough*.[4]

Today, Peacock Springs State Park, known now as Wes Skiles Springs State Park, is a beautiful and serene 280-acre park, a popular place not only for cave divers, but also for swimmers, hikers, and picnickers. People gather to enjoy the spring's natural beauty, just as the ancient peoples and the first Florida pioneers once did.

In November 2010 the park was renamed in honor of Wes Skiles, the world class explorer and cinematographer/photographer, who died in 2010 in a diving accident. Though Skiles did not perish in Peacock Springs, the park is named for him. He was passionate about protecting Florida springs, and he produced several films educating the public about the Florida aquifer.

Notes

1, 3, and 4. Exley, Sheck. *Taming of the Slough: A Comprehensive History of Peacock Springs.* Edited by Sandra Poucher. Huntsville: Published by National Speleological Society Inc, 2004.

2. Howell, Bivian Grady. "Questions Concerning Location of Dr. Calvin Peacock's Final Resting Place." Phone interview with cemetery researcher of Suwannee Valley Genealogy Society Library. 24, June, 2011.

Peacock Springs, now called Wes Skiles Springs, is located on river left. A small shoal is just before the spring. The slough is located to the left of the cypress tree pictured above. Follow a staircase leading to the park and spring. Also on river left, see a sign marking the location of Peacock Springs/Wes Skiles Springs.

A Paddler's Guide

United States Army Forts Built on the Suwannee River: Removal Declaration Causes Native American Retaliation

During the 1830s and 1840s, President Andrew Jackson was intent on removing the Seminole Indians from the area. His purpose was to capture them and relocate the native peoples to the West. However, Chief Osceola was tenacious in his decree that every drop of Indian blood would be spilled before they would relinquish to the United States' removal declaration. In 1818, Jackson had unmercifully attacked the Seminole tribe, killing braves, women, and children, as well as stealing their livestock. Consequently, the violent action further intensified Seminole Indian violence against Florida settlers.

By 1835, two formidable groups of Indians had relocated back to what is today Lafayette County. One was Halpatter-Tustenuggee, often called Alligator Chief, and another was Cotzar-Fixico-Chopee, known as Mad Tiger. These groups consisted of forty-two young warriors in the Cooks Hammock vicinity. Another sixty warriors were also present in the area. Because of the hostile climate and mortal threat to Florida pioneers, the United States government began constructing numerous forts. Some of the garrisons were located directly on the Suwannee River. In most cases, the forts were not tremendously large, some having only a two-story building, which served as a good look-out post. Troops averaged from 14 to 150 or more.

Military records reveal the forts that were once located in Lafayette and Dixie Counties on the Suwannee River. They were Fort Atkinson, once on the other side of the Suwannee River from Charles Ferry; Fort MaComb, located on a small five-acre island in the Suwannee River (erosion has made the island smaller); Fort 17 East Florida, once located north of today's Mayo, Fort Griffin, eight miles up-river from the mouth of the Suwannee; Fort McCrabb, built between Fort Downing and Old Town on the Suwannee; Fort Wool, up-river ten miles from the mouth, near Shelton; and Fort Fanning, just across the river from Old Town.[1] A fort named Twenty East may have been located at Suwannee Spring, yet no evidence of the remnants have been discovered or verified.[2] There were many other forts built, but the aforementioned ones were located directly on the Suwannee River. According to old documents, many of the forts were burned, though some were built back. All were eventually razed and the materials utilized for other practical endeavors by pioneers of the area.[3]

Not only were Florida settlers and soldiers combating the Seminole uprisings at the time, but many were infected with malaria, spread by mosquitoes. The deadly disease claimed the lives of more soldiers and pioneers than did the Native American hostilities. One physician's account reveals that 1836, 1837, 1839, and 1841 were all epidemic seasons. Dysentery and scurvy took many lives as well.

It is rumored, but cannot be fully confirmed, that Fort MaComb was a sick fort. The place, according to some stories, housed those with contagious diseases. After the Seminole uprisings, many local pioneers steered clear of the fort. They believed the contagion was still a threat.

Several fascinating stories surround Fort Macomb and Fort Downing. According to an account from a United States Army soldier named Paul A. Giroward, several soldiers were buried on Fort Macomb Island. Their names were Sergeant Edward Hessen, who drowned on April 1, 1840; Private Henry Bussy, who died of an accidental cause in February 1842 (no details of his death were provided); Private Henry Stuhlman of Company H., who starved; Edward Brown, killed by Native Americans as he attempted to protect a wagon train; Private Richard Ellis of Company H., who died of fever on September 2, 1840; and Private John Harvey, also of Company H., who perished of fever on September 15, 1839. In an effort to validate the claim that soldiers were buried on Fort Macomb, Graham and I contacted Bivian and Murl Howell, cemetery researchers in Suwannee County. They communicated to us that they have searched the island but have yet to find the burial place of any of the soldiers.

Yet another intriguing story about early pioneers and clashes with Native Americans happened at Fort Downing, located near the confluence of the Santé Fe River. Fort Downing had been under constant Native American retaliation for three weeks. Those settlers and soldiers inside were low on supplies. When peace seemed evident and the attacks had ceased, two volunteers ventured out to kill some game for food. However, the two men did not come back. A search party was formed, and the two men were discovered; their scalped bodies were left near a trail that led from the Old Town Road, located near the Dixie County line.[4]

Notes

1. and 3. Holmes, Melton Jr. Lafayette County History and Heritage. Mayo: 1974.
2. Musgrove, Eric. Reflections of Suwannee County: 150 Anniversary Edition 1858-2008. Live Oak: North Florida Printing Co., Inc., 2008
4. Moses, Grace Emerick. Footprints Along the Suwannee. North Florida Printing Company. 1981.

A Paddler's Guide

See several small islands on Section Six; the largest one makes a suitable camping spot. Some sources have called that one camp Council's Island; however, this island is not the former location of Fort Macomb, where the United States Army constructed a fort and where several U.S. Army soldiers were reportedly buried. The Macomb Island is much smaller. It is located out from the Macomb boat ramp.

Rose Knox and Graham Schorb

The Early Logging Industry in North Florida: How Area Rivers Played a Role

The harvesting of lumber in Florida dates back to small water-powered sawmills operated in Spanish Florida and spans to paper and pulp mills of today. The period of 1880 through 1930 was considered the peak of the lumbering boom. Throughout the basin, and directly upon the banks of the Suwannee River, thousands of loggers labored in the cypress swamps and piney woods during the era of colonization, providing logs for the world's demand for hewn lumber. By 1930, the loggers had almost completely obliterated the virgin forests, once existing in approximately 27 million acres. Yet, in only several mere decades of unabashed razing, only 6 million acres of virgin forest prevailed. [1] Janisse Ray, in her story "Borderline" from the book *The Wild Heart of Florida,* reverently describes a virgin forest located at Blue Spring, where County Road 143 meets State Road 6. She describes a still existent long leaf forest in Hamilton County.

> It stands out like a skyscraper in a refugee camp, suddenly tall and very green, waving at the unremitting sky. Something in the back of my mind—some old, mossy, creaky memory of what a forest looks like—and I mean the forest that used to be here, that covered this land—gets triggered . . . You'd have to drive a hundred, two hundred miles to see anything like this.[2]

After reading Janisse Ray's poetic description, Graham and I took a special trip over to Hamilton County, for we longed to stand in shades of such "green, waving" wonder. That "old, mossy, creaky memory" indeed got triggered, just as Ray vowed as we found ourselves standing in the forest trying to imagine what this place, this region, the Suwannee river basin was before the razing of the longleaf. Luckily, we did not have to travel two hundred miles!

Notes

1. Drobney, Jeffery A. *Company Towns and Social Transformation in the North Florida Timber Industry 1880 -1930.* Florida Historical Quarterly 75:2.
2. Cerulean, S, Ripple J, editors. *The Wild Heart of Florida.* "Borderline." Gainesville: University Press of Florida, 1999.

A Paddler's Guide

Man and beast worked together in the late 1800s and early 1900s in an effort to harvest longleaf yellow pines. In the present day, the large harvesting wheels are still discovered and recovered from the depths of the Suwannee River. Visit one at the Suwannee Canoe Outpost, where the giant wheel is displayed against a sycamore tree at the entrance of the building. Courtesy of State Library and Archives of Florida.

By 1930, loggers had almost completely obliterated the virgin forests once existing in approximately 27 million acres. Yet in mere decades of unabashed razing, only 6 million acres of virgin forest prevailed. Courtesy of State Library and Archives of Florida.

Logs are resurrected from the river. Courtesy of State Library and Archives of Florida.

The sawmill at Ellaville in the late 1800s. Courtesy State Library and Archives of Florida

A Paddler's Guide

Logs were once transported down-river by floating them on the Withlacoochee. People today are still recovering the sunken logs; there is demand for them in custom-built homes. Courtesy of State Library and Archives of Florida.

Logging boom near covered bridge at the confluence of the Suwannee and the Withlacoochee. Courtesy of State Library and Archives of Florida.

Troy Spring: Captain Tucker's Steamship, the Madison, Rests Here

Troy Spring, one of the Suwannee River's first magnitude springs, is seventy feet deep, making it a popular destination for scuba divers, snorkelers, and swimmers. The spectacular spring is a frequent stop for paddlers, too.[1] It is historically famous because the spring run is where Captain James Tucker of the Confederacy's 8th Florida Infantry intentionally had his steamship, the *Madison*, scuttled in the spring run in 1863. In so doing, he hoped to prevent Union soldiers from capturing his boat. The *Madison* was known as the United States Mail steamer, but she also transported general goods up and down the Suwannee River. Some of the items the *Madison* carried were chickens, hogs, hams, animal hides, and honey. The remnants of the steamer are still visible.[2] For further details on the *Madison*, refer to "Steamboats Navigate the Suwannee" in Map Section Four of this guidebook.

Look for the spring on river right. There is a deck and a sign indicating the spring's location. The park is a day-use facility only. No camping is permitted.

Notes:
1. www.floridastateparks.org/troyspring/default.cfm
2. Mueller, Edward A. *Suwannee River Steamboating*. Florida Historical Quarterly, Vol. XXV.

A Paddler's Guide

The *Madison* at Troy Spring. Courtesy of Martha J. Robinson, public information specialist with the Florida Department of Environmental Protection.

Little River Springs

Little River Springs is a second magnitude spring. It is named so because of the spring run of 150 feet in length. Within the 125-acre county park, visitors can take nature walks and may encounter a variety of wildlife. Certified cave divers are drawn to the spring to explore the 1,200-foot-long cave system with depths of over 100 feet.[1] The spring is considered by cave divers as one of Florida's most superb caverns. One underwater section is named "The Florida Room," and there is one picturesque undulating corridor called the "serpentine passage."[2] Swimmers, snorkelers, and hikers also enjoy the spring and the park.

Notes
1. www.suwanneeparksandrecreation.org/Parks.htm
2. DeLoach, Ned. Diving Guide to Underwater Florida. Jacksonville: New World Publications, 1991.

Little River Springs is a 125-acre state park. Cave divers come to the spring to explore hundreds of feet of underwater caverns.

A Paddler's Guide

Section Seven Map

Ivey Memorial Park Ramp at Branford to Wannee Ramp
Mile 76 to 49.9

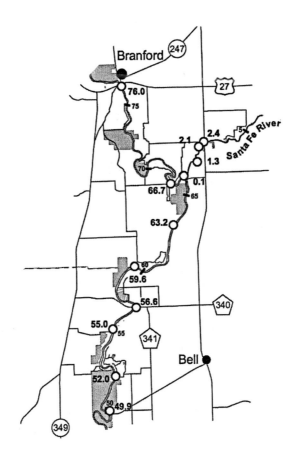

Navigation Warnings

As the Suwannee River widens, encountering motor traffic increases; from Branford to the Gulf of Mexico, large wake created by motorized engines, such as jet skis and pleasure crafts, is quite likely. Paddlers should use caution as fast-moving motor traffic can swamp a loaded canoe. In December through March there is less motorized boat traffic. Remember, too, that the wind can pick up on wide sections, and the surface waters can become choppy. Once, while paddling here, we were stopped by a polite game warden. He was checking to see if we had flotation devices for each passenger.

Camping Information

Camping is limited on Section Seven. Take note of the SRWMD public land-use areas located primarily on river right. Guaranto Spring County Park, on river right, has camping for a fee.

Topography

Many paddlers feel this section is not as naturally scenic. The river widens significantly here. See Branford Spring, Shingle Spring, Turtle Spring, Pothole Spring, Rock Bluff Spring, and Guaranto Spring, all on Section Seven. The river here has evident human development. The banks on both sides are dotted with sheds, trailers, cabins, river camps, and palatial homes, as well as docks and floating decks. The embankments are lower here. Some areas of this section offer beautiful, natural places with hardwood forests.

Wildlife Spotted

In early May 2009, after the historic flood, Graham and I spotted a wide array of wildlife, including one cormorant, one great blue heron, numerous turkey vultures, several red-shouldered hawks, and a flock of snowy egrets flying low and in formation. We also saw many Suwannee cooters sunning on logs, and one swallowtail kite soaring above head. One impressive sight was an American bald eagle flying approximately thirty feet above us; the majestic bird suddenly turned downward, dived into the river, and snatched a fish in its talons. Encountering a very light-colored oak snake swimming across the river was a surprise. We witnessed a spectacular sight as a four-foot sturgeon jumped completely up and out of the water, and we spied a male pileated woodpecker, numerous black crows, and three sandpipers.

Points of Interest

Hatch Bend was once an old pioneer homestead and the location of a Native American retaliation. The Santa Fe River meets the Suwannee just down-river from the Dorothy Land Ramp, located in the Hatch Bend area.

Restocking Supplies

At the Ivey Memorial Park ramp(s) at Branford, go up the ramp to the parking area. Head north through the parking lot to Highway 27 and go right—east. There are convenient stores with general supplies and ice, beer, and gas. See also restaurants and a motel in sight.

Another restocking option is to go under the 340 Bridge, also called the Orb Cannon Bridge; the Rock Bluff Boat Ramp is on river left. Walk up the ramp, travelling straight ahead for approximately one hundred yards. A general store can provide general supplies and ice, beer, and gas.

Rock Bluff is visible on river left, just after the 340 Bridge. Exit at the ramp and restock supplies up beyond the boat ramp.

On river left, an old craft is docked that gives the appearance of a ghost ship. She is called the Mona; her best days are well behind her.

A Paddler's Guide

On section seven, see many homes, boats, and docks. Houseboats are not an uncommon sight.

Human development is evident on Section Seven. Look on river right for two large water slides.

In the flood of 2009, many homes, docks, and properties were damaged.

The river widens on Section Seven. Be prepared to encounter high-speed boat traffic. Some boaters travel at speeds of sixty miles an hour or more. Warning: Wake from a speedboat or a jet ski can swamp a loaded canoe.

A Paddler's Guide

Section Seven offers areas of natural scenery. The bald cypress was probably struck by lightning.

Branford's Ivey Park: Named for Steamboat Captain

Once known as Rowland's Bluff, the town of Branford, as the town is known today, was once an important location on the Suwannee River. Remembered as a ferry crossing and a major steamboat landing, Rowland's Bluff was incorporated in 1886, making the place a thriving economic area in the 1800s and early 1900s.[1] The riverside park in Branford, which today has picnic tables and two boat ramps for paddlers, was named in honor of Captain Robert Absalom (Bob) Ivey, a famous river boat captain, in the late 1800s and early 1900s. His *Belle of the Suwanee* was one of the last river steamers, and was built by J.W. Ward in Branford in 1889. Ivey also captained the *Three States,* the largest steamer on the river. Serving as both freight and passenger craft, the *Three States* offered such amenities as twenty staterooms, a large saloon, and a live orchestra that played lively tunes to entertain guests.

Mrs. Berta George was Captain Ivey's daughter. According to records left by her, Ivey once owned the town of Branford, and he was instrumental in convincing Henry Bradley Plant to bring his railway system to Branford. Plant, according to Mrs. George, said he named the town after his birthplace of Branford, Connecticut. During the pinnacle of steamboats on the Suwannee River, the ships traveled routes to Cedar Key and to New Orleans. According to some accounts, the *Belle of the Suwanee* went down two miles southwest from Pepper Fish Key, in only ten feet of water. The year was 1904.[2] Note: Other accounts differ on the date of the ship's demise.

Paddlers will see the lawn and picnic tables between the boat ramp(s) on river left. Ivey Park is a day-use facility only.

Notes

1. Boning, Charles, R. *Florida Rivers*. Gainesville: Pineapple Press, Inc., 2007.
2. Moses, Grace Emerick. *Footprints Along the Suwannee*. North Florida Printing Company, 1981.

A Paddler's Guide

Ivey Memorial Park is named in honor of Captain Robert Absalom Ivey, famous riverboat captain of the steamers *Belle of the Suwanee* and the *Three States*. Both were popular ships in the late 1800s and early 1900s on the Suwannee River. See the park on river left.

Rose Knox and Graham Schorb

Swamp Cabbage: Florida's Tree, Southern Savior, and Today a Delicacy

The swamp cabbage has contributed greatly to the lives of people in North Florida. According to early pioneer accounts, the palm was used as a staple food source during the 1800s and early 1900s. It is officially known as the sabal palm, but early settlers, as well as locals today, refer to it as swamp cabbage. Because of its historical significance, Florida has declared the sabal palm the official tree of the state. Marjorie Kinnan Rawlings, in the chapter "Cornucopia of the Scrub" in her book *Cross Creek*, describes how early settlers made staples of swamp cabbage and poke weed.[1]

In 1953, the state of Florida chose the sabal palm as the official state tree. It will thrive in most any soil and is salt and frost tolerant. In the 1970s, the Florida legislature deemed that the sabal palm would take the place of the cocoa palm on the Florida State Seal.[2]

Such palms grow in the forests of the southeastern United States and on other continents of the world. Some cultures equate the tree with life because the palms not only serve as a food source, but also are used to make clothing and furniture. Early humans utilized the palm in many ways: the bud was eaten, the fibrous trunk was used to make shelters, and the fronds made sealed roofing. The chickee huts of native peoples were made from parts of the palm tree.[3]

After the American Civil War, when the South was devastated financially, the cabbage palm helped sustain hungry, desperate people, many whose lives were forever altered by new decrees of the changing societal landscape. Along with squirrel, opossum, raccoon, and fish from area rivers, pioneers ate what was available to them. Today the swamp cabbage is celebrated in a festival in LaBelle, Florida. Many restaurants in Florida still serve the palm, and "the meat of the tree" is considered a southern delicacy.[4]

The river basin should be respected and left as untouched as possible. The sabal palm is protected on Florida state lands.

Settlers used the following method to cook cabbage palm:

How to make swamp cabbage
1. Cut down a cabbage palm and remove the boots and fronds.
2. Remove the heart of the tree, the edible portion of the palm. The heart (center portion) will weigh about five pounds and can feed six to eight people.
3. There are many ways to prepare cabbage palm in delicious dishes, including boiling or frying it. One way to prepare swamp cabbage is to chop the heart and onions into pieces. Then boil the heart with onions, ham hock, with salt and pepper to taste.

4. Another popular Florida cracker dish is swamp cabbage Fritters, which is a southern favorite. Prepare your favorite batter, and dip heart of palm pieces in the batter and fry. Fritters and boiled cabbage are served as scrumptious side dishes to most any meat.

Notes
1. Ste. Claire, Dana. *Crackers: The Cracker Culture in Florida History.* Gainesville: University Press of Florida. 2006
2. State Symbols USA. Sabal Palm. www.statesymbolsusa.org
3. The Hall of Florida Fossils: Evolution of Life and Land. Sabal Palm. www.flmnh.ufl.edu
4. Williams, Winston. *Florida's Fabulous Trees.* Tampa: World Wide Publications. 1986.

The cabbage palm, known as Florida's state tree, thrives along embankments of the lower Suwannee River. Eating the heart of a cabbage palm is a southern delicacy today. Early settlers, however, called it swamp cabbage; it served as a staple for feeding hungry families. In pioneer Florida, people often visited the riverside, where they cut and prepared the heart of the palm. They enjoyed swamp cabbage with fresh fish that they caught from the river.

A restaurant in the town of Fanning Spring serves swamp cabbage.

Sam Schorb, Graham's nephew, helps cut a swamp cabbage. The tree was downed on private property.

Cooking swamp cabbage with a ham hock is a southern delicacy.

Though palms are associated with Gulf beaches, sable palms are a prevalent sight on the shores and embankments of the lower Suwannee River. *Bay Palm* Courtesy of Sue Knox

450-Year-Old Dugout Canoe Pulled from River Near Confluence of the Suwannee and Santa Fe Rivers: An Unconfirmed Find

In the winter of 1999, young Trey Owen, while strolling and exploring with his paternal grandmother, Evon, on the Owen property, spied what he thought was a "neat slide." [1] After closer examination, Evon and her husband, Bill Owen, Senior, contacted a field archaeologist. An inspection was conducted; the canoe (seemingly) was verified as that of a 450-year-old dugout canoe called a long boat. The confirmation reported the Native American artifact as 90 percent intact. The canoe measured twenty-two to twenty-four feet in length. Because the long boat had been submerged in the river, it was saturated and laden with water. The weight of the craft, after extraction from the river, was approximately five hundred pounds, according to a field report. Volunteers assisted the Owen family in carefully excavating the rare discovery from the depths of Suwannee River. The stone chippings found inside the canoe, according to the archaeologist, revealed that the boat was at least 450 years old, if not older.[2]

In researching the story to ensure the canoe's validity, I e-mailed the state of Florida and corresponded with an archaeologist there. He said that no canoe was ever recorded in their field documents at the particular location that had been named in the *Suwannee Democrat* article. The name of the person verifying the object was in question as well, for she was not even on record as an employee or listed as an archaeologist in the state of Florida. Therefore, the find is speculative; however, the idea of a long boat canoe being discovered in the Suwannee River is all the more intriguing, for the story of the canoe's authenticity may be forever shrouded in mystery.

Long boats were crafted and used by native peoples for navigation on waterways and for travelling long distances for trade.

Notes
1. Owen, Evon. Telephone Interview. January, 2009.
2. "Dugout Canoe Discovered Near Sante Fe," *Suwannee Democrat,* Feb. 1999.

Some believe that a 450-year-old canoe was found by young Trey Owen at the confluence of the Santa Fe and Suwannee Rivers in 1999. Courtesy of Bill and Evon Owen, Bill Howard, and the *Suwannee Democrat*

The Timucua dig out a longboat. Courtesy State Library and Archives of Florida.

A Paddler's Guide

A Seminole man and a child in a longboat in Florida around the 1930s. Courtesy of State Library and Archives of Florida.

Rose Knox and Graham Schorb

Hatch Bend: Settlers Versus Native Americans

Some local history books contend that Hatch Bend was named so because of its location on a river bend within the Suwannee River corridor.[1] However, other more feasible historical accounts reveal that a family with the Hatch ancestry can be traced up-river to the town of Branford. Florida State library records and other state reports list Paul Hatch as a Lafayette County judge in 1895.

An old timer, A.T. Earls, once recounted the story that he often heard told as a small child. He remembered tales spoken by his elders of a Native American retaliation on the Hatch House at Hatch Bend. The story included a plot of woe for early settlers living in the vicinity. Chronicling the story as he pieced together memories, A.T. Earls recalled that there was once an old log cabin located near the area, and the father of the household (whose name is unknown) fought off a violent Native American attack upon their homestead. During the assault, the heavy wooden planks of the home's exterior door were penetrated with Native American arrows. The cabin door was later taken from the threshold and donated to a museum as a solemn symbol of the conflicts between natives and early pioneers.[2] Encroachment by the white Man instigated the attacks, and history reminds us that the Native Americans had lived and thrived upon the contested land for thousands of years. Natives were merely attempting to preserve their way of life as they fought to protect their religion, their mores, and their cultural manner of existence from the decimation of encroaching settlers. In the approximate year of 1882, records indicate that there was a general store, a cotton gin, and a grist mill at Hatch Bend.[3]

Note: We searched area museums and talked to historians, yet no one could tell us the whereabouts of the arrow-laden wooden door. We are still searching for answers.

Notes

1. and 3. Holmes, Melton.. *Lafayette County History and Heritage*. Mayo: 1974.
2. Moses, Grace Emerick. *Fooprints Along the Suwannee*. North Florida Printing Company. 1981

A Paddler's Guide

Santa Fe River Major Tributary: Inspiration for Coleridge's Famous Poem

> And from this chasm, with ceaseless turmoil seething,
> A mighty fountain was forced:
> Huge fragments vaulted like rebounding hail,
> It flung up momently the sacred river . . .
> Through wood and dale the sacred river ran,
> Then reached the caverns measureless to man,
> And sank in tumult to a lifeless ocean.[1]

These verses from Samuel Taylor Coleridge's famous poem *Kubla Khan* may have been inspired by the Santa Fe River. The Santa Fe River is a major tributary to the Suwannee River and begins in Santa Fe Lake, located in northeast Alachua County. From there, it flows for approximately seventy-five miles, where her waters join the Suwannee River near a town called Wanamake. At O'Leno State Park, the current continues flowing underground, and this "disappearance" so awed William Bartram, the renowned naturalist, that he recorded the unusual fact in his journals. It is believed that the British poet Samuel Taylor Coleridge (1772-1834), in composing *Kubla Khan*, wrote of Bartram's reference of the underground river.[2]

John Livingston Lowes, in his work *The Road to Xanadu*, reveals that many of the origins of such references found in *Kubla Khan* and *The Rime of the Ancient Mariner* indeed came from Bartram's *Travels*. In 1774, Bartram named areas of North Florida in his journal. Some of the names were Alligator Hole and Manatee Springs, but one place went unnamed. Perhaps that nameless river was a reference to the Santa Fe River, which flows underground. In *Kubla Khan,* Coleridge speaks of chasms and caverns and references the "disappearing" river as he describes how the river eventually surfaces and flows to the sea.[3]

Notes:
1. and 3. Wright, John K. "From *Kubla Khan* to Florida." *American Quarterly*. Vol. 8, No. 1. Spring, 1956.
2. McCarthy, Kevin M. *The History of Gilchrist County*. Gainesville: 1986.

TRAVELS

THROUGH

NORTH AND SOUTH CAROLINA,

GEORGIA,

EAST AND WEST FLORIDA,

THE CHEROKEE COUNTRY,

THE EXTENSIVE TERRITORIES OF THE MUSCOGULGES

OR CREEK CONFEDERACY,

AND THE COUNTRY OF THE CHACTAWS.

CONTAINING

AN ACCOUNT OF THE SOIL AND NATURAL PRODUC-
TIONS OF THOSE REGIONS;

TOGETHER WITH

OBSERVATIONS ON THE MANNERS OF THE INDIANS.

EMBELLISHED WITH COPPER-PLATES.

By WILLIAM BARTRAM.

PHILADELPHIA: PRINTED BY JAMES AND JOHNSON. 1791.
LONDON:
REPRINTED FOR J. JOHNSON, IN ST. PAUL'S CHURCH-YARD.

1792.

Samuel Taylor Coleridge, the famous poet of *Kubla Khan* and *Rime of the Ancient Mariner*, received his inspiration from William Bartram's reference to the Santa Fe's "disappearing" river. Courtesy of State Library and Archives of Florida

A Paddler's Guide

The Santa Fe meets the Suwannee. The Santa Fe is on the left; the Suwannee is on the right.

The Rock Bluff Ferry: Often Called the "Free Ferry"

Rock Bluff is located on river left, just after the 340 Bridge. Before the first bridge was built, a ferry operated near the vicinity. Named Rock Bluff because of the topography of high bluffs in the basin, the ferry was called the Rock Bluff or "Free Ferry." Passengers crossed over the Suwannee River free of charge because Dixie and Gilchrist Counties funded the operation. Only one automobile at a time could cross. How exactly did it work? The ferry was attached to a steel cable, extending to massive live oak trees on either side of the embankments. Operation of the ferry continued year round, except during floods. The ferry service was forced to close in the flood of 1928 and the flood of 1948.

Local history reveals that a man by the name of Truman Fowler kept the ferry in operation for approximately thirteen years, until the year 1963. Later, a bridge was constructed in 1965, making the ferry obsolete.[1]

Note: Information leads and materials about Dixie County were provided by Bellot and Chavous.

Notes:
1. Palmer, Beth Ann, ed. *Precious Memories of Dixie County*. Dixie County Historical Society, 2000. Vol. 10
2. Bellot, Cindy. Personal Interview at the Dixie County Library. Fall 2008
3. Chavous, Preston. Personal Interview at the Dixie County Library. Fall 2008.

A Paddler's Guide

The ferry crossing at Old Town and a sign from the 1950s. Courtesy of State Library and Archives of Florida.

Prehistoric Fish, Eight Feet, 200 Pounds: Swimming Under Canoe!

Gulf sturgeon are prehistoric fish, dating back 200 million years, and they frequent these waters. Travelling up the Suwannee River from the Gulf of Mexico, their instincts drive them to spawn. Paddlers may get the thrilling opportunity to encounter the massive ancient fish, which can grow eight feet long and can weigh as much as two hundred pounds. Almost like something out of a futuristic tale, their features are unusual; their bodies have five rows of hard plates called scutes; their whisker-like feelers are called barbels. Feeding along the bottom, they use the barbels to identify various foods, such as marine worms, isopods, crustaceans, and other bottom dwelling animals. Sturgeon spend part of their lives in saltwater bays, such as the Gulf of Mexico, but they also travel up to fresh water rivers and consequently are known as anadromous. [1] Be on the lookout for sturgeon; they usually jump completely out over the water in the spring and summer months. In deep wide turns in the river, they often leap. At evening-tide, if someone in the camping party hears a prodigious splash, chances are a jumping sturgeon is swimming near the camp's shoreline!

In early April of 2008, I saw a strange occurrence. A large sturgeon, approximately seven feet in length, swam up to the top of the surface, only four feet from my kayak. I happened to be paddling near a deep place at a turn in the river bend, just past Suwannee Spring. My heart raced as my adrenaline pumped. To think that a large prehistoric fish was swimming under my kayak! I felt lucky to get such a close glimpse at the fish. Later in September 2008, on the river stretch from the Suwannee Canoe Outpost, to the Boy's Ranch, I saw a four-foot sturgeon jump completely out over the water. The fish was about twenty feet in front of my kayak. Later in the same month, on the river stretch from the Hal Adams Bridge to Troy Spring, Graham and I spied six sturgeon jumping. Later in 2010, when river levels were very low, Graham and his good friend Jerry stopped to admire a baby sturgeon. It was about sixteen inches long, and the young fish swam in the shallow tea-colored water.

Unfortunately, boaters and jet skiers have managed to give the sturgeon a bad reputation. Speed on the river is part of the dilemma. For example, as motorists move rapidly down the Suwannee River, they, too, sometimes encounter the prehistoric fish. When sturgeon jump and one is hit by a boater or jet skier going at high speeds, the result is often serious for the motorist. Sadly, when newspapers cover such stories, the headline usually reads something like "Sturgeon Hits Boater." Yet the prehistoric fish existed long before human beings walked the Earth. The headline should read, "Boater Hits Sturgeon." To illustrate such media coverage, according to a local newspaper within the

Suwannee River Basin, in an article dated Friday, April 20, 2007, a woman was injured in March, when a Sturgeon "knocked" her from her jet ski. The article continued to chronicle how eight people were injured by collisions with sturgeon in 2006.[2]

As paddlers make their way down the Suwannee River, they should know that, by one scientific estimate, 6,500 to 7,500 sturgeon swim these waters. Biologists are uncertain of why sturgeon jump, but some theories contend that perhaps the activity is a show of dominance, or perhaps jumping is a way for the fish to communicate.[3]

Sturgeon were once a commercial commodity and valued for their meat. Their eggs were also used for caviar. However, overharvesting the great fish led to a decline in their numbers. Today, sturgeon are a federally threatened species and cannot legally be harvested.

Canoeists should keep an eye out for wide areas of the Suwannee River or on turns where the water level is especially deep. Perhaps a sturgeon will jump. Getting a glimpse of such a large fish is a marvel.

Notes
1. Crabbe, Nathan. "Sturgeon: The Misunderstood Fish," *Gainesville Sun*, 11, May 2007.
2. "Jumping Sturgeon." *The Suwannee Democrat*, April 20, 2006.
3. "Florida Warns of Jumping Sturgeon," *Gulf Coast Fisherman*. 1, April, 2008.

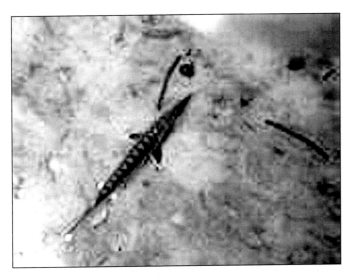

Graham and Jerry get a glimpse of a baby sturgeon. Courtesy of Jerry Long.

At many boat launches along the Suwannee River, signs warn boaters of potential dangerous encounters with an ancient fish, the Gulf sturgeon.

A sturgeon is displayed at an area Suwannee River restaurant.

Section Eight Map

Wannee Ramp to the Manatee Springs State Park Launch
Mile 49.9 to 25.1

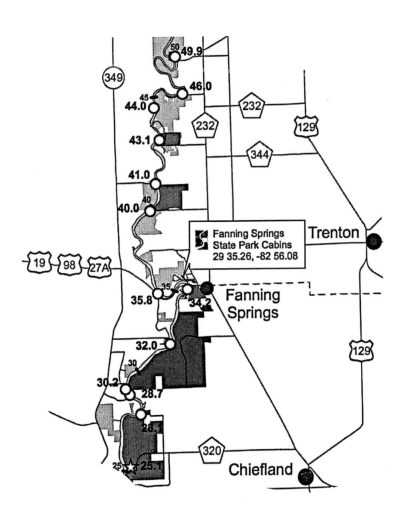

Navigation Warnings

As the Suwannee River widens, paddlers will encounter increased boat traffic. Use caution on Section Eight because the wake of motorized boats can sink a loaded canoe. Note that the wind can affect paddlers, and waters may be potentially choppy.

Camping Information

Camping opportunities are located on river left and river right on SRWMD public use lands. Hart Springs is a beautiful location for campers. The spring is found within the Hart Springs run, amid a lush hardwood forest. Campsites are fairly accessible for canoe campers. Boardwalks within the park provide excellent views of the forest, the spring run, and the river. Visitors may camp at Hart Springs for a fee. Specific directions for camping at Hart Springs are found on the following pages. Fanning Spring is located on river left, and campsites are very accessible to the river. Paddlers may camp at Fanning Spring for a fee. See detailed directions to the campsites on the following pages. Andrew Wildlife Management Area is open for public use. See the wildlife area on river left, just after Fanning Spring.

Topography

Much like Section Seven, Section Eight has evidence of human habitation. There are many homes, docks, and decks on this section. Above Fanning Spring, Highway 19 parallels the river for a stretch. Paddlers will hear automobile traffic at this camp. After Fanning Spring, there is an expansive hardwood forest on river left. The area is Andrews Wildlife Management Area. Embankments are low on river Section Eight.

Wildlife Spotted

In early May of 2009, Graham and I encountered Suwannee cooters, a sand piper, mullet jumping, one five-foot sturgeon jumping, one snowy egret foraging for food, one pileated woodpecker in flight, a black crow, and a male cardinal. In the cooler months, we encountered several West Indian manatees in the Fanning Spring run. Though we did not see any American alligators on our excursions, we did take a picture of a prominent sign at the banks of the river in Fanning Spring. The text on the sign adamantly warns swimmers to beware of large alligators in and around this particular section of river. Monster alligators swim these currents!

Points of Interest

Seminole Indian artifacts were once discovered at Old Town. The *City of Hawkinsville* is a steamship that was abandoned in 1922. The steamer rests at the bottom of the Suwannee River and today is designated as an underwater archaeological preserve. Be on the lookout for underwater divers exploring The *City of Hawkinsville* and her watery remnants. Fanning Spring was once a United States Army Fort location. History reveals that several soldiers drowned in the river near the fort. Historical markers within the park offer more information about the area. West Indian manatees visit Fanning Spring in colder months.

Restocking Supplies

Downriver from the Greenways Trail and the archaeological preserve of the *City of Hawkinsville*, see a motel located on river right. After exiting the river at the Suwannee Gables ramp, walk across Highway 19. There is a convenience store with general supplies of ice, beer, and gas. Several restaurants and motels are in the vicinity.

There are river-accessible campsites at Fanning Spring. Take out before the spring run. Campsites are situated to the left.

Be on the lookout for manatees during winter months; they take refuge at Fanning Spring. They are often seen congregating in social groups.

Hart Springs: Enjoy Nature Trails and Camping

According to local historians, Hart Springs was named for a Seminole Indian man. He once lived at the spring in the 1850s. He remained at Hart Springs, although most of his people had been forced out of Florida during the Seminole Indian Wars. Yet Hart stayed behind, choosing to live with white pioneers of the vicinity.

Near this location was once McCrabb's Ferry, which transported wagons, livestock, people, and later, automobiles across the Suwannee River to Dixie County. There was also another ferry near the area; locals referred to it as Coon Bluff.[1]

Hart Springs run is located on river left. Paddlers will see the sign and the boardwalk toward the left. Camping is allowed for a fee. To camp, or to visit the serene tributary, paddle up the spring-run to the canoe launch. While paddling upstream, notice the half mile river boardwalk; the wooden walkway loops and later runs parallel to the spring run on the left. Hiking the boardwalk on a one mile wooded trail loop is an option. Both trails are surrounded by thick oak hammocks and beautiful cypress trees. Camping for paddlers is located at the canoe launch to the left. Hart Springs boat ramp is down-river from the spring run. It is situated approximately 150 yards down-river from the Hart Springs location.

Notes
1. McCarthy, Kevin M. *The History of Gilchrist County*. Gainesville: 1986.

Hart Springs was named after a Seminole Indian.

Seminoles on the Suwannee River: History Discovered at Old Town

Rivers whisper age-old symphonies of celebration, laughter, sorrow, and death. Lend an ear to the music of rivers, to hear humanity's story. Unraveling the many mysteries of the Seminole culture has been difficult for anthropologists, mostly due to the understandable reluctance of the mighty Seminole Nation to share their rich history. Historical and cultural information that exists today mostly comes from narratives by early travelers, including William Bartram, journalists, sportsmen, and those who had contact with the Seminoles throughout various times in history. Other ways of learning about Seminole culture has been derived by analyzing and admiring their jewelry, crafts, and clothing. In addition, stories of the Seminoles themselves, taken from songs, folklore, and oral histories have provided a vivid account of the mighty and creative Seminole Nation.[1]

Through those various sources, anthropologists have been able to take historical accounts as they attempt to chronicle the rich ancestry of the Seminoles, who came forth from the Creek Indians. During the late seventeenth and early eighteenth centuries, Englishmen in the southern colonies began using the term Creek to identify a great variety of autonomous peoples that spoke numerous languages and practiced diverse cultural ways. However, the natives called themselves Coosas, Cowetas, Yuchis, Alabamas, Tuskegees, Shawnees, and many other names. It is from these peoples that the Creek Confederacy emerged, and from that diverse ancestral culture that the Seminole Nation ultimately burgeoned.

The word Seminole springs from Spanish origin. *Cimarron* means wild or untamed. The name was directed at uncooperative non-whites and Africans whom the Spaniards had to combat in their quest for wealth in a new land.[2] The Seminoles evolved as a strong and unified nation, by the Second Seminole Indian War, which lasted from 1835 to 1842. Their steadfast, ferocious solidity was created and necessitated by the attempts of the United States government to forcibly remove them from their home in Florida. Because their only desperate choices were to surrender, fight, or flee, they stood resolute and found strength in a new nation. We know them today as Seminole.

Clues to their way of life have been discovered on the Suwannee River as well; Seminole villages existed near Old Town. In the 1960s, anthropologist John M. Goggins recovered a large collection of Seminole pottery from the depths of the Suwannee River via scuba exploration. Goggins brought up many remarkable artifacts, including sixteen vessels intact, or mostly intact, and other significant pieces large enough for anthropological research. The important find revealed much about the lives of the

Seminoles. For instance, the small-round bottomed bowls may have been used to serve china-briar root soup, while the larger bowls were probably used to serve dishes of oil-dressed venison. The large pottery bottles, anthropologists surmise, were used to store honey and bear's oil for sea trade with Spanish Cuba. The trade by the Seminoles was most likely accomplished by way of large ocean-going canoes, sometimes called long-boats.[3]

Complex farming methods helped sustain the nation as they farmed crops of corn and rice; they also relied on wild plant foods. These peoples were a prominent presence on the Suwannee River, and the years between 1812 and 1858 were dominated by continuous hostilities between the Seminoles and early pioneers, soldiers and the United States government; all were foes intent on removal and extermination of Indians in the Eastern United States. Billy Bowlegs, known by his followers as Holata Micco, established a town in 1818, called Bowlegs Town. It was situated directly upon the banks of the Suwannee River. Micco and his followers fled to the banks of the Suwannee after being driven from an area near Payne's Town, which today is called Payne's Prairie. (See Billy's Island and Billy's Lake in Section One of this book. Bowlegs also lived in the Okefenokee Swamp in the 1830s before he was driven out by the United States army.)

Bowlegs' village, near Payne's Town, suffered great losses in the raid of 1812, at the hands of United States soldiers and volunteers. In that three-week raid, 386 houses were burned, 300 horses and 400 head of cattle were captured, approximately 2000 bushels of corn were consumed or destroyed, 2000 deerskins were seized or destroyed, 20 Seminoles were killed, and 9 Seminoles and blacks were captured. The raid sent Bowlegs fleeing to the banks of the Suwannee River, where he established a settlement. Near Bowlegs Town was a village known as Nero. The settlement, located on the west bank of the Suwannee, thirty-five miles from the mouth of the river, was inhabited by three hundred to four hundred escaped slaves from Florida and Georgia. Andrew Jackson moved against both of these Suwannee River settlements, driving the occupants deep into Florida's peninsula.[4]

Later, during the Second Seminole War of 1835 to 1842, the United States government spent $20 million to fund the efforts to rid the land of Seminoles. In those seven years, 1,500 soldiers died, but no one knows the human toll to civilians or Seminoles.[5] What is known is that in less than fifty years—due to raids by the Georgians, by Andrew Jackson and his Tennesseans, and by the United States Army—the Seminole Nation was driven out of North Florida; they fled in terror to the south. By 1858, at the conclusion of the last Seminole Indian War, only two hundred Seminoles survived.

Yet another famous Seminole was the legendary and tragic figure of Osceola, known as William Powell. He strategized many successful battles against five United States generals in the Second Seminole War. He also stood valiant and is reputed for his tenacious spirit of non-surrender.[6] When Osceola was asked to sign the Indian Removal Act—a decree which asked for the Indians of Florida to be relocated to other states, such as Oklahoma and Arkansas—he reportedly stabbed his knife into the document. Later, Osceola was tricked by General Thomas Jessup who took Osceola into custody under a flag of truce. Jessup was greatly criticized for the act and spent the entirety of his life explaining the deed.[7]

From those Seminole ancestors, several thousand descendants live today. They run a multi-million dollar cattle industry, as well as one of the most financially successful citrus packing houses in Florida. They, too, are politically active, and in the 1980s were prominent contributors to statewide political campaigns.

The Seminole Nation of Florida today is divided into two distinct, federally recognized nations. One is the Seminole Tribe of Florida, recognized in 1957, and the Miccosukee Tribe of Indians of Florida, established in 1962. Two specific southeastern Native American languages are spoken by them.[8]

Notes

1. and 3. Weisman, Brent Richards. *Unconquered People: Florida's Seminole and Miccosukee Indians.* Gainesville: University Press of Florida, 1999.
2. Wright, Leitch J. Jr. *Creeks and Seminoles: Destruction and Regeneration of the Muscogulge People.* Lincoln: University of Nebraska Press, 1986.
4. Covington, James W. *The Seminoles of Florida.* Gainesville: University Press of Florida. 1993
5. Ste. Claire, Dana. *Cracker: The Cracker Culture in Florida History.* Gainesville: University Press of Florida, 1998.
6. http://www.seminoletribe.com/history/index.shtml
7. and 8. Clark, James C. *200 Quick Looks at Florida History.* Sarasota: Pineapple Press Inc., 2000.

The portrait of Osceola was painted by George Catlin (1796 – 1872) from life, at Fort Moultrie, South Carolina. Osceola was imprisoned there, but died a few months later, in January 1838. Photographs and caption information courtesy of State Library and Archives of Florida.

A Paddler's Guide

Chief Billy Bowlegs was one of the most significant figures in the Third Seminole Indian War. (1855 – 58). He lived on the Suwannee River in the early 1800s and established a town thirty-five miles from the mouth of the Gulf. He was driven from the Okefenokee Swamp by the United States Army in the 1830s. Billy's Island and Billy's Lake in the Okefenokee Swamp are named for him. Courtesy of State Library and Archives of Florida.

Lottie Shore, a Seminole woman, chooses beads to weave for her Seminole dolls. White Springs, Florida, 1984. Courtesy of State Library and Archives of Florida.

A Paddler's Guide

Seminole crafts and traditions live on in White Springs, at the Stephen Foster Folk and Cultural Center located directly on the banks of the Suwannee River. Courtesy of State Library and Archives of Florida.

A chickee dwelling provided shelter for the Seminoles. Expansive Seminole villages existed on or near the Suwannee River in the 1800s. The Seminole families were driven from their homes by Andrew Jackson's militia. Courtesy of State Library and Archives of Florida.

Andrew Jackson and the United States government were intent on removing the Seminoles from Florida. Under The Indian Removal Act, a law that furthered the nation's ultimate relocation, thousands of Seminoles were forced to move to reservations. Courtesy of State Library and Archives of Florida.

A Paddler's Guide

Myths of the Southeastern Native American Tribes

According to Joseph Campbell, the world's foremost authority on mythology, in his *Power of Myth*, mythic tales are simply stories of peoples' quest through the ages for meaning, significance, and truth.[1] Because human beings must come to grips with death and must accept death as destiny, we must create a way to express those cosmic curiosities. Not only the demise of this "mortal coil" must we address, but also the life experience needs clarification. "Life is hard," I always heard Mama say. Campbell reveals that just as we need help in coping with death, our varied challenging life journeys, from birth to life, and then ultimately to death, need explaining. Through myths, these clues to our potential as spiritual beings shine through; therefore, mythic stories portray cultural values and mores that can depict clues to ancient belief systems of indigenous peoples. The southeastern native tribes were rich in myths, legends, songs, and ceremonies; many themes, situations, symbols, and archetypes parallel other belief systems of the world, including Catholicism and Buddhism. These aspects can tell what a culture knows or reveres regarding history, archaeology, geography, botany, arts, animals, phonetics, people, supernatural happenings, medicinal cures, farming, home life, and religion. Colonizers may easily call a native nation savage or pagan, but myths convey many truths, uncovering the complexities of the original peoples of the southeastern region. The following are brief excerpts and summaries from James Mooney's comprehensive study of southeastern native tribes, *Myths of the Cherokee*. These stories include Creek tales; some of those mythic stories filtered into Seminole lore. In Mooney's text, some animal names were sometimes capitalized. For consistency, I have capitalized all animal names.

From a Creek Myth

Origin of Indian Corn

The corn plant is actually a transformed body of an elderly woman. She has but one son who is empowered with magical abilities. Her son has emerged from one drop of her blood [perhaps menstrual blood].

Deer Confined in a Hole

A widespread belief of Native Americans is that game animals were originally confined within a cave but set free by an accident or some sort of trickery.

How the Turkey got his Beard
The Turkey was once a mighty warrior and would display his last scalp about his neck. Another version of the tale says the scalp is that of a man, which the Turkey took from the Terrapin, but accidentally swallowed it; so the scalp grew from the Turkey's breast.

The Rabbit Lover
There was once a beautiful maiden who would not surrender to her lover, the Rabbit. The Rabbit would hide near a spring, and using a blowgun as a trumpet, he would scare the girl into consent by singing this song: "The girl who stays single will die, will die, will die."[2]

From many southeastern tribes

The Bear
Because the Bear can stand upright, and its tracks resemble human prints, there was a pervasive belief among many native tribes that the Bear was half human. Much reverence was given to the animal and many stories were told involving the Bear.

The Snake Tribe: The Rattlesnake
Native Americans held a sacred custom of asking forgiveness of slain or injured animals. Their reverence for the Rattlesnake was universal and much dread accompanied offending one. Similar tales have been often repeated throughout varying tribal communities about such reverence for the snake. In fact, William Bartram, the naturalist, recounts a story of the Seminoles around the year 1775. Bartram records how the natives were intent on never killing a Rattlesnake or any other reptile. According to Bartram, the Seminoles believed that if killed, the spirit of the snake could inflict influence over the killer's living relatives as the spirit was intent upon revenge. Some tribes referred to the Rattlesnake as Grandfather, to endow it with a name of respect and of honor.

From the Cherokee

The Underground Panthers
The following is a condensed, summarized version of the tale from Mooney's text.

A hunter was in the forest on a cold winter's day, when he spied a Panther walking toward him. Preparing to defend himself, the man was on the verge of shooting, when the great cat spoke, and at that instant it seemed to the hunter as if there was no difference between them; they both were of the same nature. The animal inquired of the man about where he was headed, and the hunter replied he was searching for a deer. The Panther said that he and others were preparing for a Green-corn dance and were also out to get a buck. He invited the man to join their hunt. . . . After killing a large deer without any problem, the Panther wrapped his tail around the animal and tossed it over his back. He then invited the hunter to join him at the townhouse.

The Panther took the lead, with the deer upon his back, heading up a small stream until they reached the spring head. It seemed like a door on the side of a hill opened, and they both stepped in. Within the townhouse, the hunter noted green trees and warm air. A crowd was preparing for the dance; they were all Panthers, but the scene did not appear unnatural to the hunter. Other Panther hunters gathered with their deer and the dance started. After the hunter danced for several rounds, he remarked that the day was growing old and he must return home. The Panthers opened the door, and the hunter exited, but immediately he found himself alone in the forest in a cold winter snowstorm. Finally, he arrived at his settlement where he discovered a search party just going out to find him. They wanted to know where he had been off to for so long, and he relayed to them that he had been invited and had stayed in the townhouse of the Panther for several days (not a few hours as he initially thought). The hunter died within seven days of his return, because he had already begun to transform into a Panther nature, and therefore could not abide again with fellow humans. If the man had remained with the great cats, he would have lived.[3]

Notes

1. Campbell, Joseph. *The Power of Myth with Bill Moyers*. Edited by Betty Sue Flowers. New York: Doubleday, 1988.
2. Mooney, James. *Myths of the Cherokee*. New York: Dover Publications, Inc., 1995.
3. Ibid.

Rose Knox and Graham Schorb

Underwater Archaeological Preserve: Steamship Abandoned in 1922

The *City of Hawkinsville* was once a prominent steamboat operating on the Suwannee River in the late 1800s and early 1900s. Built in 1886, the steamer was used to transport timber upon the Suwannee River. However, in 1922 the ship was abandoned in the midst of the river; today her remnants rest near the Greenways Trail, at the Old Town landing. The site is marked by buoys. The *City of Hawkinsville*, though submerged in the river, still attracts curious tourists as she did years ago; for where she ultimately went down is today a famous wreck site, drawing in many visitors and scuba divers. The steamship is part of an official Florida Underwater Archaeological Preserve.[1]

Notes
1. Florida State Archives

The *City of Hawkinsville* was a prominent steamship once traversing the Suwannee River. She was abandoned in 1922. Paddlers can see remnants of the old ship near the Greenways Trail, at Old Town landing. The site is marked with buoys. Courtesy of State Library and Archives of Florida.

Fanning Spring State Park: Once a Paleo-Indian Gathering Place, Fort Location, Ferry and Steamboat Landing, Tourist Attraction, and Manatee Refuge

Fanning Spring has a rich and diverse history. The first inhabitants of the spring were the Paleo-Indians. They lived approximately thirteen thousand years ago. Much later, the name Fanning Spring originated from Alexander Campbell Wilder Fannin. Fannin lived from 1788 to 1846 and was a military figure in the Second Seminole Indian War. The fort was built in 1838 in the area near the spring, in order to guard a highly used crossing upon the Suwannee River. The initial fort, however, was called Fort Palmetto. Because the structure was not made of stone, but made of wood, any evidence of the building has since disintegrated.

Federal soldiers occupied the fort for approximately five years. Historical records indicate that thirty-one soldiers perished in or around the fort's vicinity, while serving duty. They met their demise in different ways. Twenty-seven died from disease, two died of wounds, one was shot, and one drowned in the Suwannee River. The soldiers

Fanning Spring was an important place on the Suwannee River in the 19th and 20th centuries. In the 1800s, the Fort Fanning Ferry transported people and horses over the river. Later, a steamboat landing was built. In the 1900s, a railway transported goods to and from the area. Courtesy of State Library and Archives of Florida.

After WWII, Marx Chaney established a tourist destination, Suwannee River Jungle Drive, at Fanning Spring. The attraction offered many sights and amenities for the traveler, including restaurants, tourist cottages, gift shops, boardwalks through the swamp, boat rides up the Suwannee River, and horse-drawn carriage rides into the Florida wilderness. Courtesy of State Library and Archives of Florida.

were probably buried in the fort's vicinity, in the area located approximately two hundred yards north of Highway 19.[1]

The fort was renamed for Colonel Fannin, who served under General Andrew Jackson in the First Seminole Indian War. When the Second Seminole Indian War began, Fannin had risen to lieutenant. He was honored by the United States government for his military service against the natives. History reveals he was responsible for leading a charge in a battle, which took place near the Withlacoochee River. Fannin's ultimate military goal in the Second Seminole Indian War was to capture members of the Seminole Tribe and relocate the natives to the West.

Fanning Spring (Fannin is now spelled with a "g" at the end) was a bustling trade site on the Suwannee River in the 1800s, first as a ferry landing, transporting people and horses over the river. The spring was also the location of a steamboat landing, serving area cotton plantations. Later, in the 1900s, a railway crossed the river, making trade at the spring vigorous, with lumber, cotton, and turpentine being exported, while farming and living essentials were being imported.[2]

Tourists seeking thrills in wilderness areas flocked to the spring after WWII because Marx Chaney had created a nature-themed Florida attraction located near the area. He advertised the park as Suwannee River Jungle Drive. Fanning Spring, because of Chaney's promotion of the unique Florida attraction, became a popular tourist destination, bringing visitors in to partake in varied amenities, such as restaurants, tourist cot-

Warning sign at Fanning Spring.

tages, gift shops, and a boardwalk. Visitors experienced the jungle-like atmosphere as they lolled along the boardwalk, which passed through a swamp. The more adventurous traveler marveled at the blankets of thick, grey Spanish moss within green hardwood forests while riding in horse-drawn carriages.

When Interstate 75 was built, travelers no longer used U.S. 19 as a major north-south thoroughfare. Consequently, Fanning Spring, once a thriving tourist economy, had devolved into a secluded ghost town. In fact, Tim Hollis, in his fascinating book about early Florida tourist destinations, reveals the dire forecast for the once-crowded attraction. For example, boats that previously traversed up the Suwannee River, full of excited tourists, were no longer in operation. The gift shop that had been in the Jungle Drive complex was being used as a church, and the carriages, which once had taken eager tourists for rides in the Florida forest, now stood rusting amid tall weeds and overgrown grass. The decline in tourism had an immediate economic effect on the Fanning Spring area, for the thirty-three-room Suwannee Gables Motel and restaurant went up for sale; nearby gas stations and another restaurant went out of business.[3]

Today, Fanning Spring is a state park and is noted for its natural beauty. The spring and river attract water sports enthusiasts for swimming, fishing, canoeing, and snorkeling. As one of Florida's thirty-three first magnitude springs, the aquifer is continually pumping forth approximately 65 million gallons of water per day. In colder winter

The *City of Hawkinsville* rests on the riverbed near here. Photo courtesy of State Library and Archives of Florida.

months, the spring attracts manatees, and within that time frame, swimming areas for tourists are closed. Camping is available at the location for a fee.[4]

Tips for Paddlers: Paddlers should notice a sign for the park on river left, just before the Fanning Spring run. Before the spring tributary, the embankment serves as a canoe launch. The camping spot, which has a large fire ring, is located just up the path to the left, approximately thirty yards from the river launch. The open field near the fire ring can accommodate many campers. Also, there on the shores of the river, is a warning sign for swimmers and paddlers to beware of strong currents and speeding motor boats. One sign is designated specifically to warn people of enormous alligators traversing the waters. Beware the words, and hold strictly to such warnings!

In the park is a place designated in memory of the old fort. The memorial honors all of those people on both sides of Florida conflicts; those violent times which took place during the Seminole Indian Wars. A multitude of people suffered and died in those years. They were Native Americans, early pioneers, and United States soldiers.

See the unique roundish wooden sign made from a live oak tree section, which informs visitors of a former steamboat landing. Read there about the history and the location of the old steamer, the *City of Hawkinsville*.

Notes
1. McCarthy, Kevin M. *The History of Gilchrist County.* Gainesville, Florida: 1986.
2. and 4. www.floridastateparks.org/fanningsprings/History.cfm
3. Hollis, Tim. *Glass Bottom Boats and Mermaid Tails: Florida's Tourist Springs.* Mechanicsburg: Stackpole Books, 2006.

Inside the spring run, the Suwannee River is visible in the background. Late afternoon lighting in the photograph does not reveal the crystal-clear nature of the aquifer. A swimming area is designated; surrounding the spring is a cement boardwalk. Marveling at aqua blue water against a white spring bed, Graham and I spied six manatees resting within the run. One was a Mother with her baby.

Signs warn of monstrous alligators at Fanning Spring.

A Paddler's Guide

The majestic great blue heron. Courtesy State Library and Archives of Florida Postcard Collection.

A Seminole Indian Village Named Tallahascotte

Clay Landing was once referred to as Tallahascotte by the Seminole Indians. Some scholars believe the natives established a settlement in the vicinity upon the Suwannee River. However, the exact location of the Native American village is still under debate. Primary documents from early travelers—such as the famous naturalist William Bartram, within his journals and later book *Travels*—often can tell a story of past settlements. According to Bartram, who visited the town on the Suwannee River, the village was once located on the eastern embankment. He noted that the settlement was three or four miles up-river from Manatee Springs, and he stated that the location of the village was situated upon a high bluff.

The debate continues about the exact location of the bluff. The first bluff on the Suwannee River was above Manatee Springs at New Clay Landing. At the edge of the river, the bluff is only ten feet high; however, the topography at this place rises considerably—approximately twice that height. The next bluff is also considered in the question. This particular bluff is situated at a place called Ross Landing, about three miles further up-river. Many people in the area of Old Town believe that this bluff, near the Ross Landing site, was the true village settlement of the Seminole natives in the 1800s.[1] The Seminole name Tallahascotte is derived from the Seminole word *talwa*, meaning town; *ahasse* means old, and translates to "little" or "Little Old Town."[2] Paddlers should seek out high bluffs on this section of river for clues about the location of the once-thriving Indian settlement.

Notes:
1. Bartram, William. *Travels*. New Haven: Yale University Press, 1958.
2. Holmes, Melton. Jr. *Lafayette County History and Heritage*. Mayo: 1974.

The Loggerhead Musk Turtle: A Prodigious Climber

Musk turtles are often seen basking on limestone outcroppings, cypress knees, overhanging branches, or small tree trunks. They are determined climbers, and some species have even been known to scale to heights of 6.6 feet! Because they are water turtles, their shells are infested with leeches and covered with algae. Why do they love living around the Suwannee? The slow moving current and soft river bottom of the Suwannee River provide an ideal habitat for their foraging needs. Be on the lookout for loggerhead musk turtles near springs or as they sun on limestone walls. Often they will fall from their high perches before paddlers pass them. In fact, paddlers may only hear a splash, but they might never actually get a glimpse of the prodigious climbing turtle.[1]

Loggerhead musk turtles bask on limestone outcroppings. They are known as prodigious climbers. Scientific identification courtesy of David Cook, biologist with the Florida Fish and Wildlife Conservation Commission.[2]

Notes:

1. Orenstein. Ronald. Turtles, *Tortoises & Terrapins: Survivors in Armor.* Buffalo: Firefly Books Inc., 2001.; Cook, David. "Identification of the Loggerhead Musk Turtle," e-mail to the author. May, 2009.
2. Cook, David. "Identification of the Loggerhead Musk Turtle," e-mail to the author. May, 2009.

Muskogean Tribes Merge with Escaped Plantation Slaves: Black Seminoles on the Lower Suwannee

During the 1700 and 1800s, North Florida drew refugees from several southeastern states such as Georgia, Alabama, and South Carolina. These Native Americans of the Muskogean tribes fled persecution from ever increasing European occupation. They often ran with escaped black slaves from area cotton plantations. In the spring of 1818, General Andrew Jackson marched three thousand militia and "friendly" Creeks through North Florida to the Suwannee River basin. After battling two hundred warriors along the Ecofina River, Jackson's Creek scouts, under Lower Creek chief William McIntosh's command, fought Red Stick chief Peter McQueen's band of warriors. McIntosh recounts a battle in a "bad swamp" and relates the skirmish endured for three hours; in that time, thirty-seven warriors perished and ninety-eight women, children, and men were taken captive.

Raids on cattle and storehouses gave Jackson's side seven hundred head of cattle, many hogs and horses, and an abundance of corn—all of the bounty gained in the raid. McIntosh's forces lost three warriors, and five were injured. After the Ecofina basin conflict, Andrew Jackson's forces moved toward the Suwannee River near Old Town, descending upon the large Seminole and maroon villages nestled along the lower Suwannee. Just before the sun set over the horizon, Jackson's men came up on a band of Black Seminoles. Fire from muskets lit the dusk, and though the Black Seminoles were vastly outnumbered, they were using a rearguard strategy to ultimately hold off Jackson's attack as their loved ones fled the invasion and made their way across the Suwannee River. Later, as night fell, the warriors, too, swam across the expanse of the river to safety. Because Jackson felt he had been successful in his raids to disband the Seminoles on the Lower Suwannee, he did not pursue the Black Seminoles across the river. However, his forces in the raid burned village structures and food storehouses and took nine hundred head of cattle. During that same time, two British traders were captured and killed for helping the Seminoles of the lower Suwannee River.[1]

Notes
1. Alderson, Doug. *Waters Less Traveled: Exploring Florida's Big Bend Coast*. Gainesville: University Press of Florida, 2005.

A Paddler's Guide

Section Nine Map

Manatee Springs State Park Launch to the Gulf of Mexico
Mile 25.1 – Mile 0

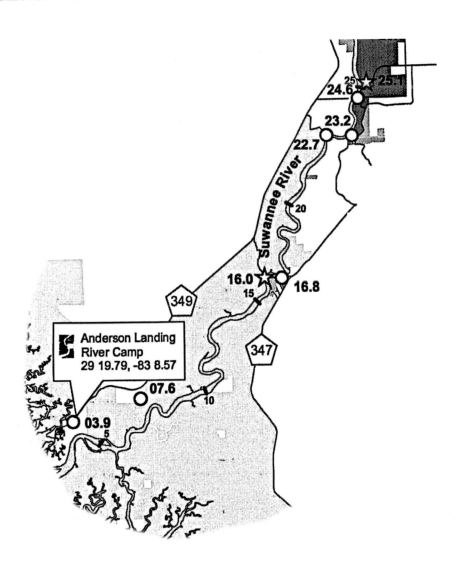

Navigation Warnings

Navigation: The Suwannee River widens on section nine, winding ever closer to the Gulf of Mexico. Beware of motor craft such as jet skis and cigarette boats; high-speed motor craft can swamp a loaded canoe. Tides also affect the river as it nears the Gulf of Mexico, and the wind can pick up, making waters choppy.

Take Out: When paddlers see stilted homes in the distance, they should begin heading for the inlet on the right, located at mile 3.9 on river right. Commercial signs for a marina and a fish camp are posted. When you see the commercial signs, paddle to the right, directly into the inlet. Then take the first left, leading to the Town of Suwannee. Follow the commercial signs for the marina and the fish camp. Paddlers will also see a sign for Anderson Landing, where you can camp for a fee or rent a room with advance notice.

Camping Information

Paddlers may camp at Manatee Springs for a fee. See it located on river left. Paddlers who choose to camp at Manatee Springs must travel up the spring run. The boat ramp

In the Lower Suwannee Wildlife Refuge, hardwood forests line the river on both sides.

The heavy, sweet fragrance of roses wafted over the river, beckoning us to the pink delicate petals.

is on river right, about a quarter of a mile up the tributary. However, the campsites are a long way from the spring run; canoe campers may find the trek an arduous journey in transporting gear. Down-river from Manatee Springs, approximately two miles, is a public land use area on river left, called Camp Azalea ramp. Camp Azalea is located within a gorgeous hardwood forest. A privately owned camping area is located on river right, just below Camp Azalea. Camping is prohibited in the Lower Suwannee National Wildlife Refuge. Anderson Landing is located at the Town of Suwannee. It is a state-owned facility. There are campsites for a fee and rooms for rent there.

Topography

Manatee Springs has a winding spring run. Great stands of bald cypress trees shade the tributary, and the spring is lovely and serene. From Fowler's Bluff to the Town of Suwannee, paddlers will encounter wild and natural areas in the thick hardwood forests of the Lower Suwannee National Wildlife Refuge. There are numerous creeks, undulating back into deeply shaded places. Lilly pads were growing in one creek where we explored.

Once paddlers see the commercial signs, they will move forward into the inlet where houses and docks line the canal.

Wildlife Spotted

In early May of 2009, Graham and I encountered many wildlife species amid a variety of trees. We saw magnolias, bay trees, bald cypress, laurel and live oak, loblolly pine, and sabal palm. On the section was a variety of wildlife, too. We saw two wood ducks in flight, a little green heron on the shore, numerous mullet coming to the river's surface, and a Suwannee cooter sunning on a log. We heard the delightful chatter of songbirds and the piercing cry of a red-shouldered hawk. As we approached the Gulf of Mexico, near the Town of Suwannee, we were thrilled and much surprised to see a school of dolphins; three of them swam very near to us! The notebook I was using to write field notes was drenched! Across from the inlet to Anderson Landing, over near the hardwood forest, we passed an American alligator; it was approximately ten feet long. The large reptile was cruising across the river. In a shady stand of bald cypress trees, near an array of cypress knees, we witnessed an otter fishing for mullet. We stopped to marvel at his enthusiastic hunt! Once we arrived in the channel, following the channel markers to the Gulf of Mexico, we passed vast, breathtaking salt marshes, dotted with stately

A Paddler's Guide

sabal palms and bald cypress trees. The river widens significantly on section nine, and stilted homes line the banks on river right. In the salt marsh, our gaze turned upward to tall cypress trees; we marveled at two magnificent osprey nests built in spindly branches. Both sets of parents were diligently guarding each huge twig nest. We also spied one brown pelican, one sandpiper, several turkey vultures, a red-winged black bird, and a grackle. We saw a five-foot sturgeon jump up completely over the river's surface. Stopping for a break on one of the channel salt marsh islands, we took pictures of pieces of twisted driftwood until the horseflies and the sand fleas chased us away! We also explored several winding channels within the salt marsh, on river right; we encountered a great blue heron foraging for food there. We finally completed our journey, which had originated in the Okefenokee Swamp! We had finally made our way to the Gulf of Mexico.

Points of Interest

Manatee Springs is a splendid natural setting within hardwood hammocks. The boardwalk parallels the spring run. Paddlers may very likely get a glimpse of manatees

At the Town of Suwannee, paddlers may camp in the inlet at Anderson Landing. There are campsites available for a fee; rooms also may be rented with advance notice.

as these docile mammals congregate in the spring for warmth and protection. Divers also are often seen exploring the spring tributary. Fowler's Bluff is another place of interest. Located on river left, the site is famous for an intriguing tale about a man who, on his deathbed, gave away a treasure map. The pirate's treasure, legend recounts, was left here and may still be somewhere in the vicinity. One landowner is actively searching for treasure with modern-day equipment and with the assistance of scuba divers. Paddlers will canoe through the Lower Suwannee National Wildlife Refuge, a wild and scenic place.

At River's End

There is a fish camp and a marina in the Town of Suwannee. Anderson Landing is located at the site. Ice, beer, and restaurants are available in the Town of Suwannee.

Paddlers who wish to go all the way to the Gulf of Mexico (paddling past the inlet) will see vast, awe-inspiring salt marsh islands.

A Paddler's Guide

Nearing the Gulf of Mexico, paddlers will encounter a directional sign.

Here, the Suwannee River finally meets the Gulf of Mexico. I was reminded of the Steve Miller song when I saw the view. "Wide river, carry me down to the sea. . . . She runs like a river that has never been won, Runs like a river to the setting sun. . . ." —The Steve Miller Band

Rose Knox and Graham Schorb

Manatee Springs: Gulf Sturgeon and Manatees

When William Bartram journeyed through the Suwannee River Basin in the late 1700s, he encountered the magnificent spring he named Manatee. The spring still bears the name that Bartram jotted in his journals.[1] Approximately 64 million gallons flow forth from the aquifer daily, making Manatee Springs a first magnitude spring. Manatees today still congregate within the spring's tributary and spring area, from November through April as they search for warmth that a constant 72-degree temperature of spring water provides. The place is a wonderland for nature lovers, too; there are eight-and-a-half miles of hiking trails meandering through hardwood hammocks and cypress swamps. The lush, exquisite spring run is a quarter of a mile long and winds into a gorgeous hardwood hammock and swamp. The tributary can be seen on river left. The run supports many species of wildlife, including manatees, turtles, birds, and fish. Today the spring area is a state park.[2]

The manatees visiting the spring may have originated from Caribbean stock, as their ancestors migrated to the Gulf approximately twelve thousand years ago. Scientists and archaeologists have discovered ample evidence that the Seminole Indians hunted manatees for food and oil. They also used the bones for crafting tools. The first state protection of the manatees came in 1893, and punishment for disturbing or harming them included fines and prison sentences. In Florida, manatees are up against fierce challenges which threaten their very survival, such as ever increasing motorized boat traffic, and uncaring people harassing the docile, trusting mammals. The decline of their winter habitat, because of potential power plant losses, is another concern in protecting them from extinction.[3]

In the past, people have also witnessed Gulf sturgeon jumping out over the surface water of the Suwannee River near Manatee Springs. When paddling these waters, be on the lookout for the endangered and affectionate manatee; seek, also, the prehistoric Gulf sturgeon. Camping is allowed in the park, with a reservation and a fee.

Notes:

1. Bartram, William. *Travels*. New Haven: Yale University Press, 1958.
2. www.floridastateparks.org/manateesprings/-57k-
3. Bonde, Robert K. and Roger L. Reep. *The Florida Manatee: Biology and Conservation*. Gainesville: University Press of Florida, 2006.

Scientists and archaeologists have discovered ample evidence that the Seminole Indians hunted manatees for food and oil. The natives also used the bones for crafting tools.[3] The nurturing nature of the manatee is depicted sweetly upon Poali's canvas. Artwork courtesy of Linda K. Della Poali of Steinhatchee, Florida

A sign on river left alerts paddlers to Manatee Springs and run. The tributary meanders a quarter of a mile up though hardwood hammocks and cypress swamps. Boats with motors are banned from the run.

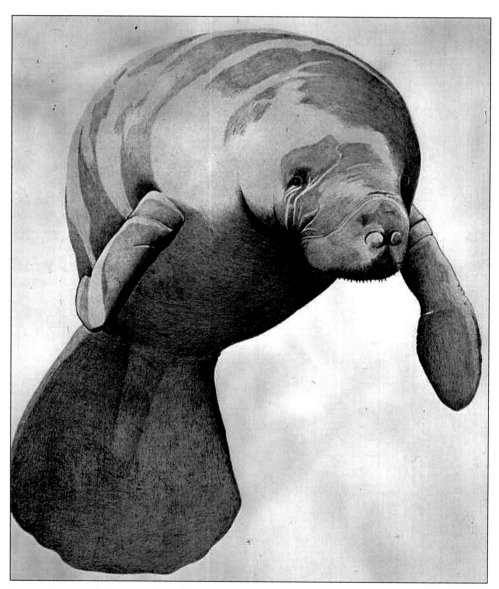
Manatees may be seen congregating in spring areas on the Suwannee River. Courtesy of State Library and Archives of Florida.

A Paddler's Guide

Fowler's Bluff and Pirate's Treasure

Could chests filled with gold still lie somewhere within embankments of the Suwannee River? Might pirate's treasure, hidden here centuries earlier, await discovery of some lucky person? In December 2008, on the lower Suwannee River, Graham and I pondered these questions. Weeks later, as I began the academic research of the area, I came across numerous articles pertaining to the legend of pirate's treasure at the Fowler's Bluff location. Graham had always heard about stories of pirate's treasure in the vicinity, and one article offered specific information about how the legend has prompted a search for gold. What I uncovered in research gives credence to such fascinating and legendary stories, for pirates may truly have been here!

According to *National Geographic* News, in March 2007 Tommy Todd, owner of the property, revealed that flecks of gold and mahogany wood samples, perhaps from an old chest, had been discovered at Fowler's Bluff. Currently, Todd is using scuba divers and a large excavating crane in his attempt to find the treasure. The scuba divers searching for treasure come to the surface covered in gold flecks after diving in the excavated hole, which is thirteen feet deep and four meters in diameter. Workers drilling the site reported that they found a sheet of gold surrounding the drill bit as the bit was withdrawn from the site. Todd and his excavation crew may be close to finding a treasure, which, according to local legend, was buried in the vicinity some two hundred years ago by Jean LaFitte.[1]

Lore reveals that in the early nineteenth century, LaFitte cruised up the Suwannee River from the Gulf of Mexico. He was known as a smuggling pirate to the greater society. He, however, insisted in defining himself as an entrepreneur; he claimed he was intent on defending American freedoms. Other characters deemed infamous by the culture were supposedly affiliated with LaFitte. They were Jose Gaspar, Billy "Bowlegs" Rogers (not the Seminole chief), and Black Caesar. Todd believes that he is close to unearthing the pirate's treasure, but at the time of the *National Geographic* news report, he could not (or would not) offer real evidence to the reporter.[2]

In February 2009, I called Mr. Todd to ask him a few questions concerning the location of his search for gold. He openly shared with me details concerning his continuous quest. He said that the place of digging is located inward on his property, and the land is positioned directly on the Suwannee River. He conveyed that the excavation is performed using a steel Kasson pipe and a coffer dam. Getting to the supposed treasure has proven difficult; he has had to hire scuba divers to search within the area. During the phone interview, he also confirmed the *National Geographic* report that evidence

See a boat ramp and mileage sign at Fowler's Bluff on river left. The distances posted may not be exactly accurate.

of old wood pieces and charcoal pieces had indeed been recovered in his modern quest for gold. I ended the conversation by inquiring if he was still currently looking for LaFitte's treasure. He replied, "My crew is still actively searching for the lost gold; I think it is only a matter of time before we find it."[3]

Todd is not the only person seeking out treasure here. Three or four other excavations have been made in the vicinity of Todd's search area. One was conducted by Bill Wise, who owned the land until 2000, where he once ran a small bar. Wise, with the help of a Baptist preacher, searched in vain several times using metal detectors. Growing weary of treasure hunters, who were continually dropping by unannounced and asking questions about the lost gold, Wise finally sold the property in 2000. He explained to the *National Geographic* reporter that though legend of pirate's treasure was good for bringing customers into his place of business, he had no expectations of ever finding any treasure there.[4]

Yet another story of an excavation surrounded a sawmill operator named Emmett Baird. He may have discovered gold on Wise's former property. According to a 1945 article in the *Saturday Evening Post*, Baird heard of the pirate's gold from a man who was on his deathbed. The story reveals that in 1897, Baird's dying acquaintance offered Baird a map. Baird promptly traveled to Fowler's Bluff on the Suwannee River, where after three months, he withdrew from the excavation. However, soon after that, some people believe that he may have indeed discovered gold, for Baird went to Gainesville where he invested in several businesses, including a bank and a hardware store. The store eventually burgeoned into one of the most prominent in the state of Florida. Also in the 1900s, he purchased one of Gainesville's most expensive mansions. These sudden, flamboyant financial activities created a flurry of controversy around Baird that continued to follow him throughout his lifetime. The legend of gold does not end at edge of the Suwannee River, however. The home in Gainesville is still frequented by curious inquiries of hidden gold. Baird supposedly buried gold at the Gainesville estate.[5]

The question about lost gold still intrigues people today. Does there remain buried treasure at Fowler's Bluff? As paddlers pass, might they be floating over valuable pieces of eight left centuries before by a pirate named Lafitte? Experts think so, as *Coin World*, a publication for coin collectors, lists Fowler's Bluff as a "productive site for the seeker of pirate treasure."[6] Remember the fantastic legends of undiscovered treasure while paddling past Fowler's Bluff, as you ponder the unsolved mystery of a treasure chest filled with gold.[7]

Notes

1, 2, 4, 5, 7. Drye, Willie. *Clues to Pirate Gold Unearthed in Florida, Treasure Hunter's Claim* . National Geographic News 15 March 2007. 31 January 2009 http://news.nationalgeographic.com/news/2007/03/070315-pirate-treasure.html

3 and 6. Todd, Tommy. Telephone Interview. February, 2009.

The owner of a nearby property has been on a long, diligent quest in search for pirate's gold. Legend has it that gold was abandoned somewhere in the vicinity in the early 19th century, by a pirate named Jean LaFitte. The river widens as it approaches the Gulf of Mexico. Imagine how pirate ships might have navigated up into the Suwannee River, searching for a secluded, convenient embankment where they could hastily bury treasure.

Pirate's Treasure and a Ghost Story: Unconfirmed Tales of the Suwannee River Basin

Legends surround the Suwannee. One story often told by locals is about a pirate ship that sailed along the coast of the Gulf of Mexico. The pirates needed to bury treasure chests, and they supposedly did so near a place called Shell Mound, a Native American site located in the Suwannee River basin, near Cedar Key in the Lower Suwannee National Wildlife Refuge. Towering over the horizon, about twenty-eight feet above sea level, stands an impressive shell mound that was once used by Native Americans.[1] Strange stories have arisen in modern times about the ancient gathering spot. Often it is difficult to discern what is true and what is not concerning the fascinating tales. Like many stories, however, there may be some historical accuracy to the intriguing yarns. For instance, a treasure hunter from Saint Petersburg, Florida, confirms that he did, in fact, discover pieces of old falling-apart chests. Metal detectors were used in the area around the mound, and coins were discovered there, too.

Knowing the information about the pirates and their hidden treasure makes the ghost story intriguing. Not one, but many versions of the account about a ghostly woman and her dog, prevail at Shell Mound. One recollection is from a woman named Anna Ray Roberts. She talks of her weird encounter with a spirit, saying that she spied a beautiful girl with long dark hair in the woods. So detailed were her specific remembrances of that night in 1969 that they made the story almost believable. She said the season was mid-January, and she had pulled her automobile down to Shell Mound, located near the water. As she sat in the car in the dark, she noticed a light that was nine inches around and floating five feet above the ground! The apparition was wearing a light-colored top and a dark skirt. Beside her was a dog that looked much like a wolfhound. The illumination moved forward slowly toward her as it continued to hover in the air. Then the light moved toward the nearby hardwood forest.

Another ghoulish tale recounts how an eight-year-old child ambled toward the same hardwood forest near Shell Mound. When her mother realized that the wandering child was walking too far away, she called for her daughter. The child, upon her return, reported that someone had been calling her, beckoning her into the shadows among the trees.

What are the truths behind the tales and strange sightings? Could there be some validity behind the ghost stories? Perhaps so, for locals tell an old narrative about a woman named Annie Simpson and her dog. Simpson came upon some pirates as the men buried their treasure. According to the accounts, they murdered her to keep hidden the secret of their riches. Matching fact with lore, not only have pieces of chests and coins been found near the location, but the complete skeletal remains of a dog were unearthed there too. However, Annie Simpson's bones have never been recovered.[2] Bizarre tales like these are compelling; yet paddlers must decide for themselves. Do they dare believe in ghosts at Shell Mound? Is there a ghost of a beautiful woman and her dog truly roaming the twenty-eight-foot mound? Graham and I like to keep to the facts. But as the sun started to set on Shell Mound, we were looking intently for our own chance to see the ghosts!

Notes

1. Kiosk at Shell Mound in the Lower Suwannee National Wildlife Refuge in the Suwannee River Basin.
2. Moore, Joyce Elson. *Haunt Hunter's Guide to Florida: Thirty Three of the Most Bone-Chilling Places in the Sunshine State.* Sarasota: Pineapple Press, 1998.

Shell Mound towers twenty-eight feet high, offering breathtaking views over expansive salt marshes.

A Paddler's Guide

Another impressive vista is gazing from Shell Mound boat ramp across the wild expansive saw grass landscape.

Mystery and intrigue envelop Shell Mound, for the midden not only was an ancient gathering ground for Native Americans, but also is the setting of a strange story of pirate's treasure and ghosts.

A Paddler's Guide

When the "Lazy" River Rises: The Mighty Suwannee Turns Deadly

"This is the worst disaster that we've ever had to deal with."[1]

Many find it hard to believe that a gentle river can become an uncontrollable monster in only a few days. Paddling the Suwannee River when currents are low is a relaxing experience. Some have even called the Suwannee a "lazy" river. I have been guilty of that. On April 4, 2009, my twenty-year-old daughter and her fiancé, Doug, paddled a seven-mile trek on the middle Suwannee River with me, while water levels were low. Sandbars peeked up from the riverbed. They rose from the tannic water; we maneuvered around them like we were zig-zagging an Olympic obstacle course. Doug commented that he just could not imagine the river levels ever rising up over the banks. I told him, "We've been out here when the river was flowing over those treetops." Doug just kept shaking his head in disbelief.

As the two paddled ahead of me, I remembered the symbolic scenery in the movie *Stagecoach*. There was my Jessica, in an orange and yellow kayak, and Doug, in his blue sit-on top, cruising past tall limestone walls. They seemed to me like the miniscule people in the movie; they, too, were dwarfed by the expanse—the all encompassing presence of Nature. They almost looked like they were paddling in a puddle. I saw how this river gets the reputation of being "lazy." But I know this river well. Those who live upon these shores do too. Oh, and how fickle are those currents!

Less than a week after our day trip down the "lazy" and low Suwannee, the flood waters came; they arrived with a vengeance. Jim Stanley, of Madison County Emergency Management, commented that the flood was the river's "worst disaster" he had ever seen.[2] Standing upon the old Highway 90 Bridge at Ellaville, Graham wanted to get some pictures of what would later be called a "record flood." He called me on his cell phone as he walked the expanse of the bridge, describing the rising currents as "swirling and churning." A friend walked the bridge too, and she said that the rushing river reminded her of the muddy Mississippi. A few hours later, I made my way from Madison County to Suwannee County via detour, so I, too, could witness the continuous rising. The dark water was fast flowing and treacherous. If a river can exude human qualities, I would characterize her as angry, restless, and undaunted.

In April 2009, the National Weather Service in Tallahassee predicted flooding along the Suwannee River and its tributaries—the Withlacoochee, the Alapaha, and the Santa Fe rivers. Their dire proclamations were correct, and by April 6, the rising Withlacoochee River had surpassed the flooding record of the 1973. It too, beat the infamous all-time flood record of April 5, 1948! On April 11, 2009, the Suwannee had risen at

The vacation home of Kathy and Jim Sale of Madison, Florida, was severely flooded in April 2009. Josh, their son, canoed in to assess damages; he stood upon the home's roof, looking down at the rising river. Courtesy of William French.

Ellaville to the level of 63.83, cresting one foot below the 1973 flood and two feet above the 1998 flood.[3] As a result, approximately 270 roads and 40 bridges were closed in the North Florida area. So devastating was the damage that Governor Charlie Crist signed an executive order declaring a state of emergency to the affected North Florida counties. By the time river levels began to recede, several people had lost their lives, hundreds of homes had been damaged, many of those completely destroyed.[4] Some of my friends had homes that were flooded, and they were greatly saddened over the event. Because of the cresting, lives were altered forever.

Nature will have her way, though. While the rising of the river causes such turmoil in our human lives, it serves a purpose. The uncontrollable currents, cresting over embankments, seem to have a life of their own; yet the rising keeps people from over-developing. In many places along her 242-mile corridor, the legendary Suwannee River remains untouched by Man's development. Though the virgin forests have virtually disappeared since they were destroyed during the logging era of the 1800s and early 1900s, the new growth forest gives us a glimpse of the way a river and an embankment should look. The ancient and "lazy" river can be deceiving and unpredictable, but perhaps the lesson is Nature's way of teaching us—her way of humbling us. The rising is like an

A Paddler's Guide

unexpected guest, and one with no manners. But the flooding over embankments keeps developers from ruining the beauty that is the Suwannee River.

Notes

1. Burlew, Jeff. "Updated: At Least 100 Homes Impacted by Flooding in Madison County." *Tallahassee Democrat*, 8 April 2009.
2. Ibid.
3. Suwannee River Water Management. "River Levels, Crest Predictions, Flood Warnings," e-mail from Efrain Bonilla. North Florida Community College via Victoria Brown Program Coordinator, Madison County Emergency Management.
4. Ibid.

A railroad employee inspects the bridge at Ellaville, assessing any damage as the Suwannee River rises in the flood of 2009. He told Graham that if the river rose one more inch, his supervisor would have to close passage of the bridge.

The raging river.

A Paddler's Guide

Pollution on the Suwannee River: The Human Toll

The water quality of the Suwannee River has been rated as very good according to state scientists. The land, which encompasses the basin, is owned by private individuals and multiple government agencies. Because of flooding, and because many miles of land are owned by government agencies, development on the river has been deemed by some as mostly insignificant. Yet the river is polluted in many ways. Nitrate concentrations (caused by fertilizer and animal waste), boaters (which spill gas and oil into the river), and human litter, all are contributing factors of unnatural waste to the Suwannee River's water quality. Also, irrigation needs, and other water demands, have slowed the Suwannee River's current.[1] Only a culture that reveres natural places can save them. The future of the river is in our hands. What will we do?

Notes
1. Boning, Charles, R. *Florida Rivers*. Gainesville, Florida: Pineapple Press, Inc., 2007.

A plastic chair dangles from an overhanging branch.

A refrigerator is lodged in an overhanging branch after the river's flood. Humankind's irreverent capacity to litter a pristine river basin with obsolete appliances and inventions speaks volumes about what we, as a culture, value and revere. Litter we have seen dumped in the river (or swept away by flood waters because items have not been responsibly secured) includes a shopping cart, a golf cart, a computer monitor, plastic chairs, lawn umbrellas, plastic flowers, rubber rafts, and balls, to name only a few.

Fragmentation and Wholeness: Isolation and Community

> The world is too much with us; late and soon,
> Getting and spending, we lay waste our powers:
> Little we see in Nature that is ours . . .
>
> —William Wordsworth

> Fragmentation is the separation of habitat in a landscape. It means chopping a wild place into pieces, or slicing bites off its edges, or putting a road or other divider through the heart of it so that it becomes a conglomerate of smaller, less functional pieces. . . . Any time a human construct—house, building, field, road, parking lot, power line, pipeline, mine, clear cut, food plot, canal, levee, embankment—destroys anything of nature, it fragments the landscape. . . . The worst part of fragmentation is that it leads to isolation. For humans isolation is the place of hopelessness, depression, of despair . . . we know community to be a place of hope, of possibility, of wholeness. Human community, wild community.[1]
>
> —Janisse Ray

Nature provides a way out of the modern world—the fake construct of which we have been forced to live—a world that chops our lives into pieces—where we must always hurry to divide time; but on the river, we can find solace, continuity. We can begin to heal our fragmented selves as we come to know our True selves, escaping the mad world of Man and machines and "progress." It is here that our souls can connect with the energy and power of Nature.

Between white sand beaches and towering limestone walls, and beneath ancient cypress trees, we are allowed time to shed the artificial world. Like detoxification, the gentle whisper of wind, the rhythm of each paddle stroke, or the supreme silence transports us to a place of Truth, where we rediscover wholeness. Here, there are no light and pixels emanating from plasma computer screens or television sets. On the river, we are not prodded to buy anything, do anything, or be someone we are not. Here, we are not ushered into a false self. We are merely allowed to just "be." So come to the river and "be."

James Dickey, a prominent Southern writer, and one of the major American poets of this generation, who authored the novel and screenplay *Deliverance*, echoes Janisse

Ray's lament when he comments on how the natural world has been ravaged, and the losses are not just to the landscape—these losses affect humanity to the core. He says, "We're never gonna be able to get *out* of the mad world, if we don't have any place to go *from* the mad world. That's why we need these rivers, streams, creeks, woods. . . . You need to be in contact with Nature as it was made by somethin' else than Men."[2] John Boorman, the director of the film, echoes the loss of natural places as well, and his statement can remind us that we must do our best to preserve the Suwannee River. He says, "When you see that river, and you realize what this country used to be—then you weep for the destruction."[3]

The river offers silence to still a fragmented mind. It begs us to escape from our inauthentic selves—selves that have been craftily molded by commercial and political interests. Yet, I read once that there is death in silence. The silence of wild places frightens us, for we come to know our primordial selves as we realize our frailty, and with that knowledge, we know our mortality; but I say there is life in silence, too. For only in silence can we hear our own thoughts. We come to know what is real, what is important, what Truth is, and ultimately what is whole. That is living!

Notes

1. Janisse Ray, *Pinhook: Finding Wholeness in a Fragmented Land*. White River Junction: Chelsea Green Publishing Company, 2005.
2. James Dickey, *Deliverance*. New York: Houghton Mifflin, 1970.
3. *Deliverance*. Dir. John Boorman. Warner Brothers, 1972.

A Paddler's Guide

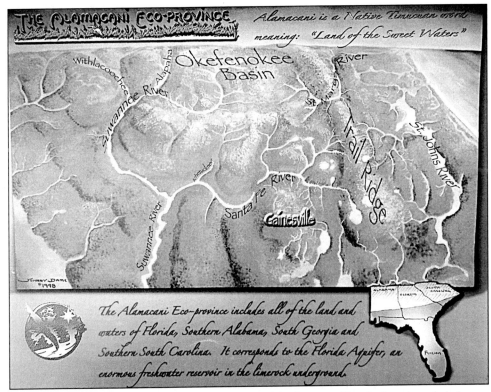

Johnny Dame, a spiritual naturalist and noted local artist of the Suwannee River basin, paints of wholeness in a landscape. His Alamacani Eco-Province depicts un-fragmented river basins. Courtesy of Johnny Dame.

A Paddler's Guide

Graham's Outdoor Kitchen: Recipes for Camp Cooking

Fargo Flapjacks, Ham Steaks and Cane Syrup

Choose a pancake mix and follow directions for appropriate serving sizes. (Graham prefers water-only mixes.)

Ingredients
Cane Syrup
Ham steaks

Fry ham steaks in cast-iron skillet. Remove from skillet, wrap in foil, and place at the back of the stove. Heat oil in skillet. Prepare pancakes according to mix. Cook until golden brown and serve with cane syrup.

A breakfast of flapjacks, scrambled eggs, fresh fruit, and peach preserves is an ideal way to relish moments of camp life.

Eggs Roline

Serves four.

Ingredients
1 medium onion, chopped
1 small can chopped mushrooms
8 eggs
1 tablespoon butter
1 cup shredded cheese

3 – 4 splashes Louisiana hot sauce

In a large cast-iron skillet, sauté onions and mushrooms in butter until desired tenderness. Add more butter. Then put eggs directly into the hot skillet with onions and mushrooms. Stir vigorously in order to scramble eggs until cooked. Remove from heat. Splash three to four times with hot sauce. Sprinkle on shredded cheese. Cover three to four minutes off of the heat.

Suwannee Fish Fry: Fried Redbellies
1. Catch a mess of red bellies.
2. Clean and scale.
3. Season fish with dried oregano, garlic powder, and black pepper (or use seasoning mix of choice).
4. Dredge fish in flour and cornmeal mix of your choice. (Packaged mixes are also available.)
5. In a cast-iron skillet, add one inch oil and place on camp stove at medium-high heat.
6. Fry fish until golden brown (about 7 to 10 minutes for each side). The skin will easily peel away from meat.
7. Serve with coleslaw, baked beans, cheese grits and hush puppies.

Suwannee Chili Pie
Serves four, using 12-inch Dutch oven.

Hot ashes smolder and simmer. They are used to prepare warm, delicious meals. Scrumptious aromas rise around camp when Dutch ovens are used to cook a variety of meals, including chicken, steak, pork, bacon, eggs, bread, pizza, and desserts of cobbler or cake.

Ingredients
2 medium onions
Fresh garlic to taste
1 tablespoon oil
1 tablespoon chili powder
1 pound ground meat
1 12-ounce can chili beans
1 12-ounce can diced or crushed tomatoes
1 12-ounce can kidney beans
1 12-ounce can tomato sauce
1 package corn muffin (Graham prefers water only mixes.)

Sauté onions, garlic and ground meat in the Dutch oven on hot coals until meat is cooked. Add beans, tomatoes, and chili powder. Stir well. Put lid on and simmer 45 minutes to one hour. (No coals on the lid at this point) After the chili has simmered for the appropriate time, combine muffin mix with water, then remove lid and pour directly on the chili. Replace lid and cover lid with hot coals. Bake for 20 to 25 minutes.

Dutch oven recipe titles are available online and in many bookstores. Graham has been cooking in a Dutch oven for decades. He often experiments with his own recipes, altering spices and sauces. Here, he is concocting a batch of scalloped potatoes.

Dad's Scalloped Potatoes
Serves four, using 12-inch Dutch oven.

Ingredients
4 medium onions
4 large potatoes

1 lb. block cheese
1 lb. canned ham
4 tablespoons butter

Slice onions, potatoes, ham and cheese. Put one tablespoon chipped butter on the bottom of the Dutch oven. Next, layer with potatoes, ham, onion, cheese and chipped butter. Repeat the same layering process two to three more times. Proportion each layer equally. Place lid on and cover the lid with coals. Allow Dutch oven to cook on a bed of medium-hot coals. Cook for 30 to 40 minutes.

Hearty River Stew

Serves four, using 12-inch Dutch oven.

Ingredients
1 lb. beef or venison stew meat
¼ inch cooking oil
2 large onions, quartered
4 potatoes
4 carrots, chopped
Broccoli (you choose portion size)
Mushrooms
Seasoning of choice, e.g. salt, pepper, oregano, garlic cloves, curry powder (to taste)
Soy sauce or Worcester sauce (to taste)
Flour or cornstarch
Water

Put cooking oil in the Dutch oven. Place oven on ready hot coals. Heat oil, add stew meat and onions, and cook until meat is browned. Drain excess oil (optional). Chop carrots to smaller size as they need more cooking time. Add potatoes, carrots, broccoli, and other desired fresh vegetables. Season the ingredients to taste with salt, pepper, and other seasonings of choice. Add soy sauce or Worcester sauce. Add sufficient warm water to cover vegetables. Put Dutch oven on ready coals and cook until vegetables are tender. When vegetables are cooked, thicken broth by mixing flour or cornstarch and water. Cook 30 to 40 minutes until all vegetables are tender.

Piney Woods Pork Chops with Potatoes and Gravy

Serves four, using 12-inch Dutch oven.

Ingredients
4 boneless pork chops

¼ inch cooking oil
2 medium onions
4 potatoes
1 small can of cream of mushroom soup
Salt and pepper or other favorite seasonings

Put cooking oil in the Dutch oven. Place oven on ready hot coals. Brown boneless pork chops until almost fully cooked and set aside. Brown potatoes and onions. Drain oil and return pork chops. Add cream of mushroom soup and water to cover the pork and vegetables. Cook 35 to 45 minutes on medium-hot coals until potatoes and pork are done.

Paddler's Pineapple Upside-down Cake

Ingredients
1 box yellow cake mix
Egg, water, oil Follow directions according to specific box brand.
1 can sliced pineapple
8 – 10 almonds or walnuts

Grease bottom and sides of 12-inch Dutch oven with vegetable oil. Arrange pineapple slices on bottom of the Dutch oven. (Important: Save the canned pineapple juice.) Place nuts in the center holes of the pineapple. Mix cake mix according to box directions, replacing water or milk with pineapple juice. Pour batter over pineapple slices. Place lid on Dutch oven and place oven on coals (5 coals on bottom and 6 coals on top for medium-hot coals). Bake at 350 degrees for 30 minutes.

Fireside Fruit Cobbler

Ingredients
Vegetable oil, butter, or margarine
1 cup flour
1 cup sugar
1 cup milk
1 to 1½ cups fresh or canned fruit of choice

Grease a 12-inch Dutch oven on the bottom and sides. Mix flour, sugar, and milk. Pour the mixture into the Dutch oven. Sprinkle fruit in the mixture. Place Dutch oven on medium-hot coals and add coals to the top (5 coals on bottom and 6 coals on top for medium-hot coals). Bake at 350 degrees for 30 to 35 minutes.

Dutch oven cooking can render hearty meals and delectable desserts. Using his own handpicked berries and a box of cake mix, Graham prepares a blackberry treat.

Graham, a river guide and outdoor cook, encourages campers to get creative using the Dutch oven. There are many recipes on the internet, and Dutch oven cookbooks are available in major bookstores as well.

Suggested Reading

Not only do Dutch Oven Cookbooks offer delicious recipes, but many also provide directions for selecting, using, and caring for the Dutch oven. Some give temperature charts and recipe planning. The following are recommended:

National Museum of Forest Service History. *Camp Cooking: 100 Years.* Salt Lake City: Gibbs Smith Publisher, 2004.

Juanita, Mike, Pat, and Wallace Kohler; and Pat and Dick Michaud. *World Championship Dutch Oven Cookbook.* Logan: Watkins Printing, 1989.

Woody Woodruff. *Cooking the Dutch Oven Way.* Guilford: The Globe Pequot Press, 2000.

For Cracker recipes to try at home:

Janis Owens. *The Cracker Kitchen: A Cookbook in Celebration of Cornbread-Fed, Down-Home Family Stories and Cuisine.* 2009.

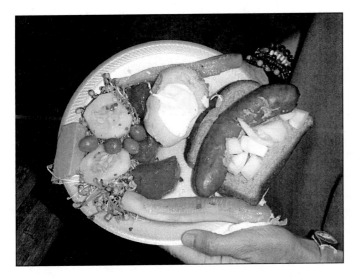

Fresh vegetables, link sausage, and a slice of cheese on fresh bread make a diversified snack after a morning of paddling.

Bacon sizzles and potatoes fry on a camp stove.

Camp stove cooking.

Camp dogs Marley and River wait for a tasty treat.

A Paddler's Guide

Rose and Graham take a scouting trip on the middle Suwannee.

A Paddler's Guide

Boat Ramp and Launches

Upper Suwannee River

242.0 Stephen C. Foster State Park Ramp: From Fargo, travel south on US 441 to CR 177; turn left and travel to Stephen C. Foster State Park.

235.0 Griffis Fish Camp Ramp: From Fargo, travel south on US 441 to CR 177; turn left and travel ten miles northeast; Griffis Fish Camp is on the left.

221.0 Fargo Ramp: The boat ramp is on the northeast side of US 441 and the Suwannee River.

202.0 Roline Launch: From White Springs, travel north on SE CR 135; cross over SE CR 6 onto NE 180 Boulevard (Woodpecker Route); travel north to NE 25 Way; turn right and follow road to ramp.

197.7 Turner Bridge Ramp: From White Springs, travel north on SE CR 135; cross over SE CR 6 onto NE 180 Boulevard (Woodpecker Route); travel north to NE 38 Trail; turn right and follow road to ramp.

195.7 Highway 6 Bridge. Travel east from Jasper; launch is on the north side of the bridge.

186.5 Cone Bridge Road Ramp: From Lake City, travel north on US 441 to NW Cone Bridge Road; turn left and follow road to ramp.

177.1 Big Shoals Tract Launch: From White Springs, travel north on CR 135 to SE 94 Street (Godwin Bridge Road); turn right and follow road to Big Shoals.

171.0 Suwannee River Wayside Park Ramp: From White Springs, travel south on US 41 to the river; the ramp is on the south side in the town park.

168.3 Stephen Foster Folk Culture Center State Park Launch: Canoe launch is in Stephen Foster Folk Culture Center State Park in White Springs.

163.2 Blue Sink Launch: From Live Oak, travel northeast on CR 136; cross over I-75 to 27 Road; turn left and continue north to 64 Terrace; follow road to canoe launch.

158.0 Woods Ferry Tract Launch: From Live Oak, travel north on US 129 to CR 136A; turn right; travel east to 57 Drive; turn left and continue north to Woods Ferry Path; follow Woods Ferry Path to canoe launch.

150.0 Suwannee Springs Launch: From Live Oak, travel north on US 129 to 93 Drive; turn right; travel north to 32 Street; turn right and follow to park area.

148.5 Spirit of Suwannee Music Park Ramp: From Live Oak, travel north on US 129 to Spirit of Suwannee Music Park; turn left on 95 Drive and follow road to boat ramp.

147.3 Deese-Howard Ramp: From Live Oak, travel north on CR 795 to 24 Street; turn right on 24 Street; travel east to 107 Road; turn left and follow road to boat ramp.

135.4 Gibson Park Ramp: From Jasper, travel southwest on SW CR 249 (road becomes SW 67 Drive) to SW CR 751; turn left and find boat ramp on the right in Gibson Park.

130.4 Road 141 Ramp: From US 90, turn right onto NE Myrrh Street; cross the Withlacoochee River (road becomes CR 141); turn right on SW 74 Street; turn right on SW 44 Lane; travel south to SW 77 Street; turn left and follow to boat ramp.

127.7 Suwannee River State Park Ramp: From Live Oak, travel west on US 90 to CR 132; turn right; cross railroad tracks and turn into Suwannee River State Park entrance.

115.6 Boundary Bend Ramp: From Dowling Park, travel west on CR 250; turn left on NW CR 101; travel north on NW CR 101 (road becomes SE Waccamaw Avenue); turn right on SE Boundary Bend Trail and follow to ramp.

113.0 Dowling Park Ramp: The boat ramp is on the north side of CR 250 at the Suwannee River.

111.2 Sims Landing Ramp (North Lafayette County): From Dowling Park, travel west on CR 250; turn left on NW CR 251; travel south on NW CR 251; turn left on NW Sims Landing Road and follow to boat ramp.

110.2 Christian Tract Launch: From Live Oak, travel southwest on CR 250 to 225 Road; turn left; travel south to 136 Street; turn right and travel west; crossover 233 Road onto Christian Path; follow road and turn right on Shirley Springs Trail; follow road to canoe launch.

106.5 Charles Spring Ramp: From Live Oak, travel south on SR 51 to 152 Street; turn right on 152 Street; travel west crossing 237 Drive; find boat ramp in the county park.

106.4 Ezell Landing Ramp: From Mayo, travel north on US 27 to CR 292; turn right on CR 292; travel north to ninety degree turn; continue straight on Ezell Landing Road and follow to boat ramp.

103.3 Lafayette Blue Springs State Park Ramp: From Mayo, travel west on US 27 to CR 292; turn right and go north to NW Blue Springs Road; turn right and follow road to Lafayette Blue Springs State Park.

98.2 Hal W. Adams Bridge Ramp: From Mayo, travel north on SR 51 to the river and find the ramp on the right.

97.4 Telford Springs Ramp: From Live Oak, travel south on SR 51 to 180 Street; turn left; travel east to 203 Road; turn right and follow to boat ramp.

92.9 Hardenbergh Ramp: From Mayo, travel east on US 27 to NE CR 361; turn left; travel north to NE CR 354; cross over to NE Pecan Avenue; turn right on NE River Road and follow to boat ramp.

90.4 Hugh Byron Hollingsworth, Sr. Ramp: From Live Oak, take SR 51 south to CR 349; turn left on CR 349; travel south to 198 Terrace; turn right and travel west to 157 Lane; turn left and follow road to 198 Trail; turn left and travel east to 157 Drive; turn right into park.

86.6 Fort MaComb Ramp: From Mayo, travel east on US 27 to CR 410; turn left on CR 410; follow to boat ramp.

83.7 Walker Tract Launch: From Branford, travel west on US 27 to NE CR 425; turn right and travel north; at the end of the pavement, where the road becomes NE Jeff Walker Road, turn onto the first dirt road to the right and follow to canoe launch.

82.0 Ruth Springs Launch: From Branford, travel west on US 27 to NE CR 425; turn right and travel north to NE Ruth Springs Road; turn right, take the first dirt road to the left, and follow to canoe launch.

Lower Suwannee River

79.0 Patrician Oaks Ramp: From Branford, travel west on US 27 to NE Lantana Road; turn right and follow road to boat ramp.

76.0 Ivey Memorial Park Ramp: Boat ramp is located in Branford on the south side of US 27 at the bridge in Ivey Memorial Park.

66.7 Dorothy Land Ramp: From Branford, travel US 27 west to CR 349; turn left and travel south to SE CR 480; turn left and travel east to SE CR 500; turn left and travel north to SE CR 490; turn right and follow to boat ramp.

63.2 Sims Landing Ramp: From Branford, travel US 27 west to CR 349; turn left and travel south to SE CR 500; turn left and travel to SE S: N: Hill Road; turn right and travel to SE R: M: Mears Road; turn right and follow to ramp:

59:6 Hirsh Landing Ramp. From Branford, travel US 27 west to CR 349; turn left and travel south to SE CR 500; turn left and travel to SE Leopard Road; turn right and travel to SE Foster Drive; turn right and find ramp on the left.

56.6 Rock Bluff Ramp: From Bell, travel north on US 129; turn left on CR 340; travel west to county park on the left at the river.

55.0 Gornto or Guaranto Spring Ramp: From Branford, travel south on CR 349 to NE 816 Avenue; turn left and follow road to boat ramp.

52.0 Log Landing Ramp: From Trenton, travel north on US 129 to CR 232; turn left and travel west to SW 70 Avenue; turn right; travel north to NW 7 Place; travel west to NW 6 Street; turn left and follow road to boat ramp.

49.9 Wannee Ramp: From Trenton, travel north on US 129 to CR 232; turn left and travel west to SW 70 Avenue; turn right; travel north to SW 10 Street; turn left; travel west to SW 80 Avenue; turn right and follow road to boat ramp.

46.0 Eula Landing Ramp: From Trenton, travel north on US 129 to CR 232; turn left and travel west to SW 70 Avenue; turn right; travel north to SW 25 Street; turn left; travel west to SW 25 Place; turn right and follow road to boat ramp.

44.0 Turner Point Landing Ramp: From Old Town, travel north on CR 349 to Ne 410 Avenue; turn right; follow to sharp left curve; road becomes NE 835 Street; continue north to NE 453 Avenue; turn right into park; the boat ramp is at the end of the road.

43.1 Hart Springs Ramp: From Trenton, travel north on US 129 to CR 344; turn left and travel west to CR 232; turn right; travel north to CR 344; turn left and travel west to SW 90 Avenue; turn right and follow road to ramp.

41.0 Purvis Landing Ramp: From Old Town, travel north on CR 349 to NE 272 Avenue; turn right and follow road to boat ramp.

40.0 Sapp Landing Ramp: From Fanning Spring, travel northeast on SR 26 to CR 232; turn left; travel north to SW 70 Street; turn left and follow road to boat ramp.

A Paddler's Guide

35.8 Suwannee Gables Ramp: From Fanning Spring, cross the river on US 19; travel west and find Suwannee Gables Motel on the right.

34.2 Joe Anderson, Jr. Ramp: From Fanning Spring, cross the river on US 19; turn left on SE 989 Street; travel south to SE 155 Avenue; turn left and the ramp is at the end of the street.

32.0 Hinton Landing Ramp: From Old Town, travel south on CR 349 to SE Cr 346; turn left; travel east to SE CR 317; turn right and follow road to boat ramp.

30.2 Old Pine Landing Ramp: From Old Town, travel south on CR 349 to SE 295 Avenue; turn left; travel east to SE 837 Street; turn right and follow road to boat ramp.

28.7 New Pine Landing Ramp: From Old Town, travel south on CR 349 to SE 311 Avenue; turn left; travel east to SE 849 Street; turn left and find boat ramp on the right.

28.1 New Clay Landing Ramp: From Chiefland, travel west on NW 115 Street to NW 110 Avenue; turn right and travel north to NW 129 Place; turn left and travel west to NW 130 Street; turn left and follow road to ramp.

25.1 Manatee Springs State Park Launch: From Chiefland, travel west on NW 115 Street to Manatee Springs State park.

24.6 Usher Landing Ramp: From Chiefland, travel west on NW 115 Street to NW 107 Terrace; turn left and travel south to Usher boat ramp sign; turn right and follow road to boat ramp.

23.2 Camp Azalea Ramp. From Chiefland, travel west on NW 115 Street to NW 107 Terrace; turn left and travel south to Camp Azalea; turn right on NW 128 Court and follow road to boat ramp.

22.7 Yellow Jacket Ramp: From Old Town, travel south on CR 349 to SE 477 Avenue; turn left; travel east to SE 752 Street; turn right and follow road to boat ramp.

16.8 Fowlers Bluff Ramp: From Chiefland, travel on SW 4 Avenue (CR 345) 6 miles; turn right on CR 347; travel 9 miles; turn right on NW 46 Lane and follow to boat ramp.

16.0 Weeks Landing Launch: From Old Town, travel south 17 miles on CR 349 to unmarked Lower Suwannee National Wildlife Refuge Road; turn left and follow road to canoe launch.

7.6 Munden Creek Ramp: From Suwannee, travel north on CR 349 to SE 371 Street; turn right, travel east to SE 374 Street, and follow road to boat ramp.

Rose Knox and Graham Schorb

3.9 Anderson Landing Ramp: Located in the Town of Suwannee on CR 349

Notes
Map information courtesy of Suwannee River Water Management District.

Bibliography

Akerman, Joe A., and Mark J. Akerman. *Jacob Summerlin: King of the Crackers.* Cocoa: The Florida Historical Society Press, 2004.

Akerman, Joe. *Florida Cowman: A History of Florida Cattle Ranching.* Kissimmee: Florida Cattleman's Association, 1976.

Alderson, Doug. *Waters Less Traveled: Exploring Florida's Big Bend Coast.* Gainesville: University Press of Florida, 2005.

Bartlett, R.D., and Patricia Bartlett. *Florida Snakes: A Guide to Their Identification and Habits.* Gainesville: University Press of Florida, 2003.

Bartram, William. *Travels.* New Haven: Yale University Press, 1958.

Bonde, Robert K., and Roger L. Reep. *The Florida Manatee: Biology and Conservation.* Gainesville: University Press of Florida, 2006.

Boning, Charles, R. *Florida Rivers.* Gainesville: Pineapple Press, Inc., 2007.

Browning, Edwin, Jr. "Ellaville Stood by Confederacy." *The Tallahassee Democrat,* 25 June 1970.

Burch, Betsy, et al. *Echoes of the Past: A History of Suwannee County.* 1858-2000. Saint Petersburg: Southern Heritage Press, 2000.

Burlew, Jeff. "Updated: At least 100 Homes Impacted by Flooding in Madison County." *Tallahassee Democrat,* 8 April 2009.

Campbell, Joseph. *The Power of Myth with Bill Moyers.* Edited by Betty Sue Flowers. New York: Doubleday, 1988.

Cerulean, S., and J. Ripple, eds. *The Wild Heart of Florida.* "Borderline." Gainesville: University Press of Florida, 1999.

Cerulean, Susan, Laura Newton, and Janisse Ray, eds. *Between Two Rivers: Stories From the Red Hills to the Gulf.* Tallahassee: Heart of the Earth and the Red Hills Writers Project, 2004.

Ceryak, Ron, and David Hornsby. *Springs of the Suwannee River Basin, Florida: Water Resources Special Report 10-98.* Live Oak, Florida: Suwannee River Water Management District Department of Water Resources, 1998.

Chambers, Virgil, and Robert Kauffman. Brochure. American Canoe Association Inc., Newington VA.

Chance, Martha, et al. *A Brief History of Hamilton County, Florida.* Jasper: The Jasper News.

Council, Clyde C. *Suwannee Country: A Canoeing, Boating, and Recreational Guide to Florida's Immortal River.* Sarasota: J and G Printing Inc., 1988.

Covington, James W. *The Seminoles of Florida.* Gainesville: University Press of Florida, 1993.

Crabbe, Nathan. "Sturgeon: The Misunderstood Fish," *Gainesville Sun,* 11 May 2007.

Curtis, Emily B. *Tales from the Suwannee River Country.* New York: Writers' Club Press, 2002.

Davis, Margaret Lewis, et al. *The History and People of Hamilton County.* Saint Petersburg: Southern Heritage Press, 2000.

DeLoach, Ned. *Diving Guide to Underwater Florida.* Jacksonville: New World Publications, 1991.

Deliverance. Dir. John Boorman. Warner Brothers, 1972.

Dickey, James. *Deliverance.* New York: Houghton Mifflin, 1970.

Drobney, Jeffery A. *Company Towns and Social Transformation in the North Florida Timber Industry 1880 – 1930.* Florida Historical Quarterly 75:2.

Drye, Willie. "Clues to Pirate Gold Unearthed in Florida, Treasure Hunter's Claim." *National Geographic News,* 15 March 2007.

"Dugout Canoe Discovered Near Santa Fe." *Suwannee Democrat,* Feb. 1999.

Ervin, William R. *Let Us Alone.* W and S Ervin Printing Publishing. 1983.

Exley, Sheck. *Taming of the Slough: A Comprehensive History of Peacock Springs.* Edited by Sandra Poucher. Huntsville: Published by the National Speleological Society Inc., 2004.

Fergus, Charles. *Swamp Screamer: At Large with the Florida Panther.* Gainesville: University Press of Florida, 1998.

Fletcher, Hodges, Jr. *The Swanee River and A Biography of Stephen C. Foster.* White Springs: The Stephen Foster Memorial Association, Inc., 1958.

"Florida Warns of Jumping Sturgeon," *Gulf Coast Fisherman.* 1 April 2008.

Folkerts, George W. and Lucian Niemeyer. *Okefenokee.* Jackson: University Press of Mississippi, 2002.

Garrison, Webb. *A Treasury of Florida Tales.* Nashville: Rutledge Hill Press, 1989.

Gingerich, Jerry Lee. *Florida's Fabulous Mammals: Their Stories.* Tampa: World Publications, 1999.

Hinton, Cora. et al. *Early History of Hamilton County, Florida: A Bicentennial Project.* Jasper: The Jasper News.

Hollis, Tim. *Glass Bottom Boats and Mermaid Tails: Florida's Tourist Springs.* Mechanicsburg, Pennsylvania: Stackpole Books, 2006.

Holmes, Melton Jr. *Lafayette County History and Heritage.* Mayo, 1974.

Housewright, Wiley. *An Anthology of Music in Early Florida.* Gainesville: University Press of Florida, 1999.

"Jumping Sturgeon." *Suwannee Democrat,* April 2006.

McCarthy, Kevin, M. *The History of Gilchrist County.* Gainesville: 1986.

Malloy, Johnny. *From the Swamp to the Keys: A Paddle Through Florida History.* Gainesville: University Press of Florida Press, 2003.

Milanich, Jerald T. and Theodore Morris. *Florida's Lost Tribes.* Gainesville: University Press of Florida, 2004.

Moore, Joyce Elson. *Haunt Hunter's Guide to Florida: Thirty Three of the Most Bone-Chilling Places in the Sunshine State.* Sarasota: Pineapple Press, 1998.

Mooney, James. *Myths of the Cherokee.* New York: Dover Publications, Inc., 1995

Moses, Grace Emerick. *Footprints Along the Suwannee.* North Florida Printing, 1981.

Mueller, Edward A. "Suwannee River Steamboating." *Florida Historical Quarterly 45* (January 1967): 271-288.

Musgrove, Eric. *Reflections of Suwannee County: 150 Anniversary Edition 1858-2008.* Live Oak: North Florida Printing Co., Inc., 2008.

Nelson, Megan Kate. *Trembling Earth: A Cultural History of the Okefenokee Swamp.* Athens: University of Georgia Press. 2005.

Orenstein, Ronald. *Turtles, Tortoises & Terrapins: Survivors in Armor.* Buffalo: Firefly Books Inc., 2001.

Palmer, Beth Ann, ed. *Precious Memories of Dixie County.* Dixie County Historical Society, Vol. 10: 2000.

Ray, Janisse. *Pinhook: Finding Wholeness in a Fragmented Land.* White River Junction: Chelsea Green Publishing Company, 2005.

Revels, Tracy J. *Sunshine Paradise: A History of Florida Tourism.* Gainesville: University Press of Florida, 2011.

Russell, Franklin. *The Okefenokee Swamp*. Alexandria: Time Life Books Inc., 1973.

Royal, Captain Ron. "Fresh It Is." *Nature Coastlines*. Nov/Dec 2005.

Sims, Elizabeth. et al. *A History of Madison County, Florida*. Madison: Jimbob Printing Inc., 1986.

Smith, Patrick D. *A Land Remembered*. Sarasota: Pineapple Press, 1984.

Ste Claire, Dana. *Cracker: The Cracker Culture in Florida History*. Gainesville, Florida: University Press of Florida, 2006.

Strawn, Martha A. *Alligators Prehistoric Presence in the American Landscape*. Maryland: The Johns Hopkins Press Ltd., 1997.

Thoreau, Henry David. *Walden and Other Writings*. New York: Bantam Books Inc., 1962.

_____. *Walden and Other Writings*. Edited by Joseph Wood Krutch. New York: Bantam Books, 1981

United States. County Commissioner's Meeting. "Proposal to Construct a Dam at Suwannee Springs." Live Oak: 1964.

Weisman, Brent Richards. *Excavations of the Franciscan Frontier*. Gainesville: University Press of Florida, 1992.

Weisman, Brent Richards. *Unconquered People: Florida's Seminole and Miccosukee Indians*. Gainesville: University Press of Florida, 1999.

Williams, Winston. *Florida's Fabulous Trees: Theirs Stories*. Tampa: Worldwide Publications, 1984.

Worth, John E. Timucuan. *Chiefdoms of Spanish Florida: Volume 1: Assimilation*. Gainesville: University Press of Florida, 1998.

Wright, John K. "From Kubla Khan to Florida." *American Quarterly*, 8:1 Spring, 1956.

Wright, Leitch J. Jr. *Creeks and Seminoles: Destruction and Regeneration of the Muscogulge People*. Lincoln: University of Nebraska Press, 1986.

Historical Kiosks

Shell Mound in the Lower Suwannee National Wildlife Refuge in the Suwannee River Basin.

Suwannee River State Park, Live Oak.

Suwannee Springs, Live Oak.

Internet Sources

Defenders of Wildlife. "Black Bear" http://www.defenders.org/

Drye, Willie. "Clues to Pirate Gold Unearthed in Florida, Treasure Hunter's Claim." *National Geographic News*, 31 January 2009. http://news.nationalgeographic.com/news/2007/03/070315-pirate-treasure.html

E Movie National Geographic. http://news.nationalgeographic.com/news/2006/10/0610-10suwanee-video.html

http://www.floridastateparks.org/fanningsprings/History.cfm

Florida State Parks. "Stephen Foster Folk and Culture Center State Park." http://www.floridastateparks.org/stephenfoster/

http://www.floridastateparks.org/manateesprings/-57-

www.seminoletribe.com/history/index.shtml

http://www.floridastateparks.org/troyspring/default/cfm

http://www.suwanneeparksandrecreation.org/Parks.htm

Hall (The) of Florida Fossils: Evolution of Life and Land. Sabal Palm. www.flmnh.ufl.edu

Info@bigcatrescue.org-more

National Geographic. "Alligator Snapping Turtle." http://www.animals.nationalgeographic.com/animals/reptiles/alligator-snapping-turtle.html

"San Juan Catholic Mission History." http://www.sanjuanmission.org/missionhistory.html

State Symbols USA. Sabal Palm. www.statesymbolsusa.org

U.S. Fish & Wildlife Service. "Okefenokee National Wildlife Refuge." http://www.fws.gov/okfenokee/

E-mails

Cook, David. "Identification of the Loggerhead Musk Turtle," e-mail to the biologist with the Florida Fish and Wildlife Commission. May, 2009.

Cook, Dr. Karen. "Lee Family Photograph," e-mail to archivist at University of Kansas. September, 2011.

Harper, Robin. "Permission to Use Questions Concerning the Lee Family Photograph," e-mail to Robin Harper. June, 2011.

Howell, Bivian Grady. "Questions Concerning Location of Ivey Cemetery-Pioneer Cemetery," e-mail to cemetery researcher of Suwannee Valley Genealogy Society Library. 08, May 2011.

Howell, Bivian Grady. "Questions Concerning Conflicting Accounts of Rueben Charles' Death," e-mail to cemetery researcher of Suwannee Valley Genealogy Society Library. 10, September 2008.

Ilene, Frank. Tampa Library Reference Archive Department provides information concerning local archival maps: e-mail correspondence. Fall, 2008.

Musgrove, Eric. "Questions Concerning Captain Robert Ivey and his Resting Place," e-mail to local historian and author. 10, May 2011.

Suwannee River Water Management. "River Levels, Crest Predictions, Flood Warnings," e-mail from Efrain Bonilla. North Florida Community College via Victoria Brown Program Coordinator, Madison County Emergency Management.

Interviews

Akerman, Joe. Personal Interview(s) at his Home: Confederate Cow Cavalry and Alligator-Snapping Turtle Artwork. March - April 2010.

Bellot, Cindy. Personal Interview at the Dixie County Library: History Leads of Dixie County. Fall 2008.

Birdsong, "Chip" Vincent. Phone Interview with Database Administrator at the Division of Historical Resources in Tallahassee, Florida Concerning Archaeology of the Suwannee River. Winter 2009.

Burkhart, Jim. Phone Interview with Ranger in the Okefenokee Wildlife Refuge Concerning History and Questions of the Sill. Fall, 2008.

Camp, Paul. Telephone and e-mail correspondence: Tampa Library Reference Archive Department assists with old maps. Fall, 2008.

Chavous, Preston. Personal Interview at the Dixie County Library: History Leads of Dixie County. Fall, 2008.

Dame, Johnny. Personal Interview upon the Middle Suwannee River: His life, Work, and Philosophy Manifested in Artistic Expression. March, 2008.

Griffis, Dot and Al. Personal Interview at their Home Near the Okefenokee Swamp: Pioneer Georgia and Early Excursions within the Okefenokee Swamp. March, 2008.

Goss, Marvin. "Use of the Lee Family Photograph." Telephone conversation with archivist at Georgia Southern University of the Zach S. Henderson Library. August, 2011.

Howell, Bivian and Murl Grady. Personal Interview in the Charles Cemetery: Life of Ruben Charles' Family and Leads on Pioneer Papers. April 2008.

Owen, Evon. Telephone Interview: Story of Dugout Canoe on Owen Property. January, 2009.

Pharr, David. Personal Interview at the Suwannee Canoe Outpost on the Middle Suwannee River: Native American Carving and Construction of Floating Barge. May, 2008.

Price, Dennis. Telephone Interview Conducted by Graham Schorb: Hawthorne Layer and Topographical Questions Concerning Big Shoals. May, 2011.

Schorb, Graham. Personal and Telephone Interview (s): Camping and Cooking Tips and Navigational Directions for 242 Miles of the Suwannee River Corridor. April 2008 –August 2011.

Smith, Randy. Personal Interview at Graham's Cabin: Bizarre Stories of a River Guide. August, 2008.

Todd, Tommy. Telephone Interview: Quest for Pirate's Gold is Still Underway Upon the Suwannee River. February, 2009.

Wheeler, Ryan. Telephone interview and e-mail correspondence: Chief archaeologist of Florida attempts to help validate the authenticity of a dugout canoe found on the Suwannee River. Fall, 2008.

Maps
Suwannee River Water Management District

Related Reading: People of the Swamp and Suwannee River Basin
Exploring the Okefenokee: Letters and Diaries from the Indian Wars, 1836-1842 by C.T. Trowell

Okefinokee Album by Francis Harper and Delma Presley

Jackson's Folly: The Suwannee Canal Company in the Okefenokee Swamp by C.T. Trowell

Confederate Florida by William Nulty

Florida Indians and the Invasion from Europe by Jerald T. Milanich

Indian Mounds You Can Visit: 165 Aboriginal Sites on Florida's West Coast by Mac Perry

River Without End: A Novel of the Suwannee by Pamela Jekel

There Let Me Live and Die by Eric Musgrove

Suggested Reading for Graham's Outdoor Kitchen

Kohler, Juanita, Mike, Pat, Wallace, and Pat and Dick Michaud. *World Championship Dutch Oven Cookbook*. Logan: Watkins Printing, 1989.

National Museum of Forest Service History. *Camp Cooking: 100 Years*. Salt Lake City: Gibbs Smith Publisher, 2004.

Owens, Janis. *The Cracker Kitchen: A Cookbook in Celebration of Cornbread-Fed, Down-Home Family Stories and Cuisine*. New York: Scribner, 2009.

Woodruff, Woody. *Cooking the Dutch Oven Way*. Guilford: The Globe Pequot Press, 2000.

About the Authors

Rose Knox

Rose Knox began her secondary education at North Florida Junior College in Madison, Florida, and received her Associate of Arts degree in 1981. She finished her Bachelor of Arts degree at the University of Montevallo in Alabama in 1983. She concluded her formal studies in 2000 at Valdosta State University in Valdosta, Georgia, with a Master of Arts in English Studies. She is currently teaching writing and literature at a rural college in North Florida. As an avid reader, she gravitates to subjects concerning pioneer Florida. She also is immensely intrigued in parallel symbols and stories found within spiritual rituals and myths of the world. Southeastern authors that have influenced her writing include Patrick D. Smith in *A Land Remembered*; Joe and Mark Akerman in *Jacob Summerlin: King of the Crackers*; Marjorie Kinnan Rawlings in *The Yearling*; and Janisse Ray in *Ecology of a Cracker Childhood*. Eckhart Tolle and Joseph Campbell have widened her world view on spiritual and cultural belief systems found within their works *The Power of Now* and *The Power of Myth*.

The Suwannee River is her sacred place. As a native Floridian, Rose appreciates and reveres what remains of wild North Florida. She encourages those around her to paddle these currents. When she is not teaching, she is practicing yoga, kayaking, or hiking. She has recently begun a new work about the Okefenokee Swamp.

Photograph courtesy of Parker Schorb.

Graham Schorb

Graham Schorb is a native Floridian. He attended Pinellas Vocational Technical Institute and received a two-year certificate in Horticulture Studies in 1980. Like Henry David Thoreau, he wanted little of the modern world with its many frivolous distractions. Consequently, in the 1980s, he was drawn to North Florida, went into the woods, and built his own cracker cabin. The pioneer lifestyle of early Floridians intrigues him, and Graham strives to live as closely to Nature and as true to pioneer Florida as possible. As a river guide and outdoor enthusiast, he has explored the Suwannee River and Suwannee River Basin and the wild areas of North Florida for over twenty-five years. He loves to read books about early pioneer exploration, and some of his favorites include William Bartram's *Travels*; *The Wilderness World of John Muir*; Joe and Mark Akerman's *Jacob Summerlin*; and Patrick Smith's *A Land Remembered*. His photographic contributions and his expertise as a river guide have made this paddler's guide a reality. Preserving the culture and history of the legendary Suwannee River would have been impossible without his supervision, knowledge, and guidance.

Index

A

Adams Tract 218
Akerman, Joe and Mark 131
Alapaha River confluence 110, 136, 139
alligator
    American 24, 33, 37, 61, 72–74, 81, 111, 184, 218, 268, 300
    industry 73, 74
    nesting 72
    poaching 73
alligator-snapping turtle 107–108
antebellum 51, 88, 94–98, 154
Apalachee 1, 53, 88, 189, 190–191, 194
artifacts 2, 107, 195, 255, 269, 273

B

baptisms, modern day 215
Bath House. See White Springs.
beginners 5, 21
Bellamy Trail 184, 206–207, 208, 210, 213
Belle of the Suwanee, steamboat 161, 163, 164, 203, 248, 249
Belle of the Suwannee, paddleboat 98
Big Shoals 18, 50, 59, 79, 80, 81, 82, 83, 85–87, 106, 110
Billy Bowlegs 2, 29–30, 274, 277
Billy's Island 29–30, 65, 274, 277
Black Seminoles. See Seminoles.
boar, wild 24, 184, 196–198, 199
Bowlegs Town 274
Branford 12, 116, 148, 161, 166, 204, 217, 219, 241, 242, 243, 248, 258

C

Camino Real 51, 208, 213
camping tips 19, 21
carillon, bell tower 95
Cedar Key 160, 190, 248, 311
Charles Springs 51, 53
chickee 250, 279
City of Hawkinsville 166, 269, 284, 288
Cofa, Village of 213
Colonial Hotel 88, 91
Columbus Cemetery 156–158
Columbus, Town of 111, 151, 156–158, 160, 167, 226
Confederate Army 153, 154
Confederate covered bridge 153
Confederate Earthworks 152, 156
confederations, Native American 1, 189
cooking tips 15, 325
Cow Cavalry 154
Creek Confederacy 273
cypress, bald 2, 24, 27, 36, 44, 50, 61, 145, 219, 247, 299, 300, 301

D

Dame, Johnny 39, 81, 82, 93, 99–106, 111, 127, 323
De Bry 189, 190
de Leon, Ponce 199
de Soto, Hernando 51, 52, 145, 196, 197, 198, 206, 211, 212
Devil's Elbow 113
Dowling Park 180, 184, 185, 186, 197, 199–200
    Park Hotel 199, 200, 202
Drew Bridge 220, 226, 227
Drew Cemetery 111, 170, 171, 174, 175
Drew Mansion 111, 167–171

E

Edgewood Hotel 88
Edison, Thomas 2, 163
Ellaville 149, 167, 171–173, 226, 236, 315, 316, 317
Ellaville Shoals 110
Exley, Sheck 229

F

Fannin, Colonel 285, 286
Fanning Spring 252, 268, 269, 270, 285–291
Fargo, Georgia 14, 24, 27, 28, 38, 41, 48, 49, 55, 198
   Visitor's Center 24, 27, 48–49
ferries 148
fire, building a 21, 38
fish camp 41, 298, 302
fishing 15, 43, 61, 69–71, 141, 287
Florida panther 24, 36, 103, 111, 131–133, 142, 199
Florida Trail 50, 80, 81
Foster, Stephen 2, 3, 36, 50, 53, 81, 82, 94–98

G

Ghost Bridge 218, 226, 227
ghost story 311
Gibson Park 110, 111, 136, 137
Goggins, John M. 273
gold, search for 2, 228, 307–310
gopher gumbo 2, 119
gopher tortoise 61, 63, 81, 111
GPS navigation 13, 18
Griffis Fish Camp 24, 36, 38, 41–47, 57
Gulf sturgeon 111, 218, 264, 266, 304

H

Hal Adams Bridge 218, 223, 264
Hart Springs 268, 271–272
Highway 6 Bridge 61, 63
hiking 81, 145–147, 171, 176, 271, 304
hogs, wild 61, 197

Holton Creek 110, 113
Hotel Jackson 88, 91
hunting 73, 197

I

Indian Removal Act 51, 275, 280
Irvine Ferry 225
Irvine, Colonel Washington 204, 223, 228
islands 31, 218, 233, 301, 302
Ivey Park 248
Ivey, Captain Robert 203, 204, 248, 249
Ivey-McIntosh Cemetery 203

J

Jackson, Andrew 51, 231, 274, 279, 280, 286, 295
Jungle Drive 286, 287

K

Knox, Lunita Parrish 66

L

Lee family 65
Little River Tract 218
Little Shoals 80, 81
Lodeaver 44, 47
logging 149, 167, 170, 175, 202, 234, 237, 316
longboat 256, 257, 274
Lower Suwannee National Wildlife Refuge 299, 302, 311, 312

M

Madison County 154, 167, 169, 171, 315
Madison, Florida 122, 152–155, 316
Madison, steamship 160–161, 163, 164, 219, 238–239
Malloy, John 63
manatee 268, 269, 270, 288, 289, 301, 304–306
Manatee Springs 259, 267, 292, 297, 298, 299, 301, 304–306

Micco, Holata 29–30, 274
missions 2, 191, 213, 219
Mixon's Ferry 44, 47
Mooney, James 281, 282
Morris, Theodore 192–194
Myths of the Cherokee 281

N

Narrows, the 24, 26
Native Americans 31, 34, 48, 52, 56, 64, 88, 118, 132, 136, 184, 188–195, 206–209, 211, 228, 231–232, 258, 281–283, 288, 295, 311, 314
   Christianized 185, 190–191, 213–214, 216
New Clay Landing 292
Noble's Ferry 77, 110, 136, 137, 140, 141, 142

O

oak hammocks 7, 271
Oaks Hotel 88
Okefenokee Swamp 17, 24, 25, 26, 29, 30, 31–35, 36, 37, 41, 43, 44, 46, 48, 50, 64, 65, 66, 72, 103, 196, 274, 277, 301
   Sill 17, 24, 26, 33–34, 35
Old Folks at Home 2, 3, 53, 94
Old Stagecoach Road 148, 156
Old Town 231, 232, 263, 269, 273, 284, 292, 295
Olustee, battle of 153, 154
Osceola, Chief 231, 274, 275, 276
Outpost 55, 77, 85, 107, 110, 111, 112, 113, 127, 128, 129, 132, 134, 179, 235, 264

P

paddleboat 98
Paleo-Indian 1, 50, 88, 188, 192, 195, 228, 285
Panther (The Underground Panthers) 282–283
panther. See Florida panther.

Paxton Hotel 88
Peacock Slough 218, 229
Peacock Springs 218, 219, 228–230
Peacock, Dr. John Calvin 228–229
permit 17, 24, 33, 35, 49, 57, 73
Pharr, David 85, 127, 129, 179
pioneers 32, 34, 36, 46, 48, 64–65, 95, 118, 131, 133, 184, 203, 207, 229, 231–232, 250, 258, 271, 274, 288
poke weed 250
portage 18, 80, 81, 85
Powell, William 274

R

rapids, Class III 18, 50, 81, 85, 87
rattlesnake 176
Rattlesnake (The Snake Tribe) 282
Rawlings, Marjorie Kinnan 38, 250
Ray, Janisse 101, 234, 321, 322
Rebel's Refuge 88
recipes 15, 325–330
restocking supplies 14, 81, 111, 185, 219, 243, 269
river camps 13, 184, 218, 242
River of Deer 1, 52
River Rendezvous 221
River Saint Juan Vignoles 53
Rock Bluff 242, 243, 244, 262
Roline 23, 59, 61, 62, 71
Rowland's Bluff 248
Royal Spring 219, 221

S

San Juan de 53, 213
Schorb, Graham, river guide 6
scuba diving 228, 229, 238, 284
Seminoles 46, 273–280, 282, 295
   Black Seminoles 2, 51, 295
   crafts 278, 279
   First Seminole Indian War 286
   Second Seminole Indian War 118, 208, 273, 285, 286

Seminole Nation 2, 32, 273, 274, 275
Third Seminole Indian War 277
villages 51, 273, 279, 295
Shell Mound 311, 312, 313, 314
sill. See Okefenokee Swamp.
Skiles, Wes 218, 228
slave plantations 32, 48, 191, 295
Smith, Patrick 197–198
snakes 31, 33, 48, 61, 65, 126, 176–181
   See also rattlesnake
Spanish silver coin 219
steamboat landing 89, 156, 248, 285, 286, 288
steamboats 160–166, 203, 248
Stephen C. Foster Park 33
Stephen Collins Foster Folk Culture Center 94–98
sturgeon 77, 242, 264–266, 268, 301, 304
Suwannee River
   names for 52
   Water Management District 13, 60
Suwannee River Diner 99, 101, 102
Suwannee Spring 79, 104, 108, 109, 110, 111, 118–126, 197, 231, 264
   bridge 111, 123, 126
   experimental dam 116–117
   hotels 119, 123, 200
swamp 234, 286, 287, 295, 304, 305
   See also Okefenokee Swamp.

T

taxidermist 43
Telford Inn 81, 82, 89, 90, 92, 102
Three States, steamship 165, 248, 249
Timucua 1, 53, 74, 88, 188–191, 193, 206, 213, 216, 256
   village 213, 214
Tom's Creek 61
trembling earth 31
Troy Spring 161, 163, 218, 219, 238–239, 264
Tucker, Captain James 160, 161, 162, 238
Turner Bridge 61, 62, 63

U

Union army 167
United States Army forts 51, 231–233
University of Florida research 74

W

Wakulla River 72
Walker Tract 218
walking tour 79, 81, 90, 93
weather 15, 18, 21
White Springs 12, 18, 61, 79, 80, 81, 82, 88–93, 95, 99, 101, 102, 103, 106, 116, 118, 164, 200, 278, 279
   Bath House 81, 82, 89, 90, 93